Leap Year's Revenge

Neil J. McCurry

1

Leap Year's Revenge by Neil J. McCurry
Copyright 2022 La Maison Publishing
ISBN 978-1-970153-37-8
Library of Congress Catalog Number: 9781970153378
Distributed through Ingram Book Company

Cover Image – Shutterstock

Maison
La Maison Publishing
Vero Beach, Florida
The Hibiscus City
lamaisonpublishing@gmail.com

Chapter One

As they walked home from school, a car pulled beside Lewis and his friend, Phil.

"Hey, what are you two lovers doing on this street, getting it on?" Jerry Alfonso yelled, getting a roar from the Gallagher brothers.

"Just keep walking, Phil. Don't even look at them." Lewis said.

Simon Gallagher wheeled the GTO in front of them, and the boys jumped out.

"I asked you, Dunce. What are you doing here?" Jerry reiterated.

"None of your business, Alfonso!" Lewis said.

"Hey, city boy, didn't you get our message spray-painted on your house?" Jeff addressed Phil.

"It's going to take a lot more than a few words of hate to chase our proud family from this town. I know I'm not the same color as you, but you're too chicken to mess with me and my father, aren't you?" Phil said.

"It's your move, Jerry. Every time I see you, Simon and Jeff are by your side. Is it for your own protection?" Lewis stated as he clenched two fists at his side.

Jerry looked at the Gallagher brothers. "C'mon, let's go. We'll settle this with you later, Lewis." The three aggressors got back in Jeff's car and showered Lewis and Phil with pieces of hot rubber and dust as he peeled out.

"Thanks for getting me out of another jam, Lewis. But I don't think our family can take any more of these prejudiced assaults just because we're black." Phil confessed.

"Why did you move out of the city anyhow?"

"There was too much drug use, violence, and gangs," Phil said.

"Yea, lotta good it did you moving here, didn't it! Hey, I'll catch you tomorrow at school, right?" Lewis asked apprehensively.

"Just a few more weeks to go!" Phil tried to sound optimistic.

Lewis nodded and smiled as he left. He made it a block away and heard Simon's car pull up behind him again. The door opened, and Jerry stormed out, pointing a gun at Lewis. "Get in, now, you fairy!"

Simon blindfolded Lewis and threw him into the back seat. They drove for twenty minutes and took a hard turn onto a dirt road. The car came to an abrupt halt as it skidded sideways. Lewis thought he'd be dead soon, for sure. The door opened.

"Get out!"

Lewis slid from the car seat and heard a gun chamber spin.

"Take off your shirt!" One of the Gallaghers yelled.

"What? Take off my?"

"Then your shoes and pants, nice and slow." Lewis felt a gun barrel press into his back.

"Off with those tighty-whities too!"

"Oh, come on, hasn't this gone...?" Lewis begged.

"Do it!" Jerry ordered. "My, he is one fine specimen, isn't he, boys?"

Lewis felt a warm liquid pouring over his body. At first, he thought it was gasoline, but some dripped into his mouth. It was sweet and smelled like candy. Syrup! It was maple syrup! He didn't move. Lewis felt something light falling on him, like tree leaves. All three were laughing hysterically at him.

"He looks like a big damn chicken!" Jerry boasted. "Cluck, cluck! Don't take that blindfold off until we're gone. You've got a long walk home! See ya, Dunce!"

Lewis heard the car doors open and slam shut. They drove off quietly. He didn't dare move.

He waited until he couldn't hear the car anymore and removed the blindfold. He looked at his body. Feathers! They completely covered him with sticky maple syrup and feathers! He could hardly move as the mixture dried on him. He looked around and tried to get a bearing on where he was. He started walking, naked and humiliated, toward an exit at the far end of the sand pit, fuming and cursing. From that moment on, Lewis thought very carefully about the painful demise of the Gallagher brothers. He smiled devilishly as a plan was loosely coming together to end a twelve-year run of bullying from Jerry Alfonso. Never again.

Chapter Two
Seventeen Years Ago

February 27, 1972, 1 a.m. A vast nor'easter was brewing in the seas far from the tranquil sands of Cape Cod. The skies were damp and grey. A frozen mist was blowing across Nantucket Sound. Radio and TV stations urged Cape residents to prepare for a catastrophic storm. All public and DOT employees were sent home early that day, expecting to be called back to work when the storm subsided. The National Guard was on standby for extra help to clear snow-packed roads with heavy equipment available from Otis Air Force Base.

Bruce Duncan was one of many Guard reservists waiting for the impending arrival of snow and ice. He was pacing the floor at his day job as an accountant, almost reaching the end of an eight-hour grueling day and was ready to spring into action.

Jen Duncan, Bruce's wife, was eight months pregnant and quite excited. It was their first to be born and the only grandchild on both sides of the family. Surely this meant the newborn was guaranteed to be spoiled and fought over by both sets of grandparents, already secretly competing to outdo each other with gifts for the new baby. Bruce and Jen knew this and prepared for the pair of domineering mothers-in-law.

The day passed with no accumulating snow. As Mother Nature had her way, a full moon and high tide combined with strong winds took a toll on pristine ocean-front homes and vacant hotels. The National Guard was engaged in a futile attempt to stop those raging waters from reclaiming beaches that led to valuable cranberry bogs and swampland. Bruce was one of many front-end loader operators trying to halt the ocean's tidal rise up the Bass River in Yarmouth.

*****

February 27, 8 a.m. It finally began to snow sideways right from the get-go. The storm got off to a slow start but was just gearing up. Low pressure in the Gulf of Maine teamed with a moisture flow moving up from the Gulf Stream. The storm redeveloped, with an eye wall circulating southeast of Cape Cod. It wasn't moving at all. The meteorologists on TV were ecstatic about the enormity of the storm. Residents and public safety employees knew outages were certain from the heavy, wet snow that could rip power lines down and clog roads for days.

Jen, who had been at home sixteen hours alone, was deeply concerned about Bruce plowing in the blinding storm, working so long with no sleep and little food on the snowy, icy roads. Her abdomen was tingling, and she felt unsteady on her swollen feet. Jen called and left three messages for Bruce at the armory but had not heard back from him. This made her nervous, too. She passed the time away by putting some final touches on the new baby's room.

11 a.m. The phone rang; it was Bruce. "Hi, hon. I got your messages just now. We were stuck in a six-foot drift off High Banks Road. How are you doing? Are you okay by yourself?"

"My God, Bruce. I'm scared to death here and worried about you. The house is creaking like no tomorrow from the wind, and there's water leaking in from three windows. My stomach and back feel funny. Can you come home before it ends?" Jen pleaded.

"We're in lockdown at the armory for a few more hours. Visibility is about ten feet, and two loaders are missing already," Bruce told her.

"Well, can't you drive one of them here? It's only two miles, and I'm terrified. I can't even reach you if something happens!" Jen said in desperation.

"Nothing's going to happen, dear, and you're not due for five or six more weeks, so don't worry. This isn't the first storm that old rack of timbers has gone through. It's a hundred and thirty years old! I'll take the commander's bag phone when we hit the road again so you can call me on his dime, okay?" He tried to reassure Jen.

"I just watched the forecast. The snow isn't going to stop until tomorrow afternoon. Three to four feet of snow is predicted, with eight-foot drifts. If we lose power here, I'm screwed, Bruce."

"Well, get out all the candles and flashlights now. Fill the tub and sinks with water and stoke the fireplace. Believe me, if anything happens, I'll go

AWOL and take one of the loaders home to get you. You're a rugged, ol' Cape Coddah sea salt, remembah?" Bruce and Jen both laughed. "And don't forget you have Rex the Wonder Dog to protect you!" Rex, their Jack Russell, wasn't good for much except begging for food, humping legs, and destroying furniture.

"All right, I feel a little better now. Rex weighs only twelve pounds, but he's better than nothing," Jen said reluctantly. "Call me when you go back on the road and every hour after that—you hear me? No excuses!"

"Aren't you going to get some sleep later?"

"Are you kidding? This box of shingles you call a house is making so many noises I doubt I'll ever sleep! As long as the TV stays on, I'll be fine, I guess. Call me, got it?" Jen firmly reminded Bruce.

He gave Jen the typical, "Yes, dear, I'll call you later. I have to go. I'm getting the high sign from everyone waiting to use this phone. Love you!"

Bruce hung up so quickly Jen didn't even get a chance to say goodbye. Mumbling to herself, she went to make a sandwich.

Moving from one room to another, Jen kept one eye on the TV and the other peering out the windows at the accumulating snow sticking to everything in sight, which was not a good sign. The ocean side of the house had three inches of snow cemented onto it. The opposite side didn't have a flake. Massachusetts and Rhode Island declared a state of emergency. All police cruisers and ambulances from Yarmouth were fitted with chains for any emergency calls from residents. No vehicles were allowed on the streets until the storm was over, which meant tomorrow afternoon at the earliest.

Jen settled into a recliner with her sandwich and skimmed milk to wash it down. Rex was by her feet, looking up at her, already begging for a treat as usual. "You should weigh a hundred and forty pounds like I do, you little mooch!" She caved into Rex. He had the last corner of her sandwich. She tried to watch *The Price Is Right*, but TV programs were canceled and replaced by celebrity meteorologists. They were on fire about the storm, hunched over weather maps on TV with their hands imitating the circular direction of damaging winds and snow.

This is unreal, Jen thought. *They didn't even know about this friggin' storm two days ago!* She tried to clear her head with a cat nap in the recliner, but howling winds and pelting ice worried her as more snow accumulated on the poor roof.

February 27th, 11 p.m. Over three hours had passed since Jen last talked with Bruce. At first, he was good about calling her every hour, but Jen knew the storm's intensity had picked up. A mixture of snow and ice was coming down heavily. She hoped he would at least call with the number from his commander's bag phone. She'd tried to call the armory earlier, but the line was busy again. At least she had a working phone and power. What a blessing, she reminded herself again and got to watch Johnny Carson without being interrupted by storm coverage. When the lights and TV started flickering, she thought she had jinxed herself.

"Oh no. Please, please, just let me get through tonight!" she begged aloud while looking at the blinking TV screen. While she was scrambling for a flashlight, the house went black.

"I don't believe this. Why me?" Jen moaned. She had difficulty maneuvering her large stomach around and used two hands to support it while walking to light the candles. Jen was on her knees readying the fireplace when the phone rang in the kitchen. It took about eight rings for her to answer.

"This better be you, Bruce!" she yelled into the phone.

"Are you okay? Where have you been?"

"We've lost power. I lit the fireplace on my hands and knees and felt like a whale trying to get up. Rex tried to mount me as usual while I was down, but I was okay. Where are you?"

"I'm still at the armory and just got the word. We lost our power here too, but we're on a generator. The storm is lightening up, so we're heading out to clear some main roads. I just wanted to give you Brigg's number."

"Wait a minute. I have to grab a pen." She rummaged through the drawer. "All right, go ahead."

"It's 617-438-6854. It'll ring about ten times before the call goes through, so be patient."

"Oh, great! I'm just full of patience right now, Bruce!"

"I know, I know. I'm sorry. This wasn't good timing for either of us. I'll make it up to you when I get home. The storm is picking up some of its punch, so look for me in about twelve hours, but I'll call you in one hour, I promise."

"You'd better! Don't leave me hanging here. I can't sleep a wink. Oh, great! It seems Rex has to go out. He's scratching at the door. I'll talk to you in one hour, right?"

"Be careful outside," Bruce said. "It's pretty nasty out there."

Jen hung up the phone and shook her head while looking at Rex, anxiously waiting by the door to go out. "Boy, do you have good timing!"

Jen put her heavy coat on, took Rex's leash from a peg on the wall, and hooked him up. She went to the kitchen door. It was frozen shut. She tried to kick it open, but it didn't budge. She couldn't see through any of the kitchen windows, either. "C'mon, Rex, out the other door we go." She wiped the frost off the side porch door and opened it. There wasn't any snow on that side of the house from the wind blowing, but the back had about three feet of snow and ice. The front was bare, typical signs of a true nor'easter.

Rex led her down two short steps to the side yard on his leash when his feet went out from under him. Jen's legs crumbled over her head, and she fell flat on her back. The walkway was covered with ice. She lay there momentarily, trying to regain her wind and senses. Her back and rear end stung with immense pain. The wind gusted and showered her with small ice pellets as Rex licked her face. "I don't believe this," she said to him. "We're going to die out here!"

Jen slowly moved her toes and fingers. Rex was still attached to her arm by his leash, a miracle in itself. She rolled onto her side and struggled to her knees. Jen was soaked from a mixture of ice, snow, and rain. Rex had icicles dripping from his tiny frame. He was shaking uncontrollably.

"Okay, Rex, we're going into the house just like this, on our hands and knees."

Jen crawled to the steps with Rex at her side. Laboring heavily, they made it to the side door. "I hope you have a key!" She tried to laugh at herself as she reached up to turn the knob. It opened.

Rex scampered in with the leash still attached to Jen. "Hold it, hold it, you little pecker!" She unhooked the leash from her arm and crawled to the fireplace, which was in a full roar. She leaned against the couch and started to cry. "Bruce, where are you?" she asked in vain. Once again, she checked her fingers and extremities for movement and winced as feelings returned from the numbing cold. She took off her soaking-wet jacket and her pants. Jen huddled with Rex next to the fire for a few minutes.

Emotions of every sort were running through her head as she sat by the crackling fireplace to warm up. She knew an attempt to get to the kitchen phone to call Bruce was a priority. She regained her strength and cautiously rose from her knees while holding onto the couch. Inching along the furniture, Jen grabbed a door into the kitchen. She smiled, seeing the telephone number she had written down earlier.

Everything's going to be all right. As Jen walked across the kitchen floor, a warm sensation came from between her thighs. She stopped walking and looked down. There was a puddle of fluid on the floor.

"Oh, my god. That's all I need. I think my water just broke!" She barely reached the kitchen table and collapsed into a chair, frantically pushing the numbers written on the notepad. The phone rang and rang for what seemed an eternity. Finally, Bruce answered.

"Bruce Duncan, here."

"Bruce, get home! I think my water just broke. I had a fall. Get here quick, please!" Jen said, crying uncontrollably.

"What, are you kidding me? I'm six miles from the house, and I think I'm the closest one! There's five feet of snow between us!"

"It doesn't look good. Get here soon!" Jen said weakly.

"I'll radio the fire station for an ambulance. I'll drag them with a chain if I have to! Don't move. We'll be there as fast as we can!"

Bruce called the police and the fire station. It proved impossible to get close to because of the large snow drifts. Bruce detoured and started to clear roads to his house for an ambulance. His payloader strained its way through the mountainous, heavy snow. Fallen tree limbs, downed wires, and washed-up boulders on roads slowed his progress. It took almost an hour to reach Jen.

The ambulance crew and Bruce exploded through the door to find Jen sitting in a chair by the phone. She was shivering and wet. The fire had gone completely out. "I'm so sorry," she said while looking up at Bruce as if apologizing.

"Put her in some blankets on that stretcher and move it!" the EMT ordered his assistant. "Let's get a body temp," he yelled. A few moments passed. It was total mayhem in the kitchen. Rex got stepped on a few times and yelped loudly.

"Ninety-five core temperature, Wayne! Mild hypothermia!" the EMT stated loudly.

"Don't worry, baby. I'll stay with you for the whole ride," Bruce said, trying to comfort his wife.

"Bruce! You'll have to clear everything out of the way to Hyannis. Got it? Hyannis is the opposite way from where we came, remember?" Wayne ordered him. "We're at least an hour from the hospital!"

"Oh man, you're killing me, Wayne!" He realized he couldn't be with Jen until he cleared the snow.

"C'mon, what are you waiting for? Let's move some snow!"

Jen was wrapped in a heated blanket and placed in the ambulance. The heat inside was cranked up to ninety degrees.

Bruce attached a chain to the front bumper of the ambulance and climbed into the loader. He looked back and saw Rex standing on the kitchen table, gazing at him with total bewilderment as he scratched his paws on the window.

"Hold on tight, Wayne!" Bruce yelled from the window of his loader. He matted the throttle and smashed through a seven-foot drift at the end of his street.

Wayne put his foot on the gas pedal to the floor. The ambulance fishtailed its way, chained to the loader. They made it to the hospital in less than an hour.

February 28, 5 a.m. Jen arrived at the hospital safely after a very harrowing ride. She was stabilized, in satisfactory condition, and resting after a short nap. The water she felt coming from her body earlier was from her soaking wet sweater dripping onto her legs. She had a complete physical and showed no other signs of labor. The unborn baby had a strong heartbeat and made it through just fine. Her family obstetrician was snowbound in Yarmouth and could not drive to the hospital. Bruce was at her side next to the bed.

"You both gave us quite a scare, Jen. The doctor said you'll be fine. Your body temperature is back up to where it should be."

"I thought I was going to die out there, Bruce. Is the storm over?"

"Not yet, but it lightened up a little coming here. It's changed over to all rain. The snowbanks were pretty heavy, but nothing was going to stop me. I think I ripped the front bumper off that ambulance, though!"

Jen smiled and said, "My eyes are heavy. I can't keep them open."

"You get some rest, hon. I'll be right here."

"What happened to Rex? Did I leave him outside?"

"Heck, no, he was right by your side when we burst in. It scared the daylights out of him!"

Jen laughed. "Yeah, but I wish he would stop humping my leg every time I sit down!"

"Poor thing's never been the same since we got him fixed! You get some rest now, okay?" Bruce bent over and kissed her on the cheek as she closed her eyes. He went to the canteen, got something to eat, and stretched his legs on a chair in the waiting room. He fell into a deep sleep that lasted almost all day.

Chapter Three

February 28th, 10:15 p.m. Jen awoke with sharp, shooting pains in her abdomen and back. She pressed a call button for the nurse. By the time a nurse arrived, the pains were subsiding.

"You rang? Are you okay, Jen?" Amanda, the night nurse, asked.

"I just woke up and had some sharp pains deep inside," she replied. "I'm not sure if I was dreaming or what."

"Let's get a temperature on you." Amanda removed a thermometer from her pocket and placed it in Jen's ear. "And let's get your blood pressure, too." The nurse put the cuff on Jen's arm. "Both are slightly elevated, but I'll check on you in twenty, okay? You aren't due for at least five weeks, right?"

"Yes, March 30th. I must have startled myself as I woke. Is my husband still here?"

"He left for a while, but I think he's in the waiting room, Jen. Do you want me to get him?" the nurse asked.

"Don't bother. He's been through the wringer today. He could sleep in a shoebox if he's tired enough!" They both shared a laugh.

"You keep that call button in your hand and buzz me if you feel anything else, okay?"

"Thanks, Amanda. I'll turn the TV on and see what's happening with the storm."

Amanda returned to her station and made some notes on Jen's chart. She was seated for only fifteen minutes when the call button lit up from Jen's room. She hustled down the hall.

"What do you need, darling?" Amanda asked.

"I landed on my back pretty hard," Jen said. "I had more of those weird pains again, but I don't want to take anything for pain."

"Why don't we slowly get up from that bed and take a trip to the lady's room, okay?" Amanda took her by the arm and shoulder and assisted Jen to the toilet. She closed the door within an inch of being shut. "I'll be right outside until you're done."

"Thanks, Amanda."

Amanda could hear some grunting and a heavy sigh of relief.

"Guess I did have to go pretty bad," Jen said through the crack of the open door. "I can make it back to bed myself."

"Oh, no, you won't!" Amanda said. "You'll keep your arm right in mine until I say so, you hear me?"

With her assistance, Jen carefully slid under the sheets and found the call button buried under the pillow. She kept a tight grip on it. "Thanks, Amanda. Sorry to bother you just for a potty run."

"No problem at all. That's my job, sweetie."

Amanda returned to the triage desk and took notes on another clipboard. Jen flipped through some TV stations and found Johnny Carson on again. *Boy! Two nights in a row. I'm usually sound out by now!*

Ten minutes later, the shooting pains started in her back and lasted almost a minute. At that point, she rang Amanda.

"Sorry to bug you again," Jen said. "I just had those sharp pains in my back and stomach."

"I'll sit here and keep an eye on you. Fill me in on your day, you know? How you got here, okay?"

It didn't take long for her to bring Amanda up to speed. Before long, both were becoming good friends. They were laughing at how odd the whole day was.

A nurse from the head station marched down the hall into Jen's room. "Hey, you two. It's after midnight. Keep it down!" She stormed back to her desk as they both quietly laughed at her.

"Yeah, I guess we were getting a little loud, Jen. I have to get back to my paperwork. Call if you need me again."

"Yeah, I'll be fine for the rest of the night. Don't worry," Jen tried to assure her. Amanda hadn't made it halfway down the hall when she heard, "Amanda! Amanda, *please!*"

She spun around quickly and bolted down the hall into Jen's doorway. Jen was lying on the bed in a fetal position.

"Lynn, get Dr. Fields up here. *Now!*" Amanda ran over and sat on the bed beside Jen.

"Those pains are back again and stronger this time," Jen said through her clenched teeth and squeezed Amanda's arm. "Ohh," she moaned. After a minute, the pain subsided as she sat up in bed slowly and leaned against the pillow. "What's going on here?"

A smile came across Amanda's face as she leaned over. "You know what? I think you might be going into labor!"

"But I can't be! I'm over a month early!"

Dr. Fields rushed into the room and quizzed both women. He, too, confirmed Amanda's diagnosis.

"Amanda, I think my husband is sleeping downstairs. Can you wake him and bring him up here?"

"Oh, I think by the time he's up here, you'll be on the other side of the hospital in maternity, but he'll find you!"

"I don't believe this. What a day!" Jen griped as Dr. Fields wheeled her toward the birthing section of the maternity ward.

"Don't worry, Ms. Duncan. You'll be fine," Dr. Fields assured her.

"Yes, I know, Sir, I know." Jen tried to relax. She was transported to the other side of the hospital, two floors above. She looked up at Dr. Fields after the elevator door closed. "I have bad elevator dreams, you know. This one is okay, right?" Dr. Fields just smiled as he nodded, agreeing.

Downstairs, Amanda spotted three men in the waiting room slumped in chairs, snoring loudly.

Oh, great! Which one is Bruce? I think that's his name. She surmised a man dressed in green fatigues was Bruce. She tapped him lightly on the shoulder.

"Mr. Duncan, Mr. Duncan?" she whispered to him softly. He opened his eyes widely and startled her. "Are you Bruce?"

He stretched for a moment. "Why, yes. Is there anything wrong? How's Jen doing?"

"She hasn't gotten much sleep. We've had to move her," Amanda informed him.

"Move her? Why? Are you sure she's all right? What's going on?" Bruce asked as he tried to keep pace with Amanda marching toward the elevator. Amanda pushed a button for the fourth floor.

"I thought Jen was on the second floor?" Bruce asked as they both stepped into the elevator.

Amanda looked at Bruce and paused. "She's been moved to maternity! It appears Jen is in labor!" she said with an ear-to-ear smile.

Bruce was floored and just stared at her. "Are you sure about that? She's not due for over a month!"

"Yes, she's being prepped as we speak. It looks like you're going to be a Daddy sooner than you thought!"

Bruce didn't know what to say. He stood motionless for a moment, then jumped into the air spinning around three hundred and sixty degrees. He let out a yell so loud it was heard outside the elevator as it passed each floor.

Bruce smiled. "You're joking, right?"

"Nope. Follow me," Amanda said as the doors opened. He ran out the door first and turned back to her.

"Which way? Which way?" Bruce drilled Amanda. She pointed her finger toward a desk in the center of the room. He ran down the hall and came to a skidding halt as his boots squealed across the waxed tile floor. One of the doctors held out his arm to stop Bruce from sliding further.

"Whoa there, big fella," the doctor told Bruce as he saw Amanda trailing from behind. She gave the doctor a nod. "You must be Mr. Duncan, correct?" Dr. Fields asked him.

"Yes, Sir! Duncan, Bruce Duncan. That's me, all right! How's Jen?" he asked while gasping for air.

"She's fine," Dr. Fields said. "Jen had some contractions, and they're increasing, so it looks like you'll be a father shortly! She's at least four weeks early, right? The baby is being monitored and appears to be fine. Jen went through the ropes today, didn't she? Please come with me, Bruce."

"Yes, Sir! I was out plowing with the Guard when I got her call. It was a real adventure getting here for both of us!" Bruce told the doctor enthusiastically.

They walked into a room at the end of the hall. Jen yelled out in pain as Bruce walked in. He ran over to the bed. She had an intravenous in one arm and many wires hooked up to her other arm, chest, and stomach.

"Are you okay, Jen?"

"Looks like all this excitement today has gotten this little one kicking a bit early." She laughed as she talked. "I'm fine; cross my heart."

"Well, you probably can't cross your heart with all that stuff plugged into you!" Bruce said, trying to lighten the moment.

"Are you ready for this? To be a dad?"

"You bet I am! How about you?"

"After all the testing we went through to get pregnant and being fertile every other month from only one good ovary, I knew it wouldn't be easy. You bet I'm ready to be a mother!" Jen started to tear up.

Dr. Fields handed Bruce a johnny with some scrub pants to put on along with a hairnet. "Here, you'll need these soon enough. Your child is on the way!"

*****

February 29th, 1:30 a.m. Labor proceeded very quickly. This was very fortunate for Jen, being her first birth. A six-pound fifteen-ounce baby boy was born at 1:45 a.m. The doctor told Jen he was a remarkable size, considering many premature babies are born weighing only four or five pounds at eight months along. Bruce and Jen didn't know the baby's sex beforehand and tossed out a few names just two days before the storm.

"How about Paul, Paul Duncan?" asked Jen. "It has a nice ring, doesn't it?"

"I don't know. I just don't know." Bruce went into a deep trance for a few moments. "I've got it!" Bruce exclaimed. "As you said, we had such a hard time getting you pregnant and an unbelievable adventure to get here, right? Just think of the explorers and how tough they had it. They kept their noses to the grindstone like we did. How about Lewis, Lewis Clark Duncan? Remember Lewis and Clark? Those guys who explored our country with nothing but a canoe and leather moccasins?"

Jen thought in silence for a moment and then looked at her sleeping child and Bruce. "Lewis Clark Duncan, I love it!" Jen affirmed the choice. The three stayed side by side until Amanda came in to check on the trio.

"I hate to break up the party, but we have to get that little guy cleaned up and fed. You need some rest too, Jen!" Amanda told her. "You're breastfeeding, right?"

"Yes! I can't think of any other way. I hope my milk comes in with everything that's happened. Will having a premature birth affect that?"

"No, not at all," Amanda reassured her. "But we're going to get some liquids into him, so you have to give that sweet little thing up! Did you decide on a name for him yet?"

Jen handed her precious son to Amanda, holding him carefully as if she was ready to blow the seeds from a dandelion into a Cape Cod spring breeze.

"Lewis Clark Duncan," Bruce said proudly. He repeated it. "Lewis Clark Duncan. I think it fits since he was born in the middle of the largest storm on the Cape in decades! He sure had everybody scrambling within a twenty-mile radius. Six pounds, and fifteen ounces, he came into this world at 1:45 A.M., March 1st, 1972." Bruce proudly affirmed with a smile.

Amanda had a firm grip on Lewis, holding him close and rocking him. So far, he'd made barely a sound. "Well, Bruce," Amanda addressed him. "I think you might have the dates messed up a little. I know you've been plowing snow for almost two days."

He was puzzled and gave her a strange look. "What do you mean I have the dates messed up? I punched in two days ago. Today's the first. Only twenty more days until spring. I'm psyched!"

"I guess it's been a while since you looked at a calendar. Today's the twenty-ninth, the twenty-ninth of February. It's a Leap Year, remember? Every four years, a Leap Year. Sound familiar?" She didn't mean to confuse him, but it certainly seemed to.

Jen and Bruce looked at each other. "Well, I don't know if that's a stroke of luck or what, Jen?" Bruce asked her.

"I guess I don't know either, Bruce!"

"We haven't had a Leap Year baby here in over ten years. Your chances were about one in fifteen hundred. I'd play the Keno numbers tonight if I were you!" Amanda laughed, trying to break the tension. "Lewis has his first checkup with Dr. Fields. I'll be back shortly with some water for both of you." With Lewis in her arms, Amanda left the room for his first appointment.

"I guess being born on a Leap Year doesn't mean anything, does it, Bruce?" Jen asked him.

"No, I guess not. The most important thing is that you and Lewis are okay. You had us going for a while. I'm sure you were more scared than I was, being all by yourself. I forgot Rex was with you. He's probably shredded every pillow in the house by now, being alone all those hours!" Bruce tried to lighten the moment.

"And so, does this mean Lewis only gets to have a birthday – a real birthday, only every four years? What do other parents do?" Jen asked seriously.

"Heck, I don't know, Jen. We both thought the end of March was his due date. We never figured on this. It doesn't matter as long as the two of you are healthy. We can figure out what to do with his birthday later. There's plenty of time for that. You should try to get some sleep. I'll check back with the armory to see if there's anything I can clean up. I don't think Commander Briggs knows I borrowed the loader to get you here. I owe the Fire Department a new bumper for their ambulance that I ripped off, too!" Bruce laughed. "You're right. What a day! Get some sleep, and I'll call you in the morning."

"Bruce," Jen said wearily, "Don't let either of our folks know yet. I don't want to get assaulted by your mother with a thousand questions."

"I know exactly what you mean. I'll stop by the nursery to see Lewis and fill Briggs in before I get the firing squad!" Bruce chuckled as he left the room.

Bruce stopped at the nursery window and saw his new prize possession energetically downing liquid from a bottle. The nurse gave Bruce a thumbs up and an A-OK sign. He walked down the hall, got in the elevator, and pushed the ground floor button. After exiting the front sliding doors of the hospital, he looked up into a streetlight. A fine mist of freezing rain was coming down, glazing cars and everything in sight. Two inches of ice covered the loader he had driven earlier to the hospital. "Not good! Not good at all," Bruce mumbled.

He carefully stepped onto a foothold and grabbed an ice-covered handrail to climb into the loader cab. Dropping into the seat, he turned on an interior light. He opened a suitcase containing the phone and saw he had missed four calls. They were all from the same number, the armory. "I've had it now," he said to himself. "I might as well get it over with."

Bruce dialed the number. Briggs answered on the first ring. "Commander Brigg's, Armory 2."

"Bruce Duncan here. Sorry to be out of touch for so long, Sir. I hope you got my messages earlier."

There was a moment of silence from Brigg's end of the line. "Well, Bruce, I thought high tide took you out to sea! Congratulations! Hookie from Yarmouth Fire filled me in. I've dispatched Cracker and Nolan for the loader. Don't worry. You're on family leave as of now," Briggs informed him.

"Thank you so much, Sir. I'll be right inside it, waiting for them. I'll start the loader so that it will thaw before they arrive. Thanks again, Captain."

"One thing, Bruce," Briggs said. "Hookie told me an ambulance bumper is attached to a chain on your loader. Do you know anything about that?" He laughed.

"Yes, Sir, I do. I owe them a bumper, but it was worth it. I'll fill you in later."

Bruce fired up the loader and turned on its heaters to thaw the big rig. Carefully sliding down, the ice-covered steps, he began to scrape some ice. He took off his hat and tipped it to the black and threatening sky. "Happy Leap Year!" he shouted and raised his fist as he celebrated. "Look out, world, Lewis Clark Duncan is coming for you!" he declared boldly. Cracker and Nolan pulled into the parking lot. They congratulated Bruce and departed quickly.

Bruce went into the lobby waiting room and dropped into the same chair he was in hours before.

This time, he was wearing a smile as he folded his arms and hands across his chest. Once again, he fell fast asleep.

Bruce awoke in the chair to some commotion in the lobby around 8:30 a.m. He stood up and stretched. Walking around the hall corner, Bruce realized it was Jen's and his parents filling the lobby with ear-splitting rhetoric about the new baby. "Our new grandson!" they yelled to one another.

This can't be happening! Bruce thought. *There goes my day of peace and quiet.*

Armfuls of presents and flowers were placed on waiting room chairs. Hugs and congratulations were exchanged.

"We can't believe it! He's over a month early and such a big boy!" Bruce's mother, Fran, said to him. "We got the call from Nolan at 7:30. He said we'd find you here!"

I'm going to kill him, Bruce thought, even though Nolan and Bruce had gone to first grade together and shared two tours of duty in Viet Nam.

Fran reached into a bag and pulled out mimosa cocktails for everyone.

"Nolan called me at 7:15," Kay said smugly.

Fran knew she was saying, "Ha, ha! I knew before you did!"

Bruce could only shake his head. The competition had already started between the newly crowned grandmothers.

"Thanks, Mom, but I'll pass on the drink. I've had quite a day. One of those, and I'd be ready to ride home in a cruiser! I'll have one maybe later on at home, okay?" Everyone raised their glasses in a toast for Jen, Bruce, and Lewis.

Bruce's father, Gunther, led the toast. "Here's to our first grandchild. May he be the first one of many!" This thought drew a "Here, here" from everyone; even a few nurses and onlookers in the lobby cheered.

"He'll be a feisty one," Clint said. "He couldn't even wait another month to come out! He's something special, being born in this storm and all. What time yesterday was he born, Bruce?"

"Well, it seems either Jen or Lewis was a holdout. He was born about six hours ago, at 1:45 a.m. today." Bruce answered.

"Oh, my! No wonder why Jen is so wiped out!" her mother said. "Can we go see her?"

A nurse who was eavesdropping on their conversation piped in. "Sorry, ladies. Visiting hours start at 10:00 a.m. And that goes for the nursery too. All those new babies need their sleep!" she informed everyone, deflating their energetic momentum.

"We can get breakfast in the cafeteria to pass the time," Bruce said. "I'm starving. I haven't had anything to eat since yesterday morning."

Everyone finished their celebratory drinks and started down the hall toward the cafe.

Bruce's father, a retired cop, and detective, scratched his head as they all walked down the corridor. He came to a stop. He never missed a trick. "Bruce, did you say he was born six hours ago?"

"Yeah, Dad, why?" Everyone stopped walking and looked at Gunther, who still seemed puzzled.

"Isn't today the twenty-ninth, the twenty-ninth of February?"

"Yeah, I got fooled by it too. I thought it was March first. It seems we have something extraordinary here, everybody!" Bruce addressed his parents and in-laws in a shaky voice. "We have ourselves a Leap Year, baby!" He tried to sound a little enthusiastic.

"Oh no, a birthday only every four years?" both mothers said in unison.

Gunther stepped in. "I can have the hospital change the time on his birth certificate, Bruce. They owe my squad a few favors."

"Is everyone crazy here?" Bruce asked. "It's just a date! And no, we're not changing the date, Dad! I have the birth certificate already!"

"Well, when are we going to celebrate his next birthday?" Kay asked Bruce.

"I'm not sure, Kay, for crying out loud. He's been here for only six hours! That's not my priority right now!" Bruce was slightly irritated. Everyone started walking toward the cafeteria again, but at a slower pace and in complete silence.

Fran broke the tension in the food line by asking Kay what she bought for the baby. The two enjoyed some light conversation without squabbling as they sat down. Gunther and Clint brought up some news about the Celtics and the need to rebuild the Patriot's football team. Bruce picked at his breakfast and tried to drown out both conversations with his own thoughts of concern. But he knew they were right. When *was* his son's next birthday going to be?

Chapter Four

Bruce and Jen were finally alone in their room. A day of chaos at the hospital with the in-laws, friends, and relatives stopping by the nursery exhausted them.

"Dr. Fields wants Lewis and me to stay one more night to keep an eye on us. He said Lewis is doing excellently. Had I gone full term it would have been a difficult delivery. I can't imagine any more pain than what I went through. It was meant to be, right?"

"I guess so." Bruce paused, "If you believe in that kind of stuff. Luckily, I remembered to call your sister this morning to take Rex for the day. He always likes spending time with his Auntie. I'm due for a shower back home and a good meal. I think it's been about sixty hours since I've cleaned up."

"Yeah, I was going to mention that you're getting a little ripe," she joked. "I was lucky enough to get a hot facecloth around seven this morning. It felt great. We'll be ready for discharge at nine a.m. tomorrow," Jen filled him in. "Hey, wait a minute. How the heck are you getting home? You don't even have a car here."

"I'm one step ahead of you. Cracker left his truck for me when they picked the loader up last night." Bruce leaned over, embracing Jen and his new son with a long hug.

"Both of you are so beautiful," he said with tears. "I'll be here at nine a.m. sharp. See you then."

"Lewis says, Happy Leap Year to you!" Jen teased him.

Bruce turned around at the door and gave them both a smile. Walking down the hall toward the elevator, he saw Amanda at the nurse's station.

"I'm sure you realize by now that both of our families are crazy!"

She laughed. "Oh, I see it all the time. Don't worry. You guys did great. Just take good care of that little spitfire."

"Who, Jen or Lewis?" They both laughed. She leaned over the desk and looked up at Bruce with a serious look on her face.

"You have something exceptional. I've been on this floor for over fifteen years and have never seen a Leap Year baby born. It's a good thing. Don't worry," Amanda tried to reassure Bruce.

"I know. Thanks, Amanda." Bruce then turned to address some nurses behind the desk. "Thank you all. I feel like we're part of a family here."

"We are family, Bruce. We are," Amanda replied.

Bruce shuffled down the hall. He was weary from the pounding his body took from the loader and two nights of half-sleep in a chair. He couldn't wait to get home.

It had warmed up considerably, and the driving ban was lifted. The roads were just wet, but vast piles of snow were everywhere.

It was hard for Bruce to keep his eyes open for the short drive home. He shook his head, sang, and even slapped himself a few times to stay alert. He was happy to see the bay come into view as he rounded the corner onto his street. He was thrilled someone had plowed his driveway and shoveled his walkway. "ITS A BOY!" balloons were tied to his doorway. A note was attached to one of them, "Best wishes – Briggs, Cracker, Nolan, and the Armory Gang."

I don't believe it! Bruce opened the door to the kitchen and couldn't believe his eyes. There wasn't one item out of place. Rex hadn't destroyed anything, not even a pillow or shoe. He knew Jen's sister wouldn't have cleaned up after the dog. Her house was a pigpen.

"Maybe things are looking up after all." He walked to the fridge and pulled out two beers. He opened the first and downed it in one pleasurable gulp. A moment of spontaneous fun came to Bruce as he tried his best Johnny Most voice imitation. Johnny Most was an announcer for the Boston Celtics.

"Havlicek gets the pass on the run from Cowens. He dribbles, he dabbles, fakes left, and fakes right. He shoots off the rim! No, it's in! Cowen's on the rebound! Unbelievable!" He threw the empty beer can over his head into the trash can with his arms raised triumphantly. *We're pretty crazy!* Like I told Amanda. Bruce opened the bathroom door and turned on the shower. He twisted the handle as far as it would go to fill the small room with steam, then eased the cold water and slid into the shower to let it pound over his head. He felt like a million bucks. He couldn't hear the phone ringing in the kitchen over the shower noise. The phone stopped ringing as he turned the water off.

He changed into fresh clothes and went to the fridge for another beer. Bruce then opened the freezer door slowly. *Oooh yeah, come to papa.* He removed a large container of bay scallops and emptied them into the sink to thaw. He reached into the sink cabinet and pulled out a frying pan. Skimming the bottom of the pan with some butter and oil, he added a clove of garlic. He turned the burner on to a low temperature. *Someday, Lewis, you'll be fetching these beauties for me at low tide.* He grinned while stirring the pan.

Bruce looked out the kitchen window and saw his sister-in-law, Meg, pull into the driveway. Rex had his paws on the steering wheel, tickling her face with his wagging tail as she rolled to a stop. Rex always liked to think he was driving the car. Bruce zipped his coat and went out to greet them. The phone started to ring again as the door closed behind him.

Meg opened her car door. Rex jumped up three feet into Bruce's waiting arms.

"Boy, I guess he's glad to see you! I didn't even have to tell him it was time to go. He just ran to the car. "

"Thanks so much for watching the little guy. He didn't bug you too much, did he?"

"He was fine. My kids love spoiling him, but he likes to hump. You do have to break him of that nasty habit. Every time I kneel, he...."

"Yeah, yeah, I know, Meg." Bruce cut her off.

"So, how's Jen? Me and Sherry are going to catch the seven o'clock visiting hour tonight at the hospital."

"You'll be lucky if Jen's awake. She's beat."

"We'll be on the early side. I have something for her and the baby."

"I'll need a straight truck to bring home Jen, Lewis, and the presents!" Bruce told her, snorting. "Thanks again, Meg."

Bruce put Rex down, who proceeded to pee on every fresh snowbank in the driveway. "C'mon, let's go, Rex. I'm freezing my butt off!"

They walked carefully over the ice-covered steps into the house. Bruce gave Rex a cookie from the cabinet. "What are you going to do for this; speak, sit, or rollover? Oh, that's right! I forgot you don't do tricks like a normal dog. You spoiled little brat! Just wait and see what's coming home with Jen!"

Rex tilted his head and cocked his ears as Bruce spoke to him. He just wanted that cookie. The phone rang again. This time, Bruce was in the kitchen and heard it. He threw the cookie into the air for Rex to catch, but it dropped on the floor and broke into twenty pieces.

"Hello?"

"Where the heck have you been?"

"Well, it's nice talking to you also, Sonny!"

Bruce was surprised because his brother rarely called.

"If Mom didn't tell you, I've been at the hospital for fifty hours!" he exaggerated.

"I know, she told me. But I'm afraid I have some bad news," Sonny paused. "Dad's on his way to the hospital."

"What the heck happened, Sonny?" Bruce asked. "I just left him a few hours ago."

"They think he had a heart attack while shoveling the walkway and steps after he got home," Sonny said.

"Who're *they*?" Bruce asked.

"The ambulance guys and," Sonny paused. "The coroner, Bruce. Dad died. I hate to be the one to tell you on such a special day."

Bruce sat down in the kitchen chair. "Dead? You have to be shitting me, right?"

"Wish I was. When Mom looked out the door, Dad was face-down in a snowbank. He was already gone."

"Are you serious? What the heck am I going to tell Jen? She'll probably have a heart attack, too!"

"I'll come and pick you up. Mom's in shock, but her sister's already here."

"Never mind, Sonny. Just stay put at Moms. I'll fill Jen in later or tomorrow morning. She was sound asleep when I left the hospital. I have no idea what I'm going to do!"

"All right, Bruce. I'll see you in a while, but we have to go to the hospital morgue and fill out some papers later."

Bruce slammed the phone in anger and disgust. "What's next? A damn tidal wave?" Bruce yelled. He sat in the kitchen chair and rubbed his head with both hands. "No reason for me to let Jen know yet. She needs the rest," he whispered. Bruce rose from the chair slowly and got on his aching legs. He pulled a coat from the closet. Rex was at his feet, wanting to go with him.

"Oh, come on, let's go. You can go over to Mom's and cheer her up." He pointed his finger and shook it at Rex. "And no humping anyone!"

They both went outside. Bruce started the truck while Rex did his business again on every snowbank. As he was driving to his mother's, Bruce wondered. *Should I or shouldn't I call Jen?* It was dogging him.

He arrived at his parent's house. There were seven cars already in the driveway and street. He could see a few people milling about the front door having a cigarette. He made his way to the porch with Rex scampering along at his side.

It was a good idea to bring Rex. He charged through the door, wagging his tail frantically and licking everyone in sight. Bruce's family always had dogs growing up, but Mom and Dad's retriever died last year. It hurt them deeply not to have another dog around, but it was a lot of work for elderly parents.

Bruce remembered something his father once told him. "A dog doesn't care if you're rich or poor—if you have a nice car or a heap. They don't care if you're black or white but will always guard you in your sleep."

Chapter Five

Bruce walked up the steps and entered the house. He was bombarded with hugs, expressions of sorrow, and congratulations. Nobody knew what to say, and neither did he. He nodded and thanked everyone he passed, going into the house. In the living room, his mother was crying, surrounded by close friends, relatives, and even a few of his father's retired police brothers. It seemed like an eternity to make his way over to the couch to console his mother. He couldn't believe how fast the word spread. He felt awkward being congratulated by some friends and relatives and condolences from others. He sat by his mother and put his arm around her. Rex jumped onto her lap and tried to lick her tears. He knew something was up.

"Mom, I don't know what to say. He seemed fine just hours ago."

"I know, dear, I know. It was too much. It must have been all that heavy snow, the excitement. He's in God's hands now." She started crying loudly again.

"Have you told Jen yet?" she asked in between sobs. The background conversation was so loud that Bruce could barely hear anything she was saying. He leaned closer to her ear and said, "Me and Sonny are going to the hospital later. I'll decide then. We have some plans to make."

Bruce knew his father wanted an old-fashioned Irish wake with his body viewed in their living room, a keg of beer with plenty of food and booze for everyone. He'd say no crying at his wake or funeral, just a big party for everyone. Bruce hugged his mother and got off the couch. His aunt slid right in beside him to comfort Fran.

Bruce went over and gave his brother a handshake. They exchanged soft words between them. A family rift between Bruce and Sonny had torn them apart. Sonny went to Canada to avoid being drafted to Viet Nam.

"How are you holding up, kid?" Sonny asked him.

"I'm totally spent. Let's get out of here, but first, we must go to the hospital and fill out those papers, okay?"

"Not much we can do around here anyway. It looks like everything's under control or maybe out of control." Sonny tried to laugh it off.

Bruce looked into the kitchen and waved to one of Gunther's ex-police buddies, Murph, but he got no response. He had a finger in one ear blocking the chatter and a portable police scanner pinned to his other ear. He motioned for Bruce to come over. As Bruce got closer, Murph gave Bruce a "C'mon, get over here quick!" motion with his hand.

Bruce was about five feet from Murph. "Bruce, you live on Cottage Street, don't you?" Murph still had the scanner glued to his ear.

"Yeah, why? I know my neighbor left a vehicle in the street. They're not going to tow it, are they?" Bruce asked.

"Hell no. You're number 12, right? *The house is on fire!*"

"What the.... What's going on, Murph?" Bruce grabbed Murph by his shirt collar.

"One fire truck on the scene, another's on the way," Murph informed him.

"Aww, shit! I left the house in such a hurry; the stove is on with all that oil frying!" Bruce spun around and knocked everyone out of his way, leaving the house.

He jumped off the landing and ran to his truck. He tried to dive through the door window but bounced off. Murph was right behind him, running to keep up.

"C'mon, we'll take my car. It's faster!" They jumped into Murph's Chevelle. He put a portable flashing strobe on top of his car. "It's a little present I acquired from the force," he said, smiling while pointing up to the strobe. Bruce was out of his mind talking to himself. Murph couldn't figure out what Bruce was saying.

"C'mon, Murph. Put the pedal to this fucking thing!" Bruce pleaded. They made it to Cottage Street quickly. It was blocked off by three fire trucks. "I don't believe this," Bruce moaned.

Murph shifted the car into park and hit the e-brake simultaneously. It spun sideways and slammed into a snowbank. Bruce ran around the fire trucks but couldn't see any smoke coming from his house. He dashed around back and saw four or five firefighters at his door.

"What's going on here, Ed? What the hell did I do? Is there any damage?" Bruce knew one of the firemen.

"It seems some jackass left a big pan of oil cooking away on the stove, and it ignited! The fire spread to some drapes, a couple of towels, and a cabinet. It was a quick and easy out for us. Luckily, your neighbor spotted the smoke coming from the kitchen window. She saved your house from going up, Bruce. There's just some minor smoke and water damage."

"I love you guys!" Bruce yelled to the firefighters as they headed back to their trucks. "You too, Lois!" She was hanging from her second-story window, giving Bruce the naughty sign with her pointer fingers.

Murph put his arm on Bruce's shoulder. "Well, kid, look at the bright side."

"And what bright side would *that* be?" Bruce asked sarcastically.

"It's only twenty days until spring. This snow will probably be gone by then."

"I don't think so, Murph. It looks like you didn't look at a calendar today, either. It's the twenty-ninth, February twenty-fucking-ninth, a Leap Year."

"Well, you don't have to get in a huff about it, Bruce!"

"Let's see. My son was born a month early, my father died, and I almost burned my house down. I think my head is about to explode! Jen doesn't even know about Dad yet, or that I'm an arsonist!"

"Calm down, Bruce, calm down. I'll get the guys over here, and we'll clean this mess up. Let's go back to Fran's and have one for Gunther, maybe two." Murph smiled and shoved him toward the car. The last fire truck pulled out.

"Yeah, I could use a good stiff belt. Too bad all those scallops got wrecked in the sink, isn't it, Murph?"

"There's plenty more where those babies came from, pal. I'll take you to a spot where me and your dad used to go scalloping—a place nobody knows. Every scallop is the size of a golf ball! C'mon, let's get out of here."

Bruce and Murph drove back to Fran's house. The crowd had dwindled to five people. Bruce was badgered by many questions about the house fire from everyone. He tried to hold his patience until he heard his mother's sister, Aunt Rita, on the phone in the dining room.

"Uh, hi. Yes, room 438, please. Maternity."

This struck him as pretty odd. He listened in on his aunt's conversation. "Oh, she's sleeping? Well, can you tell her...."

Bruce knew what she was up to and ripped the phone cord from the wall. Rita was a busy bee, gossip queen, from seven a.m. to eight p.m. every day.

"Look, Rita, don't make this day any harder than it already is. I'll take care of this! I don't need you to tell Jen anything, got it?"

"I just thought," Rita mumbled.

"I know. Please stay here with Mom tonight. Sonny and me are leaving for the hospital."

"Okay, okay. Say hi to – what's his name?"

"Lewis Clark, Lewis Clark Duncan."

Rita and Fran looked at Bruce. "That's beautiful," Rita said, nodding. "You be on your way." Both women gave Bruce and Sonny hugs as they walked toward the door.

"Can Rex keep you company tonight, Mom?" Bruce added as a parting thought.

"We'd love to have him, dear," Fran told her son. "We don't have any dog food, though."

"He'll eat what you eat, just no chocolate. And don't kneel in front of him either!" Bruce added. Fran and Rita gave matching, puzzled looks as Bruce and Sonny left.

"What do you suppose he meant by that?" Fran asked her sister.

"I haven't the faintest," Rita replied. "Let's dig out some old pictures of you and Gunther for a memorial poster, okay?"

"You're a good sister. Thanks, Rita."

Bruce walked over to his truck and threw Sonny the keys. "Heads up, you're driving. I'm exhausted. I'm not taking any chances."

"You're not getting paranoid on me now, are you?" Sonny laughed.

"Man, I don't know what else this day holds for me."

"I've gone through hell today, too, don't forget!" Sonny said.

"Sorry, it's been very emotional having my son born prematurely and Dad dying on the same day."

"I know what you mean. Don't worry."

It was a quick ride to the hospital. Ironically, Sonny pulled into the same spot Bruce had pulled out of hours ago. "Look at this place. It's jam-packed. There must be many people getting operated on or kids being born."

"Yeah, and dying too," Bruce said. "I don't think I'd want an operation on a Leap Year. They'd probably try to fix the wrong leg and cut it off! A nurse told me Lewis was the first Leap Year baby born here in over fifteen years. At this point, I'm voting in favor of that not being a good thing."

"Oh, here you go again with that crazy talk. Today could have happened to anyone, Bruce. Hey, I lost a father, too!"

"I know, I know. I'm sorry. No more of that crazy talk, I promise."

They walked into the lobby and went to the front desk.

"Look, Bruce, I'll take care of the paperwork on Dad. You've got your hands full with Jen. I don't even know if we can see him yet. I'll take a cab back to Mom's and spend the night with the two hens. They'll like that."

"They sure will, Sonny. I'll call you in the morning." The two brothers hugged for a moment. Bruce looked at him and said, "Hey, Sonny, I'm glad we're talking again."

"Me too, Bruce. I'll see you tomorrow."

Bruce walked down the hall to the elevator. Although it was well beyond visiting hours, the head nurse did not object to a visit after being informed about his day. His mind was so frazzled that he didn't know how to tell Jen the bad news. He entered the room to find Jen wide awake in bed.

"What the heck are you doing here, Bruce? I thought you went home?" Bruce said nothing but sat on the bed and took her hand.

"How's Lewis?" he asked.

"I just finished feeding him. He's in the nursery. Bruce, what's going on?"

"After my folks left here today, Gunther was shoveling the walkway. They think he had a heart attack."

"They think? Well, is he in here? Is he okay?"

"He didn't make it, Jen. Gunther is in the morgue. He died instantly."

"Oh my, God, Bruce!" Jen grabbed him and started crying. "How's Fran taking it?"

"Tough, very tough. We all knew Gunther had a bad heart, but he just got a clean bill last month. But that's not all." Bruce paused.

"What the heck else happened?"

Bruce started shaking his head back and forth. "I almost burned the house down."

"Our house? You *what*?"

"Yep."

"How the...?"

"When I got the call from Sonny about Dad, I forgot to shut the stove off. It's not too bad. We'll be able to....."

"Our house?" Jen interrupted and collapsed onto the pillow. "You burned our house down?"

"No, no, just a little damage in the kitchen."

"I don't believe this! We're supposed to bring Lewis home tomorrow!"

"We'll still be able to. Murph and the guys are cleaning it up tonight. We just need a new stove and cabinet."

"Just a new stove and cabinet? What about the?"

"Look, Jen." Bruce interrupted her this time. "I haven't had anything to eat in over forty-eight hours. I've gotten about four hours of sleep the past two nights. I'm doing the best I can!"

She thought for a moment, "I'm sorry. Maybe the nurse could bring you something."

"Yeah, how about a twelve-pack for us?" Bruce laughed. "Let me in."

"What?"

"Let me in the bed. I'm not moving for the rest of the night. Okay?"

"You think the nurse will mind?"

"I don't care what she says. Move over. I have to get out of these boots," Bruce told her.

Jen hugged Bruce and took a deep breath. "You know, Bruce, it's kind of weird, isn't it?"

"What are you talking about?"

"Today, it seems one spirit came into this world and another one left, know what I mean?"

"Yeah, sort of. It's kind of like a trade-off. It'll be a long time before we figure this day out. Okay, let's get some sleep. G'night, hon."

They both fell asleep quickly. The nurse looked in and saw Bruce on the bed with Jen. She smiled. *Well, she has about three hours until that little bugger wakes her up again!* She shut the light off and closed the door.

Lewis slept very well that night. The nurse checked on him every ten minutes, which is standard procedure for a preemie. Even Lewis was tired from his entry into this crazy new world. Jen and Bruce got a well-deserved four-hour rest before the nurse brought Lewis in for a feeding.

"Time to wake up, Mom!" The nurse said as she handed Lewis to her carefully. Bruce awoke and stretched.

"Where the heck am I?" Bruce said when he saw the nurse standing over him. "Oh yeah, phew! What a weird dream I was having."

"He slept for over four hours. That's great, Jen. How do you feel?" the nurse asked her.

"Great! It won't be long before we're out of here, right?"

"That's right. Dr. Fields will be in to check on the two of you in about an hour for discharge. You'll be home soon."

"Thanks to me," Bruce said, laughing, "we have a few problems to take care of when we get there."

Dr. Fields arrived in the room an hour later and was very pleased with Lewis and Jen's condition. He looked at their charts and extended a hand to congratulate Bruce, sitting in a chair.

"My congratulations to you and also my condolences. It seems you've hit all the highs and lows between today and yesterday, Bruce."

"Yes, Sir. It was quite a day. It *is* finally March first, isn't it?"

"Yes, it is," he laughed. "I don't blame you for wanting yesterday to end." Dr. Fields thought for a moment. "I met your father a few times here in the hospital. Usually, he brought someone in for an emergency or the like. He was a very kind and generous man."

"Thanks. He sure was. There will be a small service at Mom's place, and if you'd like, I'll keep you posted."

"Thanks, Bruce. I'd like that. In the meantime, you take special care of Jen and your new son. I have a feeling he's going to be a handful!"

"Well, thanks, Dr. Fields!" Jen laughed.

"Take care now, and don't forget the follow-up next week with your doctor in Yarmouth, Jen. He's been briefed about your adventure," Dr. Fields told her.

"We'll be there. Thank you, Dr. Fields, and Lewis also thanks you." She held Lewis's hand up, motioning a goodbye wave.

Dr. Fields laughed and entered another patient's room across the hall.

"Come on, Jen. Let's get out of this place. We can check out my 'remodeling job' in the kitchen."

They bundled Lewis in a fortress of blankets and went to the lobby. Amanda was behind the desk. Jen walked around the counter, leaned over, and gave her a big squeeze.

"I couldn't have done it without you, Amanda. I don't know what to say."

"Just seeing the three of you together is why I'm here. You're all very special. If you guys have another one, don't be so dramatic about it!" All the nurses at the desk and Jen broke into giggles.

Bruce matched Jen's hug for Amanda. The sun's reflection from a blanket of fresh snow blinded them as they left the building."

"Wow, I can't even see!" Bruce declared. "But isn't it good to finally see a clear blue sky, Jen?"

"It's a brand-new day, Bruce," she said as he opened the truck door for her. "Let's stop at Fran's with Lewis and perk her up. I'm sure she could use it."

"Sounds good. We all could use a little cheer and some grub. We have to pick up Rex, too."

"Rex, who?" Jen joked.

Bruce looked back toward the hospital. "I hope it's a long time before we're here again, know what I mean?"

"Sure do, Bruce. I sure do."

Luckily, it was an uneventful ride to Fran's house. She was overwhelmed by their unexpected visit. Rita and Sonny were still there. All enjoyed an excellent breakfast. Funeral plans were starting to take shape. Sonny had been on the phone with the pastor and a funeral home all morning.

A good old-fashioned Irish wake was held two days later in Fran's home with a celebration of Gunther's life. Lots of good food, crying, and laughing filled every room of the small, ocean-weathered bungalow. Tears and toasts were shared for Gunther and Lewis. One of the photos on the memorial poster at Fran's house was Gunther with a grin. He was holding his new grandson eight hours after his birth and just hours before his passing.

Gunther was such a special officer that even a few ex-cons on parole stopped by Fran's house to pay their respects. Six police cars and several unmarked Chevy Impalas with blacked-out windows lined the street.

There was a full military funeral with an honor guard escort to the cemetery. The procession stretched for over a mile. They say you can tell how many friends a man has after he dies. Judging from the number of people there, he had lots of friends. Gunther always said he wanted a small funeral. He didn't get his wish.

Chapter Six

Jen and Bruce settled into their house quickly after the fire. Murph replaced the burnt-up kitchen stove and cabinet before they got home from the hospital. A new countertop was on order. Bruce repainted the kitchen ceiling and a wall. Deep down, he knew it was his fault for leaving the stove on.

They decorated Lewis's room to the hilt. New toys and gifts cluttered every inch of floor space in the small upstairs bedroom. Rex developed an immediate fondness for Lewis. That alone was quite a relief for Bruce and Jen. They heard too many horror stories about jealous pets when a new baby entered their domain. Bruce moved Rex's dog bed under the crib to sleep at night below Lewis and keep watch. He listened with sharp ears for every move Lewis made. When distressed, Rex sprinted into their bedroom and jumped on the bed with a flying leap to awaken them.

Jen loved pampering Lewis and Rex. During Lewis's feeding times, Rex also got a treat. When Lewis needed a diaper change, it was time for Rex to go outside and do his business, too. Jen always praised him as he trotted in through the kitchen door. If she played with Lewis, Rex would be fetching his ball, also.

Bruce settled back into his tedious accounting job, which he dreaded daily. The same cubicle, the same people, and the same bad jokes at the coffee pot. He loved being with the guys at the armory, and his bad attitude at work started to show. The lead supervisor called Bruce into his office in late March.

"Sit down, Bruce. Sit down, please," Dave said. "Bruce, co-workers have noticed you've had a pretty short fuse lately. Anything you want to fill me in on?"

"I guess this whole thing with my Dad passing, almost burning the house down, and Lewis coming all at the same time has finally caught up with me," Bruce admitted to Dave.

"I know, Bruce. I can't say I've known that happened to a person in one day without losing it," Dave commented. "I wish I could give you some time off, but this is our busiest time of the year. There are only three weeks before tax filing, and all our clients are counting on us, Bruce."

"Oh, I know, I know. Sorry I've been out of it."

"Look, between you and me," Dave leaned over the desk to Bruce and smiled, "I'll give you two weeks off after April fifteenth. I know we can pay you at least one of those weeks and maybe give you a bonus to get through the second week."

Bruce's face lit up. "I thought I was getting fired when I came in here!" They both laughed. "I'll get my act together and apologize to the girls."

"Heck no, they didn't want me to say anything to you. I've noticed your attitude myself. There are only four of us in this office. Everyone's important. Remember that, okay?"

"You got it, Dave. No more, Mr. Grumpy, I promise."

Bruce left Dave's office unsettled and tried to make the best of it. Sitting at his desk, he looked at a massive box of files and paperwork he had to examine. "Remember, no more, Mr. Grumpy," he whispered, shaking his head.

On the way to work the following day, Bruce stopped at a local Dunkin' Donuts and picked up an assortment of donuts, rolls, and coffee for everyone. Attempting to open the office door with both hands full, his co-worker saw him coming and opened it up.

"Whoa, look at this, Gail," Nikki declared, looking at him. "Did you get lucky at the Keno parlor last night?"

"Yeah, funny, Nikki. It's just a little something for everyone. We've got a long pull until the fifteenth. A little caffeine won't hurt," Bruce told the two girls. "It's your turn tomorrow."

"I knew there was a catch!" Gail said.

Bruce tried to knuckle down and be productive at work, but it never happened. He couldn't wait for that time off in April. He genuinely lost his edge at work, and everyone observed a change in him, not for the better either.

Jen, on the other hand, was on cloud nine. Her mornings were spent snuggling and spoiling Lewis. Kay and Fran came over daily with another gift for Lewis. Warm spring days were rare on the Cape, so she took Lewis for long walks in the stroller every afternoon on the beach whenever possible. Conscious of her figure, she wanted to get in bikini form by June. Rex felt he was doing his part on walks by pulling the stroller along while tied by his chain.

The April fifteenth vacation for Bruce couldn't have come at a better time. Everyone in the office was glad to have him take a break. On the way home, he stopped at the liquor store for a case of beer and some wine for Jen. He went to a butcher shop and bought two of the finest steaks in the market and a bouquet for Jen. Bruce pulled his truck into the dooryard of his house. Jen was in a rocker on the tiny front porch with Lewis and Rex. Bruce stepped out of the truck with the wine and flowers and walked up the steps slowly.

"Well, well! Are you fixing to get lucky tonight, Mr. Duncan?"

"That might be on my mind," he laughed. Bruce leaned over the chair and gave her and Lewis a pair of kisses.

"I probably shouldn't have any of this wine while I'm still breastfeeding, but I guess one glass won't hurt, will it?"

"Heck, my mother had three martinis every day while carrying me, and I came out okay, didn't I?" He paused. "Better not answer that!" They both laughed.

"Okay, just a small glass," Jen said.

Bruce returned to the truck for the case of beer.

"Oh sure, buttering me up with a glass of wine so you can have a few?"

"I have to get this vacation off on a right start, you know? A little wine, cold beer, some flowers for my beautiful wife, a nice steak, and then…."

"Then what?" She moaned into his ear.

"An early bedtime for Lewis, ha!" Bruce said loudly enough to startle both Lewis and Rex. He paused and looked directly at her. "I am absolutely whipped, Jen. I never want to see another spreadsheet, debit, or credit. I feel useless," he said seriously.

"Maybe you're having one of those mid-life crises – except you're only thirty-three."

"Yeah, four years of pencil-pushing is a little hard for me to take after two tours in Nam, you know?"

"Are you serious? You have it made at the office! No stress at all. That's what your doctor told you. No stress! Remember?" Jen reprimanded him.

"I miss the guys, the camaraderie. Why do you think I hang out at the armory so much? It's the machines, the tool room, and the smell of motor oil on the floor!" Bruce got excited.

Jen took it all in for a moment and smiled as she rose from her rocker. "Sit down," she said, handing Lewis to him. She broke the case of beer open and handed him a cold one. Jen sat down on the step and looked up at Bruce, then Lewis. "He has your big blue eyes, hands, and goofy feet." They both laughed.

"Sorry for ragging on you. I haven't even been through the door and into the house yet. I'll tell you what. Not one more complaint out of me for the next two weeks, not one more. Is it a deal?" Bruce smiled.

"Well, after my wine and our dinner tonight, I might make you suffer a little bit upstairs after Lewis falls asleep, know what I mean?" Jen whispered.

"Yeah, that sure doesn't sound like any debit or credit, I know! Let's go inside. That cool wind is starting to roll in from the sound. It might be a good night to leave our windows open for the first time this spring and listen to the waves."

"Like we used to in your sixty-five Mustang at Fins Landing?"

"You called it! Just like that."

They went inside and had a wonderful evening with Lewis, Rex, and each other. They found out together that after Lewis was born, they got disconnected. With all that happened, they each needed some passion.

Chapter Seven

The weather couldn't have been better. Bruce and Jen spent leisurely breakfasts every morning on the porch during the first week and a half of vacation. Lewis was shown every fishing hole and crabbing flat in a ten-mile radius. Bruce even broke out their Boston Whaler for a cruise on the Parker and Bass Rivers. They tried some fishing but didn't have any luck. It was too early for any bluefish or striper runs. Both mothers-in-law were given a stay-clear order for two weeks, which neither could understand; they still dropped by daily.

By the middle of the second week, Bruce was a little itchy and felt cooped up. "Hey, hon," Bruce yelled to Jen from downstairs. "Where are you?"

"Changing Lewis, it seems those strained peas don't agree with him much!" she answered from the upstairs bathroom. Bruce put his coat on. "Where are you going?" Jen asked.

"I hope you don't mind, but I just want to get out of here for a bit. Briggs called from the armory. The state finally came through with that last paycheck for plowing during the big storm."

"That's great. We can use the money. Don't forget we have that six-week check-up for Lewis tomorrow, just in case they try to rope you in for something." Jen walked over to Bruce for a kiss. He nodded 'yes, dear' to her instructions.

"See you, tiger," he said to Lewis and turned to kiss Jen. "You too, hon. I won't be long."

Bruce went out the side door and threw a hood over his head. It seemed the stretch of spring weather was quickly ending.

Bruce took the shore route to the armory and thought it would be nice to get his head on straight and be grounded again. The smell of a raw ocean at low tide, a seagull's call, worn docks, and the sight of tattered fishing boats always reminded him why he lived on Cape Cod.

He wheeled his truck into the parking lot of the old brick armory. Bruce couldn't wait to see the friends he had served with in Viet Nam. Upon passing through the door, he was greeted by his old pals with hugs and many questions about Lewis, his lifestyle change, and some typical ribbing of still being a pencil pusher at the office.

"Aw, come on, guys, it's not that bad. It pays the bills. That's about it," Bruce said humbly.

"Yeah, sure, Bruce," Nolan stepped in. "I've seen those two young hotties you work with. How old are they? Twenty-two? I saw them at Chill's Clam Shack last week, tying one on!"

"Yeah, believe me, they're no angels. Don't get any ideas, you old bastard! They have a stable full of stallions waiting for a date."

"I guess that puts me out of the running!" Nolan howled as they laughed into tears.

"Hey, where's Briggs? I hear he's got a check for me," Bruce asked Nolan.

"He's in his office. Where else? Better knock. You might wake him up."

"All right. Catch you guys later. How about a beer Friday night at Chills? I'm buying. Bring your ladies too. I have a sitter for the night, Jen's mom."

"How old is she? Single?" Nolan laughed.

"Yeah, you wish! Later, guys," Bruce added. He made his way around the corner to Briggs' office. Sure enough, the TV was on. Briggs was sound asleep with his feet perched on the desk.

Bruce knocked on the door.

"Oh, hi, Bruce. I guess my eyes closed for a second. Come on in and sit down. Here, let me shut that TV off." Briggs got up from his chair and stretched. "Sometimes this place is so boring. I just can't stand it."

"I know what you mean, Sir,"

"Bruce, enough of this *Sir* routine. You've been here for two years. It's Ralph from now on, okay?"

"Just seems kind of odd, Ralph." Bruce hesitated. "So, the checks came in from the state?"

Briggs handed Bruce an envelope. "Unfortunately, not much for you, Bruce. You worked only twenty-four hours until all hell broke loose on ya."

Bruce laughed. "Don't worry. It'll come in real handy with three mouths to feed."

"There is something else I'd like to discuss with you, Bruce." Briggs got serious for a moment.

"I told you I'd replace that bumper I destroyed on the ambulance, didn't I?" Bruce replied.

"No, no, Bruce, that's not it at all. Our station here is going to be…" Bruce looked at him with worry, fearing the station would close. "Bruce, we're expanding our unit." Briggs handed him a folder. "This is a list of all the job opportunities here and at Otis Air Force Base. We'd like you to come on board full-time."

"What? Let me clean my ears out!"

"That's right, Bruce. There are six open positions between here and Otis, plus I'm retiring in eight months. You have first dibs."

Bruce leaned over and looked through the folder. Each job had a printout of salary, full benefits, and duties. He was flabbergasted.

"Well, I know my decision, Sir. Sorry, but I have to fill Jen in first, okay?"

"Bruce, I hate to pressure you, but I need your decision by noon tomorrow."

"In that case," Bruce thought a moment, "Ralph, I'm in!" Bruce smiled as they both got up and shook hands. Little did Bruce know, but all of his buddies watched through a large window divider. They cheered, clapped, and banged on the office window in celebration.

Bruce left the office and got mobbed by his friends. He felt good. No, he felt great! Something was finally going his way. He didn't even have a chance to feel this good when Lewis was born. He couldn't wait to tell Jen.

She took the news with much enthusiasm. They had excellent health care coverage and a college reimbursement plan for Bruce. Jen was excited Bruce wouldn't be confined to a cramped office anymore. He couldn't wait to give notice to his employer the following morning.

Dave took the news very well. He knew Bruce was growing very unhappy at his job. Bruce returned to work and tied up the tax extensions he was working on. He was looking forward to walking out that office door one last time and starting his new job at the armory.

Thursday afternoon, Bruce and Jen had an appointment with Lewis's doctor in Yarmouth. Although it was only six weeks from his birth, Dr. Rooney kept a close eye on him. This was his second trip to the doctor. Bruce, Jen, Lewis, and Rex squeezed into the truck for a ride across town.

Bruce and Jen checked in with the nurse at the front desk and took a seat for a few minutes before they were called in.

"Dr. Rooney will see you and Lewis now," the nurse told Jen.

"Okay, if I go in, too?" Bruce asked. "I missed the first one."

"Of course, Bruce. Daddies are always welcome." She smiled at him as he went into the exam room with Jen. They took a seat. She was bouncing Lewis on her lap when the doctor walked in.

"Hi, Jen. Bruce, I haven't seen you since the pre-natal classes back in December, right?" Dr. Rooney asked him.

"Yes, that's right, Dr. Rooney. It seems Lewis had other things on his mind and wanted to check out a little early, I guess."

"He was doing great three weeks ago when I saw him, and I don't expect anything has changed. Jen, can you put him on the scale?" Dr. Rooney asked.

She took his coat and mittens off, then put him on the scale.

"Whoa, what are you feeding this little guy, spinach and seaweed?"

"No, just breast milk with some veggies a couple of times a day. He does have quite an appetite," she told the doctor.

"Veggies already? Let me take a look at his chart." The doctor sat down, scanning the first page. "Let's see, six pounds fifteen ounces when born, eight pounds ten ounces at three weeks, and now he's...." The doctor paused, scratched his head, and looked at them. "Twelve pounds at six weeks. I've never seen a preemie recover so fast!"

"Is that a good thing?" asked Bruce.

"Bruce, a baby's weight usually doesn't double until they're about four months old. Lewis is almost double his birth weight in half the time."

"Is that something we should be concerned about, Dr. Rooney?" Jen asked.

"We have to keep an eye on it, but it's probably something Mother Nature intended and nothing to be concerned with. The Patriots could use some big linebackers!" Dr. Rooney joked and relieved them of any worries. "We'll see him again in a month, okay? I'm sure he'll be just fine."

"Thank you, Dr. Rooney," Bruce said. "One month – the middle of May, right?"

"I believe so. By then, the blues and stripers will be running around the tip of Chatham and Monomoy. Do you take Lewis fishing, Bruce?"

"Oh, you bet. We're going to get Lewis broken in. He'll have sea legs before long!"

"I don't doubt it!" Dr. Rooney replied. "You two take care. See you in a month." Dr. Rooney exited the room and went into his office. Jen put Lewis's coat and mittens back on. As they walked by Dr. Rooney's office, she saw him speaking into a dictating microphone. Tempted as she was to listen in, she continued down the hall with Lewis wrapped up in his blanket.

They returned to the truck and found Rex asleep, basking on the dashboard in the warm spring sunshine.

Bruce opened the door for Jen, "Fine, watchdog you are!" He scared the crap out of Rex. "Come on out here and take a leak." He jumped out and went to a corner in the parking lot. Jen fastened the middle seatbelt around the bassinet. Rex jumped in and managed to jam between Lewis and Jen. Rex spent a few minutes sniffing and investigating Lewis's new smells from the doctor's office.

"It's okay, Rex," Jen assured him. "In a couple of weeks, he's going to be bigger than you!" Rex just tilted his head at Jen.

"You think he's overeating, Jen?" Bruce asked her. "You heard what the doctor said."

"Lewis doesn't cry much and barely whimpers when he's hungry. He's probably just making up for being born early. I'm not going to let him get all worked up, you know?"

"You've done great so far, hon. And I won't be crabby anymore when I start the new job, too, so I'll be able to help much more," Bruce tried to assure Jen.

"You've done fine so far, dear. Don't worry about it."

Bruce had one more week to finish some projects and late tax extensions in his office. Dave, Nikki, and Gail had a small party on Friday. When he walked out the door for the last time, he felt a massive burden had been lifted. Although Dave had been good to him, that job wasn't meant for Bruce. Anticipating his new career at the armory on Monday, he knew he wouldn't sleep all weekend.

*****

Bruce had his choice of jobs offered by Briggs. He chose the mechanic position. It would involve travel between the armory, Otis, Hanscom Field, and Westover Air Reserve in Chicopee. He received full diesel and hydraulic mechanics training for the first two months. Most of the equipment at the armory was left-over bones from the sixties and needed months of backlog maintenance. Bruce was diligent about tearing down any machine for repair in the garage. He roped off the area where he was working; no one dared enter his workspace.

As the next month passed, Jen started to notice some concerning behavior with Lewis. It was now the middle of May, and she had an appointment on the twenty-sixth. His inability to focus both eyes on moving objects around him worried her. He loved to throw toys from his crib but couldn't locate things very quickly unless by touch. She thought there was probably some logical explanation for this behavior and knew his appointment was the following week.

Jen alerted Bruce, and he became worried as well. He noticed Lewis's eyes didn't follow toys when presented to him or his animal mobile above his crib. Bruce wanted to go with Jen for the doctor's appointment the next day, but a critical work issue kept him away.

Bruce took his truck to work the day of the appointment. Jen dreaded asking her mother for a ride, knowing the barrage of questions she would ask. Luckily, Jen's sister, Meg, was available to give her a lift.

Meg was also worried after Jen filled her in on the way to the doctor's office. They arrived ten minutes before the appointment and checked in. Meg waited in the lobby during the exam.

Dr. Rooney entered the room with his folder of charts and sat on the table beside Jen and Lewis.

"Hello, Jen. How's our little – or should I say big fullback, doing?" Dr. Rooney asked her.

"I know he's still gaining weight. I can barely pick him up sometimes!" she replied.

"Here, let's get him on the scale again. Hmmm, sixteen pounds. No question, he's going to a big one! I haven't heard a peep from him since he's been here. Is he always this good?"

"He's always like this, Doctor Rooney. He hardly ever makes a sound. I have noticed something, though."

"What's that, Jen?"

"His eyes don't seem to follow me or focus on anything. Is that normal?" she asked.

"Normal in your son's development doesn't apply here, Jen. He was born over a month early. Sometimes a baby's eyesight isn't developed until at least six months. Lewis is already a month behind the eight-ball. At just three months, he may be seeing just shapes and colors. Keep a close watch for any excessive eye rubbing or blinking. That may indicate a problem. We can't do positive eye testing until he's six months old. I'm sure he'll grow into using his eyes just fine. Does anyone in either family have a history of eye disease?"

"No, not on my side. I'm not sure about Bruce's family. I'll ask him tonight," Jen replied. "Sometimes at night, when Lewis gets up and whimpers, I find him sitting there looking at the wall with a blank stare," Jen informed Dr. Rooney.

"What? He's sitting there?" Dr. Rooney looked at his folder and added some more notes. "Jen, most babies don't sit up alone until they're six months old. Are you sure?"

"I'm not seeing things, and I only had three glasses of wine in a year," she laughed. "It seems when he hears me coming down the hall, he stops blabbing," she added.

"Jen, come six months, we'll give him a complete eye exam and make sure everything is all right," Dr. Rooney told her. "I'll take a quick look at his eyes now, okay?" Dr. Rooney grabbed a small penlight and shone it into Lewis's left eye, then right. "They are nice and clear, Jen. His eyes act reflexively to the light. That's a good sign. We'll give him a complete eye exam at six months."

"Whatever you think is best," she said reluctantly. Meanwhile, Lewis was thrilled, gurgling and rolling around on the table. "Come on, you big ape," she said while putting his little Red Sox jacket on.

"Jen, let's see him in six weeks, okay? I'd feel better if we caught any issues early. Make an appointment with Peggy, and I'll see the two of you then."

Jen picked Lewis and his diaper bag up. "Thanks. See you then, Dr. Rooney." She left the exam room and went to the check-out desk. Dr. Rooney stayed behind, sitting on the edge of the table. He opened the folder and added a few more notes to his quickly growing file on Lewis, scratching his head again.

Humph, barely three months old and sitting up? What the heck is she feeding that bruiser?

Chapter Eight

Bruce settled into his new job very quickly. He blocked off a place in the garage as a makeshift office and used a portable chalkboard to create schedules for vehicle teardowns. The fleet of aging equipment at the armory required a lot of maintenance. It would take a month to go over one piece of machinery with its many grease fittings, oils, and filters to change. Time flew by every day. It wasn't like his previous job, where every minute dragged on. Some days, he swore the clock ticked backward there.

Jen was also enjoying her time with Lewis. It was June, and the flowers blossomed in their yard. Birds arrived back on the Cape in droves, nesting in every sunny bush or tree that wasn't already claimed. Lewis didn't have to get bundled up so tight that he couldn't move. The warm, salt air rolling off nearby beaches invigorated Jen while she took her daily walks with Lewis neatly tucked inside his stroller.

Bruce's mother, Fran, and Jen's mother, Kay, often stopped by to inform Jen of any neighborhood gossip, tips on child-rearing, and their thoughts on the phenomenon of postpartum depression. Kay and Fran were particularly good at turning any lively conversation into doom and gloom, causing Jen to frown.

As the doctor's appointment for Lewis approached, Jen observed Lewis's eye development. She noted that he didn't make eye contact and seemed to be blinking more. He occasionally rubbed his eyes but didn't notice this tendency before the last appointment. He couldn't follow a moving object very well. His other senses seemed fine, but she hoped his eye concerns would have disappeared by this checkup. As the appointment neared, there wasn't any improvement in his eyes. Jen and Bruce were both keenly aware of this.

Jen dropped Bruce off at work the day of Lewis's checkup. They still had only one vehicle.

"Now, call me as soon as you know anything, okay?" Bruce asked Jen as he started to get out of the truck.

"Don't worry, hon. I'm sure he'll be fine. I'll give you a call as soon as I get home."

Bruce tightened the seat belt around Lewis's bassinet before closing the truck door. He poked and tickled Lewis, making him laugh. "Talk to you later. Love you both!"

Jen pulled out of the armory and drove toward her doctor's office in Yarmouth. It was a quick ride to Dr. Rooney's. As she pulled into the parking lot, she couldn't help but notice there was only one car there.

This is odd, she thought. There are usually at least five or six cars here. She unbuckled Lewis from the seat and grabbed hold of him. As she got closer to the door, she saw a sign taped to the glass. It read, "Office Closed Due to Accident." She could see a receptionist sitting behind her desk on the phone. Jen pushed the door open and stood beside the counter, listening to a phone conversation Peggy was intently having.

"Yes, it's a broken leg... eight weeks? Yes, ma'am, I understand."

She hung up and turned to Jen, who was anxiously waiting.

"Dr. Rooney will be out for at least eight weeks, Jen. His new partner in Hyannis will be taking all of his appointments."

"Oh, great, Hyannis?" Jen said, getting a dirty look from her.

The phone rang again. "Dr. Rooney's office, please hold."

"What's going on, Peggy?" Jen asked. "What's with this broken leg?"

"I tried calling, but you must have already left."

"Yeah, we have only one vehicle, so I have to give Bruce a ride to the armory almost every day. What happened?"

"It seems like the clumsy Dr. Rooney slipped and fell while unloading his boat from the trailer last night, and his leg got in the way. He snapped it in two places. I didn't even find out until this morning. It's total mayhem here! Hold on, okay?" Peggy motioned to Jen with her finger.

"Thank you for holding," Peggy said into the phone. Jen walked out the door slowly with Lewis in total bewilderment.

"I don't believe this," Jen said to Lewis. "What are we going to do with you?"

Peggy opened the door from the office. "Jen, please take this card. It's the doctor in Hyannis who's taking all of our appointments. I'll get your folder ready later today for him."

"Thanks so much, Peggy. I didn't mean to get short with you. I don't know what I would do without you all these past months!" Jen said as Peggy handed her a business card. Peggy ran back in and picked up the phone.

Jen looked at the card and read it. Hmm, Dr. Fields. It rang a bell. *Dr. Fields! He delivered Lewis!* At least he was familiar with her early delivery. Jen buckled Lewis into the seatbelt and started to pull out onto Main Street but realized she didn't know where to go. Should she go home? Should she drive to Hyannis or the armory?

Jen nervously tapped the steering wheel as she drove and tried to sort it all out. She felt like her secure world was getting out of control and started talking to Lewis.

"Let's see here, Lewis. You were born a month early on Leap Year. Gunther died the same day your father almost burned our house down! Now, your doctor breaks his leg." Lewis was just smiling up at her with his big blue eyes. "I'm starting to feel a little out of sorts here, Lewis. I hope it's not that postpartum crap! Thanks, Fran!"

Jen looked down at the speedometer and discovered she was doing sixty in a thirty-five-mile-per-hour zone. *Whoa, slow it down here, Jen, slow down.* Everything's going to be all right, she thought.

"We'll just go home, Lewis. Good decision, right? I'll call Dr. Fields and get you right in there." Jen had calmed down by the time they got home and pulled into the yard.

"Okay, buddy. Let's go see what other trouble we can stir up!"

Once inside, she gave Lewis a fresh bottle of breast milk she had pumped earlier to keep him busy while she was on the phone. *Who should I call first? Bruce or Dr. Fields, Bruce or Dr. Fields? This is crazy! I can't even make a decision anymore.* She paced the floor and yelled at Rex, "Get out of my way!" He loved being under her feet. She picked up the phone and dialed Bruce's number. Commander Briggs answered.

"Armory! Briggs here."

"Hi, Commander Briggs. This is Jen Duncan."

"How's the big guy doing, Jen? I hear the Patriots have him in their sights already!"

"Oh, what a long story I have. He's okay, but can I please talk to Bruce? It's kind of urgent."

"Why certainly, I think he's got his hands full under a truck, but hold on." He transferred her call to the garage and opened up his office door. "Hey, Bruce; your wife's on line two. Sounds like some kind of emergency!"

Bruce rolled from under the truck on a creeper and scrambled to the phone.

"What is it, Jen? What's the matter? Are you all right?"

"Yes, dear. I probably was a little short with Briggs, that's all."

"That must have been a quick trip to Dr. Rooney's. What's going on?"

"We never got to see him. He broke his leg last night on a boat."

"*What*?"

"Yes, no appointments with him for at least eight weeks. I have to go to Hyannis and see Dr. Fields, of all people. Remember him?"

"Of course, I do! Well, that's good, I guess. Are you going today?"

"Heck, Bruce. I just got home here, and I'm a nervous wreck. I thought we'd find out what's going on with Lewis today. I haven't even called Dr. Field's office yet."

"Calm down. You'll be fine. I can come home for lunch if you want."

"How are you going to get here, fly? I have the truck, remember?"

"Oh, yeah, I did forget about that. Well, just call me if you get an appointment in Hyannis today. Pick me up on your way, and then I can work tonight."

"All right, hon. Sorry. I guess everything caught up with me today. I'll talk to you in a bit." Jen hung up the phone and looked at Dr. Field's business card. She hadn't noticed before, but his card featured a flying stork with a tiny baby sitting on a wing. The baby was holding a sign that read, 'Special Delivery!' Oh boy, she thought. *Here we go again.* She taped the card to her refrigerator.

Jen picked up the phone and called Dr. Field's office.

"Dr. Field's office, can you hold, please?" the woman on the other end asked abruptly.

Jen didn't get a chance to answer before the music played in her ear. "Oh, this is all I need!" Jen said into the phone. She was on hold for only twenty seconds, but it seemed like minutes.

"Dr. Field's office, sorry for the wait. How may I direct your call?"

"Direct my call?" Jen asked smartly. "I'd like to make an appointment with Dr. Fields for my son. He was scheduled with Dr. Rooney this morning."

"Why, yes. We've received about thirty calls to reschedule appointments for Dr. Rooney. Terrible shame, isn't it? This is Dr. Field's answering service. He's in conference today and tomorrow."

"Isn't this his office?" Jen asked.

"Technically, it is. I'm taking all of his calls in order and processing them. Dr. Field's secretary will call you back shortly with an appointment time, probably later next week."

"Next week? You can't be serious!"

"I'm sorry, ma'am. As I said, there are thirty reschedules ahead of you already." There was silence from Jen's end of the line. "Ma'am, your phone number, please, so Terry can call you?"

Jen tried to control her temper at this point. "It's 639-9386," she said very methodically.

"And the patient's name?" the woman asked sternly.

"Lewis Duncan. This is Jen Duncan." Jen could hear another line ringing in the background over the phone. "Sounds like you are very busy, so I'll let you go."

"Thank you. Calls will be returned in the order they are received." The line went dead.

"Well, same to you!" Jen yelled into the phone.

She paced back and forth about the kitchen for a few moments. Lewis started fussing, probably from the tone of Jen's voice. She apologized to him and picked him up. "I'm sorry, Lewis. Things aren't going so good for us today, are they?" She opened up her shirt and fed him, instantly calming him down. "Look at you go! I forgot I gave you a bottle, too!"

Jen called Bruce at work and filled him in. He urged her to show some patience. She made some tea and brought Lewis outside to sit on the bench. It was a sunny morning, but the breeze off the ocean had a bite to it. Rex was busy sniffing every corner of their small fenced-in yard for any dog bones he may have buried last fall.

"What the heck can I do to keep myself busy today?" Jen asked Lewis. He returned her question with a puzzled, blank stare. She walked around the house with Lewis on her arm and Rex charging from behind. Taking note of the dirty, salt-covered windows, she decided it was time for spring cleaning — a chore she despised.

"Ah, well. It could be a lot worse, couldn't it, Lewis?" As she went inside to get some window cleaner and rags, the phone rang in the kitchen. She raced to answer it with Lewis bouncing on her hip.

"Hello, Jen here." She answered enthusiastically, hoping it was Dr. Field's office.

"Hi, Jen. This is Terry from Dr. Field's office." She made Jen's day.

"Oh, you can't believe how happy I am you called so soon!" she told Terry.

"I've been getting that all morning, plus a few nasty words, too! So, your son had an appointment today with Dr. Rooney, correct?"

"Yes, he did. What a horrible accident Dr. Rooney had," Jen remarked. "Imagine breaking a leg at his age?"

"Terrible!" Terry commented. "Well, it looks like we can get Lewis in here..." Jen could hear pages of an appointment calendar flipping. "How's this Friday? I remember your name from a few months ago, so I've already pulled your chart."

"Oh, that'd be fantastic! The woman I spoke with earlier said it might be two weeks!"

"Yes, we've had a problem with her and have to discuss her attitude. So, see you Friday at – let's see here, eleven-thirty a.m., okay?"

"Great! Thank you so much, Terry. Bye now." Jen did a celebratory fist pump. "Yes, Lewis! Your old doctor, but I doubt you'll remember him!" She laughed for a moment. "Better call Dr. Rooney's office for your chart later, too. Lewis, do you think all mothers talk to their babies like I do? Better ask the doctor about that one, too!"

She called Dr. Rooney's office and was informed Lewis's chart would be ready in about two hours. She called Bruce to keep him abreast of the situation and spent the rest of the afternoon on the mundane task of cleaning windows.

*****

Jen picked Bruce up at work and went to Doctor Rooney's office afterward. She went into the office to grab the file.

"Hi, Peggy. I just stopped by for Lewis's file. I bet your day's been crazy, huh?"

"I'd rather forget about days like these, Jen. Here you go," she said while handing her the folder. "By the way, I have an update on Dr. Rooney," she paused.

"How is he?" Jen asked.

"It's a serious compound fracture with muscle and vein damage. He'll be in traction for at least a month, then bedrest for another two. You may want to schedule your next visit with Dr. Fields," Peggy suggested.

"Thanks for the heads up, Peggy. It'll be like old home day going where Lewis was born, anyhow. I'll send a get-well card for Dr. Rooney. Can you see he gets it?"

"Sure thing. Take care, Jen."

Jen took the inch-thick folder and got in the truck with Bruce, who waited impatiently.

"It doesn't look good." Jen pouted.

"How is he? Dr. Rooney?"

"He probably can't walk for months. It looks like I'll be going to Hyannis with Lewis for quite a while."

"Nothing against Dr. Rooney, and I know he's been your family's doctor for ages, but he is getting up there. Don't you think, Jen?"

"He's at least sixty-five, maybe more."

"Maybe it's for the better, this change."

"That's weird. I was kind of thinking the same thing too. The new appointment is only three days away. No big deal! I don't hear Lewis complaining. Do you?" she joked.

"I don't think I've heard him make a peep anyhow. What do you say we go out for dinner tonight? I cashed that mileage reimbursement check. It was a good one!"

"I'm game! Lewis will need a quick nap. We can get changed and go."

Bruce paused, "I meant just me and you. Maybe call your mother to see if she can sit tonight?" Bruce asked. "It's been ages since we've been on a date."

Jen thought a bit and looked at Bruce. "Sure, sounds good, hon."

Jen's mother jumped at the chance to spend some alone time with Lewis. She kept a record of how much time she spent with him compared to Bruce's mother's time with Lewis. Fran had spent a lot more time recently at Bruce's and Jen's house after the passing of Gunther. Kay wasn't too bent out of shape about it. Well, maybe just a little.

Chapter Nine

Eleven-fifteen a.m. Friday. Jen arrived fifteen minutes early for the appointment, knowing there may be some paperwork to fill out. She was called in to see Dr. Fields promptly at 11:31.

"Hello there, stranger!" Dr. Fields greeted Jen kindly. "I can't believe Lewis is four months old already. My, he is big!" Fields exclaimed.

"Yes, I do get that comment often. It must be the Cape Cod air or something! Nobody in my family is over five-six."

"It was probably a growth spurt. Some infants take off the first few months. We've been so busy since combining forces with Dr. Rooney's office. Let's take a look at his folder here."

"I was glad to hear your name mentioned after Dr. Rooney's accident. I didn't know the offices had merged."

"Dr. Rooney was planning on retiring next year, but I think this setback may have sped things along. Now, how about Lewis? I've looked over his chart beforehand. When you saw Dr. Rooney the last time, you inquired about Lewis's vision, any improvements?"

"I don't think so. It's like he can't focus on moving objects. He is rubbing and blinking his eyes a lot. But I might be imagining things."

"Any of those signs may indicate a problem, Jen. With Lewis coming prematurely, some issues can crop up. Being underweight is number one, but vision problems are a close second. There's a procedure called a retinoscopy. I'm sure Dr. Rooney may have told you about it."

"No, not to my knowledge."

"Usually, we wait until at least six months of age for an infant before giving a complete eye exam," Dr. Fields explained.

"I do remember Dr. Rooney telling me that."

"Let's get him on the scale and check his weight first."

Jen put Lewis on the scale and watched the dial stop at nineteen pounds.

"My, he is a little bucket of bricks, isn't he?" Dr. Fields laughed.

"Yes, my back is killing me from lifting him. I have to keep switching him from side to side when I walk."

"It's easy to throw your back out, so be very careful, Jen. Your muscles are just starting to recuperate from pregnancy. I will give Lewis a simple eye test with flashcards to see if he reacts. They're in my office. I'll be back in a minute."

Jen waited and sat with Lewis showing him everything in the room.

"Look at all these nice pictures on the wall, Lewis. Here's what's inside your ears and nose."

Dr. Fields returned to the office. "Don't mind me, doctor. I'm talking to myself a lot lately," Jen said.

"It's perfectly normal, Jen. Are you by yourself all day?"

"Yes. My mom visits twice a week for a few hours. We have only one car, so I'm kind of stranded."

"It's good to get out and mingle when you can. Now, let's see. Have Lewis sit on your lap and face me."

She placed Lewis directly in front of Dr. Fields. He had a series of cards, blank on one side and brightly colored on the other.

He held the cards in front of Lewis, turning them to the blank or colored sides. "Hmmm," Dr. Fields said as he went to his desk and made some notes on a clipboard.

"You're correct, Jen. There is little eye movement. Why don't we plan that eye test for his six-month checkup? By then, his eyes should be fully developed, and if there's a problem, we'll address it then."

"With what, eyeglasses?"

"We try not to prescribe infants with eyeglasses. That's why you don't see too many toddlers with them."

"I've never seen any!"

Dr. Fields tried to perk Jen up. "Only in rare cases do we ever issue eyeglasses for a child as young as Lewis. Let's get on with the rest of his checkup and not dwell just on his eyes. I'm sure they will develop with time."

Dr. Fields did a comprehensive exam of all extremities and checked Lewis's nose, mouth, and feet.

"He certainly is a solid little bugger, isn't he? Normal bowel movements?"

"I don't know what normal is, but it's quite a pile!" Jen laughed.

"Everything else appears to be in fine shape, Jen. Let's see him again on his six-month birthday. That will be right around the end of September. He'll probably be fishing with the guys by then!"

"I don't doubt it, Dr. Fields. We'll see you then and call if we notice any drastic change in his eyes or behavior."

"That's fine, Jen. I'll see both of you then," Dr. Fields assured her.

She made her way to the front desk and made an appointment for September twenty-fourth. It was going to be a long two-month wait.

It was a lovely summer on the Cape. The ocean warmed to a pleasant seventy-four degrees, and there wasn't an overwhelming heatwave. Most days were in the eighties, and nights in the seventies. Ocean breezes moderated any high or low temperatures. Tourists from the mainland flocked from Boston and outlying suburbs to enjoy miles of unspoiled beaches and fishing.

Bruce and Jen passed the time by taking long walks on the beach and window shopping in the ports of Yarmouth and Dennis with Lewis. They spent every Sunday at Nolan's house for delicious cookouts and horseshoes. Lobster, clam, and oyster steam wafted through his yard and onto many jealous neighbor's properties.

Jen made two new friends that summer. The wives of Bruce's co-workers were a little older than Jen and were hardy New Englanders. They each had two children who were in grade school. Page and Cheryl loved giving Jen child-rearing advice and provided a weekly report about shenanigans within the armory walls. Something Bruce never clued her in on. It seemed practical jokes were carried out weekly, and nobody escaped ridicule. Commander Briggs was often the target.

Labor Day was fast approaching, signaling the end of summer and another last-minute push for tourists to invade the Cape. Jen proposed a weekend escape to Bruce.

"Hey, Bruce? Why don't we pack the tent up this weekend and head to that little campground in Truro? Remember the one we used to go to when I told my parents I was staying at Julie's all weekend?"

"I sure do! Boy, we did have some good times there. You're lucky they never caught on."

"Oh, I think they knew. My parents just didn't want to admit it."

"This will be the last cookout at Nolan's, and it'll be the biggest one of the summer. I don't want to miss it, hon."

"We've been with your friends six weekends in a row, and you see those guys every day. How about doing something different? I could use a break from Page and Cheryl, too. I need earplugs if I go near them."

"Oh, come on, they're not that bad. Cheryl talks your ears off, but isn't it nice to have some friends in town? Since you moved here from Sandwich, you haven't met anybody," Bruce reminded her.

"I know, but those two hussies you worked with in the office weren't my style either. This neighborhood is a ghost town from now until Memorial Day."

"Hey, wait a minute. Those two hussies were good workers and just a few years younger than you. It's not my fault they were foxes and had every guy after them within a ten-mile radius."

"Even you?" Jen pointed her finger at him.

"Yeah, right! I'm looking at the only woman I've ever been with, and I mean to keep it that way!" Bruce's voice rose, startling Lewis.

"Now, look what you've done! Poor, poor baby Lewis. Daddy didn't mean to yell," Jen apologized to Lewis as he wiggled and squirmed.

Bruce's voice rose again. "I didn't yell. I can see this conversation isn't going anywhere!" He walked toward the kitchen door, forcefully turned the knob, and slammed it on his way outside.

Bruce stood on the side porch and took a deep breath. *What did I do to deserve this?*

Jen came out and sat with Lewis on the porch rocker, "I'm sorry. I didn't mean to accuse you of anything, Bruce. I'm spending too much time alone, and maybe I'm a little jealous."

"Jealous? About what?"

"You go to work, joke around with your buddies all day, and then we go to Nolan's every weekend. You guys always end up hanging by the grill, hooting and hollering all afternoon while I make small talk with Page and Cheryl."

"I thought you liked them?" Bruce asked.

"I do, but I'm certainly not going to discuss what goes on in our bedroom like they do every week!"

"You're kidding me, right?"

"Honest truth! I can tell you how often they do it each week and how many toys they each have in their nightstands."

"You didn't have to go there, Jen. I'm sorry. I never had a clue what was going on. I thought you enjoyed your time with Lewis when I was at work."

"I do, I do, Bruce, but sometimes I get a little stir-crazy. I enjoy having your mom and mine here and going to Nolan's. Maybe there is some truth about that depression thing after having a baby," Jen admitted.

Bruce looked over at Jen. She had a tear in the corner of her eye. "I'll go into the attic and get our camping stuff. You're right. We could use a break from the guys," he confessed.

"I'm okay. I don't mind going to Nolan's on Sunday."

"Nope, we're heading out to the dunes with Lewis and Rex. It'll be mobbed around here this weekend, anyhow. Let's get packed up, okay?"

"You're too much, Bruce."

"Are you sure Cheryl and Page don't know what goes on in our bedroom?"

"No way! If I did, they'd probably invite you for a threesome!"

"Yeah, sure! You're just trying to build me up after beating me down!"

Jen looked at Bruce, "I wouldn't ever tell our bedroom secrets to anyone, Bruce," she smiled at him. "Lewis is getting sleepy. Let's tuck him in for a nap and maybe take a detour to our bedroom?"

"What about packing?"

"You'd rather pack than get frisky for a bit?" Jen said seductively.

"Not at all. I'll grab a fresh blanket from the clothesline for Lewis. I think he lurched all over the other one last night!" Bruce removed the clothespins from a fresh, hanging blanket on the line. He crinkled it into a ball and smelled it. "Boy, there's nothing like an air-dried blanket, is there, Jen?" She just looked at Bruce and laughed.

As Jen opened the kitchen door, Bruce asked her, "A threesome? Really?" She gave him a smirk and politely gave him the finger.

Chapter Ten

September twenty-fourth came very quickly after the long Labor Day weekend. The Cape was packed with tourists for the last hurrah of a short summer season. Bruce and Jen's escape to the sandy dunes of Truro and Provincetown turned out to be just what they needed. Bruce took the day off from work to accompany Jen to Lewis's doctor's appointment. By now, they were both very concerned about his vision.

"Are you ready to go, Bruce? Lewis's appointment is in forty minutes," Jen yelled from the kitchen to the upstairs bedroom. "I have Lewis and Rex packed in the truck and ready to go!"

"Just a minute, it seems I'm having a little problem getting off the toilet this morning. Must have been those scallops we ate last night."

"Oh, no! I thought they tasted a little strange myself! Are you sure you want to come?"

"Yes! I already took the day off. Just a minute!" Bruce finished his business and jumped down the stairs to the truck as Jen got in on the other side.

"What's that under your arm?" Jen asked.

Bruce lifted his arm and pulled a roll of toilet paper from under it.

"Just in case of an emergency," he laughed.

"It's that bad?"

"Let's not discuss it. Do you have a list of questions for Dr. Fields?"

"Yes, they're right in my pocketbook. I'm kind of nervous," Jen said as Lewis happily chirped away.

"Yeah, so am I, hon."

Lewis was looking at Jen, smiling at her. Suddenly, a massive blast of gas shook his diaper. They both laughed. "You didn't eat any of those scallops last night, did you, Lewis?" Bruce chuckled.

Lewis responded with, "Mumma."

"Oh my God, Bruce, did you hear that?! He called me Mumma!"

"Who are you kidding? I think he called me Mumma!" Bruce was so surprised the truck tire caught the pavement's edge but quickly corrected his course.

"Watch where you're going, Bruce! It'd be nice to arrive at the doctor's office in one piece!" Jen scolded him.

"I've never heard him say anything. This is great!" Bruce celebrated.

Jen looked at Lewis and gave him a big kiss. "Mum, Mum, Mumma," Jen said as she tickled him.

Salivating, Lewis looked up at her again and said, "Da, Dada."

"I don't believe this, Bruce! He's talking!"

"He may have messed up who's who, but this is unreal! Wait until the doctor hears this!" Bruce tickled Lewis. Rex appeared to be a little perplexed, too, hearing these strange noises from Lewis.

Lewis repeated those two words along the way to the doctor's office. He certainly changed Bruce and Jen's somber moods into an absolute delight. They arrived at the office twenty minutes later and unloaded the truck.

"I'll take Lewis," Jen told Bruce. "You get his bag."

"No, I'll hold him. You take his bag."

"I'll take him!" she ordered Bruce with her hands on her hips.

"Okay, but I get to tell Dr. Fields that Lewis is talking."

"Yeah, sure, okay," Jen told Bruce to keep him quiet.

"You be good, Rex! Stay right there," Bruce said. They hastily marched to the office door and entered.

A receptionist was sitting at her desk. Dr. Fields stood directly behind her, making some notes in a folder.

"Hi, Beverly. Hi, Dr. Fields," Jen spouted upon entering. Bruce struggled to open the door for Jen while holding her pocketbook and Lewis's diaper bag.

"Dr. Fields! Lewis is talking!" Jen excitedly said. He didn't even have a chance to say hello.

"Jen!" Bruce angrily blurted while still holding the door open. "I thought I was going to tell him!" Jen ignored Bruce as he fumbled in and greeted the doctor.

"Well, well, Jen, Bruce. How are you?" Dr. Fields addressed them.

"We're pretty excited," Jen answered. "Lewis started talking on the way here today!"

Dr. Fields did not immediately share their enthusiasm but replied, "There was a cancellation, so we can squeeze you in a half-hour early."

"That's great. I'll be able to go fishing earlier!" Bruce declared while earning a sour look from Jen.

"Let me retrieve Lewis's folder. Please sit in the exam room on the left," Dr. Fields requested.

Jen sat on the exam table, and Bruce grabbed a chair. Dr. Fields strolled into the room and closed the door behind him. Lewis gave him a big smile as he pulled up a chair and sat next to Jen.

"Now, what's this? You think he's talking?"

"Yes," Bruce and Jen answered at the same time. Bruce continued, "He just started this morning on the way here, Mumma and Dada."

"Don't get too excited yet, folks. At six months, many infant noises can be construed as words and vocalizing."

It seemed Lewis had his own opinion and let another loud rumble from his diaper. Everyone got a short laugh while Dr. Fields continued. "How are his eyes? Is there any improvement?"

"We don't think so," Jen said. "I have a list of questions for you. Bruce, my pocketbook, please?"

"Sorry. Yes, dear," he replied, handing it to her.

Jen unraveled a piece of paper and looked at it.

"Lewis doesn't follow objects with his eyes and has started to blink a lot." Dr. Fields made a few notes in his folder.

"He bumps into things while he's crawling or couch cruising," Bruce added.

"Couch cruising? You're kidding me, right?" Dr. Fields asked, looking puzzled.

"He started about a month ago," Jen answered, "and he hasn't stopped since."

"Jen, most infants don't start holding onto furniture for support until they are ten or eleven months old! Lewis is only six." Dr. Fields made another note in his folder. "Let's put him on the scale, Jen."

Jen got up and placed Lewis on the scale. The dial stopped at twenty-four pounds. Dr. Fields looked at Jen and Bruce. "Six months old, twenty-four pounds. Let's get a length on him." Dr. Fields removed a cloth tape measure from a drawer beside his chair and placed one end on Lewis's foot. "Okay, Jen, stretch him a little. He's hunched up."

"C'mon, Lewis, don't fight me. Here we go," Jen said as she gently pulled his arms over his head. Bruce watched in silence.

"Wow," Dr. Fields remarked, "almost twenty-four inches." He went to his desk, sat down, and scratched some math on a pad. He paused. "I don't know what's going on, but Lewis is the size of almost a two-year-old child already. His weight and height are proportionate, but he's physically a year and a half ahead of where he should be. Now, let's get back to your questions about his vision."

"Lewis seems to have a hard time seeing things in front of him," Jen said. "He is always so happy and can hear me walking down the hall even if I tip-toe."

"It seems other senses are compensating for his poor eyesight." Dr. Fields said and noted that on his chart. "Let's schedule Lewis for that retinoscopy we discussed earlier, okay?"

"What is it? Will it hurt?" Bruce asked.

"It is a painless eye exam given to patients who cannot communicate or may be mentally challenged. Usually, when you go to the eye doctor for an exam, you look through what seems like a big set of binoculars, right?" Dr. Fields asked them.

"Yes, the doctor turns a dial on it and asks if your vision is improving or worsening. Is that what you're talking about?" Bruce asked.

"Exactly! A young child, toddler, or elderly patient may not convey what they see during a regular eye exam. This instrument takes the guesswork from questioning a patient. A scope with a light is simply shined through the pupil onto the retina. Through a series of mathematical calculations, we can determine a prescription for eyeglasses."

"That's amazing! Do you have that scope in your office, Dr. Fields?"

"I'm sorry, Jen. Boston is the only facility where the procedure is performed within two hundred miles. You and Lewis will have to see a specialist there. I've never had to recommend this exam before, but I can make the appointment for you."

"Oh, boy, what's next?" Bruce moaned. "Can we get it done right away before his eyes worsen?"

"Chances are, Bruce, this condition is probably genetic. He may simply have hyperopia, otherwise known as farsightedness. Lewis can't focus on nearby items, or far away for that matter. Don't get yourselves all worked up over this. I'll get you in as soon as possible with a little help from my associate at Mass. General."

"That would be super," said Jen. "Please let us know when Lewis has his appointment. Boston is so far. We'll have to stay over."

"Jen, it's only two hours from here. No big deal!" Bruce stood from his chair.

"Maybe for you, but we've never taken Lewis on a two-hour car ride."

"Please, please," Dr. Fields interrupted their spat. "There's something more concerning to me than Lewis's eyes."

Jen and Bruce looked at each other and then at Dr. Fields.

"His growth rate is quite alarming to me. He is bigger than any infant on record for his age here. Bruce, you mentioned Lewis was couch cruising?"

"Yes, I did, Dr. Fields," Bruce affirmed. "He also uses our dog for balance, too!"

"What kind of dog do you have?" Dr. Fields asked.

"He's a little Jack Russell. Rex just adores Lewis," Jen said.

"Lewis would probably break him in half if he fell on him!" Dr. Fields said, laughing. "My concern is, if Lewis keeps growing like this, his muscles may not keep up with bone growth."

"What could that lead to, Dr. Fields?" Bruce asked as he sat back down.

"I would be more concerned about leg muscles and bone strength supporting his weight." Dr. Fields informed them. "I'd like to see Lewis in one month to see if he is still gaining weight and attempting to walk. We'll look at a course of action for him at that time."

"I don't know what's going to hit Lewis next," Jen complained.

"These are just precautionary measures, Jen. Once again, please don't be overly concerned. Lewis is a very healthy and strong infant. Let's schedule an appointment. Dr. Fields looked through his calendar. "How's October twenty-sixth, at ten a.m.?"

"A whole month away?" Bruce asked.

"By then, Bruce, we'll have the results of the eye exam. We'll have a leg up on him by then. Here's a reminder card. At this point, you can schedule Lewis's appointments directly through me, not the front desk." Dr. Fields folded his chart and placed it in a file cabinet.

"Thank you, Dr. Fields." Bruce returned a handshake.

Jen bundled Lewis and could only manage a polite smile at Dr. Fields without saying a word. They walked down the hall and exited toward their truck. As usual, Rex was basking in the sunshine on the dashboard of the old Chevy. Jen flung the door open and tucked Lewis in his bassinet. Bruce jumped into the driver's seat and started the truck.

"Damn it, Bruce! We're leaving here with more unanswered questions than when we got here. What the hell is going on?"

"I don't know, Jen. Maybe we should've named him Clark Kent. You know, after Superman?"

"That's not funny, Bruce. I'm getting scared."

"Scared? Scared of what?"

"Haven't you been listening to the doctor? We have to go to *Boston* to see a *specialist!* We have to come back here *in a month* for another checkup! Lewis is not in the top ten percent of infant growth. He's the *biggest* kid on Cape Cod. He set the bar! What don't you see?"

"Jen, I don't know what happened on that special day, the twenty-ninth of February, but I'm not going to dwell on it and get myself down again. I'm not going to fold. It seems like forces in the world teamed against us that day and are testing us. You've been listening too much to your mother about that post-partum bullshit, anyhow!"

"Post-partum bullshit? My mother? It was your mother who started it!"

"Please, Jen. Let's just ride home in peace. I'm sure many other new parents have it much worse than us."

"Yeah, I guess you're right, Bruce. Maybe I'm just overreacting. Everything will be okay," Jen said.

Dr. Fields scheduled an eye exam for Lewis. Luckily for Jen, the exam was only two days away, with hardly any time to dwell upon making plans for the long trip and someone to watch Rex.

Chapter Eleven

On Friday, September 26th, at 6 a.m. Jen and Bruce packed the truck and left for Boston to get the retinoscopy for Lewis. Meg, Jen's sister, would take Rex for a doggie vacation. Bruce decided to make a weekend outing of their first trip to Boston with Lewis. Neither Bruce nor Jen had been to the city for at least a decade. She had many destinations to visit — the New England Aquarium, Children's Museum, and the North End for some great Italian food.

The trip on Route Three was uneventful but had its share of bad drivers and heavy traffic. Lewis heard every horn beeping on the highway and thrived on the traffic noise. They arrived at Mass. General's parking garage in about two hours before a long walk into the hospital.

"Wow, I've forgotten how crazy these busy cities are. How about you, Bruce?" Jen asked as they were hustling down a sidewalk dodging pedestrians.

"I can't believe how people live like this. They're like cattle herded into corrals. Look at Lewis! I've never seen his eyes so wide open. He's taking it all in!"

"Maybe we can ask him how to get back to our truck in a while. That'd be great!"

"I know, we've taken so many lefts and rights, I have no clue how to get back." Bruce paused for a breath of air and put Lewis's diaper bag on the sidewalk. "There's a sign for general admissions. I guess we start there. Let's get moving."

Jen and Bruce entered through some large sliding doors and looked at a directory on the wall. Jen peered at the glass case scanning the numerous choices.

"Okay, fourth floor, optometry. Isn't that what Dr. Fields said?"

"Yep, that's it. The elevator's right over there."

They hopped into the elevator as a bell rang, signaling the closing door. Lewis squirmed in Jen's arms, startled by the loud noise, and yelled out.

"I guess that woke him up!" Bruce said. "Look at him smiling!"

They exited the elevator and approached the receptionist's desk. There was an extensive directory of names on the counter. Jen let out a sigh of disgust as she shook her head.

"It's good we left so early, Bruce. We're here only twenty minutes before his appointment. We head this way, to the left. It's Dr. Bernard we're looking for, isn't it?"

"Righto!" Bruce agreed. He went in through the door to a check-in desk.

"Hi, we're Bruce and Jen Duncan for an appointment with Doctor Bernard."

The receptionist scanned her appointment calendar and gave a friendly response. "We need you to fill out these insurance forms, please. Who did you say the appointment was for?" She looked over his shoulder.

"My son, Lewis." Bruce turned around to find Jen and Lewis had vanished.

"That's weird," he replied to the receptionist and headed toward the entry door. He looked down the hall in one direction: nothing. Then, he turned and looked the other way to see Jen standing in front of a floor-to-ceiling glass window. Lewis was perched on a chair, looking out also. Hypnotized by the city view and skyscrapers, Jen eyed the tiny people on the sidewalk below.

"Jen, hey, Jen!" Bruce yelled, snapping her from a trance. "C'mon, we have to fill out this paperwork before we can go sightseeing. I'll grab Lewis."

"Yeah, sure, whatever you say, Bruce," Jen spoke as if in a fog.

They entered the office as the receptionist said, "Looks like you have everybody now!" and laughed. "Here you go. It's just one simple page of info. Need a pen?"

"That'd be great. I have one in my pocketbook, but I'll use yours."

Bruce kept Lewis busy by bouncing him around on his shoulders.

"You're here for a retinoscopy with Dr. Bernard?" the girl asked.

"Yes, ma'am. Eleven o'clock."

"Only one of you will be allowed in the doctor's office. Who should I put down as the attending parent?"

"What? Only one of us?" Bruce queried in an upset tone.

"Yes. Too many distractions can prolong a test like this for a toddler and may give false results."

Bruce and Jen looked at each other in disbelief.

"Here we go again," Jen remarked.

"Which one, Sir?" the receptionist asked.

"I'll wait out here," Bruce pouted.

"Thank you," the receptionist said politely. Jen got up and handed her the insurance form as Dr. Bernard entered from a hallway.

"You must be Mrs. Duncan and Lewis with his handsome father?" He reached out and shook Jen's hand, then Bruce's.

"Nice to meet you, Sir," Bruce said.

"And there's the future lineman for the Patriots I've heard so much about, Lewis, right?" Dr. Bernard asked Jen.

"We get that all the time. It must be the Cape Cod air!"

Dr. Bernard looked at the paperwork and addressed Bruce. "Bruce, I see you've chosen to remain here. After the exam, we'll discuss the results. We'll have them within a half-hour."

Bruce wanted to say, "I didn't 'choose' to wait here. I was told I had to." Instead, he politely said, "Yes, thank you, Dr. Bernard," and gave Jen a wink on her way down the hall.

Once Jen and Lewis entered the examination room, Dr. Bernard explained in simple detail about the test. He told Jen the results were very accurate. She had no questions for him and just wanted to get it over with.

Lewis was placed in a small chair adjoining the doctor's exam table.

"I know it's hard for him to stare in only one direction, Mrs. Duncan. But that is the key to this test. I have to shine a light in his eye while taking measurements with another scope. If you stand behind me and talk to him, I've found that his focus might remain on you."

"Let's give it a try."

Jen moved behind Dr. Bernard while he started the exam. She talked to Lewis as he sat there smiling and blabbering at Mommy.

After about one minute, the doctor said, "Great, let's give him a break. His eye is tearing up from the light. We can start on the other eye in a moment and come back to this one. Is he always this good?"

"He is, Dr. Bernard. Lewis was born a preemie on Leap Year, February 29. It was quite a day!"

"Yes, my receptionist was filled in by Dr. Fields. I don't know how both of you made it through. It was such a terrible accident that your husband burned the house down!"

"Oh, no!" Jen laughed. "It was just the kitchen!"

"I guess that's how stories get stretched," Dr. Bernard laughed. "I think Lewis is ready for his next session. Please step to my left this time and address Lewis. We'll be done shortly."

As instructed, Jen made some more small talk with Lewis. He focused his eyes on her once again and didn't move.

After another minute or so of testing, Dr. Bernard turned his scope off and breathed a sigh of relief.

"That was the easiest exam I've ever given! I believe I have enough diagnostics to process, Mrs. Duncan. Why don't you and Bruce tour the hospital for a half-hour? There's a cafeteria on the second floor if anyone is hungry. Great food there! I can't stay away, as you can tell!"

"Thank you. We skipped breakfast today to get here. I'm sure Bruce is starving."

"Meet me back here," Dr. Bernard eyed his watch. "Let's see. How's noon?"

"That'll be fine." Jen scooped Lewis up from the chair and went to see Bruce.

"How was it? How'd he do? Is there anything wrong?" Bruce asked Jen.

"Bruce, *please*! Let's go for a walk or something. He'll have the results in a half-hour."

"Well, come on, you have to fill me in!" Bruce pleaded.

"I know it may sound strange, but I think Lewis knew what the doctor was doing!"

"He what?"

"Bruce. Lewis did exactly what the doctor wanted him to do, the *whole* exam! It was like he knew why he was in there."

"Jen, I know Lewis is smart, but that's too much for me."

"Let's just go for a walk, okay?" Jen asked. "I have some apple sauce and string beans for Lewis. Let's sit in the lobby and decompress a little."

"Okay, but I can't wait to get out of here for a huge sub and a beer," Bruce replied.

"Yeah, me too, Bruce."

Chapter Twelve

Jen and Bruce arrived in Dr. Bernard's office at 11:55 a.m. and impatiently sat beside his desk. Lewis was sound asleep from a full belly of tasty treats.

The doctor entered the room and closed the door behind him.

"Did you make it to our cafeteria?" he asked.

"No, it seems Lewis is the only one who got to feast," Bruce said.

"I have the results as I promised." Dr. Bernard looked over the chart again. "Just to let you know, I've seen cases like this before in toddlers in far worse conditions than Lewis."

"I don't think that makes me feel much better," Bruce replied.

"The test results show that Lewis has hyperopia, better known as farsightedness," Dr. Bernard said. "It's not a severe case, as I said, but he will need corrective lenses to help him see."

"You mean glasses. Eyeglasses?" Jen asked.

"Yes, I'm afraid so."

Dr. Bernard tried to raise their spirits. "We've nipped this in the bud, as they say, and if it weren't for the both of you noticing his behavior, this could have turned out to be an extreme case. I commend parents like you that take an interest in their children. I see so many undiagnosed problems in this city. Sometimes I can't sleep at night."

"Well, I guess it's not that bad, Jen. It may be uncomfortable for him to wear glasses at first," Bruce said, "but we both noticed his poor vision, right?"

Jen turned her attention directly to Dr. Bernard.

"Is there any chance of this diagnosis being wrong?"

"No, not at all. I've had two other doctors confirm your son's results. We agree he needs corrective lenses right away to stop any further progression. He could easily fall behind as a toddler and first-grader if left untreated. With certain eye exercises and the possibility of contact lenses, your son can shed his glasses within a reasonable amount of time."

"What's a reasonable amount of time?" Bruce asked.

"It's hard to say exactly, Bruce. It may be five or six years."

"You're kidding, right?" Jen asked. "I've never seen an infant or toddler with glasses. He'll be made fun of!" Jen almost cried.

"That's because you live in a very rural area. I prescribe glasses to many young toddlers in the city, and they get along fine."

"Well, we live on a big sandbar called Cape Cod, and I've never seen eyeglasses on a baby before, either!" Bruce declared.

"I have already looked into a fine optometrist in Hyannis. He has an excellent reputation with several young patients. Please don't be overly concerned about this. Lewis will grow into an outstanding young man. I have sent his eye prescription to Dr. Mulvey already."

Jen adjusted herself in the chair. "Thank you for all you've done, Dr. Bernard. You're right. It could have been a lot worse. It's not like he's going blind or something."

"Nothing like that at all. I'm sure he will outgrow this condition with time. My best wishes to both of you." Dr. Bernard smiled at Lewis. "Come back anytime. You can show some of those crabby patients how to be good!"

Everyone laughed and tried to lighten up. Jen and Bruce picked up items left in the waiting room and walked toward the elevator, not saying anything. Lewis was fast asleep in his stroller. Bruce pushed the button on a panel outside the elevator. A bell rang as the door opened up. He looked to his side, but once again, Jen was nowhere to be found. This time, he knew right where she was.

He left the diaper bag at the elevator door and took Lewis. As he turned the corner, there she was! She was looking out the large window at the city. Jen broke her gaze and looked at Bruce and Lewis.

"Can we go up to the maternity ward?" Jen asked Bruce.

"You're not getting any crazy ideas, are you? I think one is enough to handle for now, don't you?"

"I just want to see what it's like, a big city hospital ward? Hopefully, we'll never have to come here again, right?"

"I guess so. Lewis is still sound out."

Jen and Bruce took the elevator to the sixth-floor maternity ward. The elevator door opened. There was a large desk with four clerks directing visitors in every direction. Over fifty rooms were dedicated to new mothers. They strolled to a large glass viewing area overlooking a massive sleeping room for newborns.

"Holy Moses!" Bruce declared. "They're stacked up like candlepins!"

"Unreal, isn't it?" Jen decided when she looked at the room filled with babies. "There were only two other kids with Lewis when he was born!"

Suddenly, Lewis started to fuss and reached for Jen to pick him up from his stroller.

"Okay, okay. You can have a peek too, Lewis," Jen said.

She lumbered to untangle him from a jumbled mess of blankets. A big grin came across his round face as she brought him nearer to the glass. He put his hands on the glass and started to gurgle. "Ba, ba, babies."

"Oh, c'mon, Jen, that's too much! Supposedly he can't see two feet in front of him. How can he see the babies?"

"Maybe he doesn't see them; he can smell them. Don't you miss the smell of a new baby?"

"You're crazy. The only smell I know is from changing diapers!"

"You're missing it all, Bruce. Look at him."

Lewis was mesmerized. By what, they didn't know.

"Let's get out of here and get something to eat. I'm about ready to pass out," Bruce complained.

"Me too, hon. What do you think? Hit up the Aquarium after a bite to eat?"

"That sounds good. I feel like Jed Clampet from the Beverly Hillbillies coming from the country into the big city," Bruce joked.

"Yeah, at least we got one thing straightened out today with Lewis. I'm not too concerned about that checkup for him next month."

"Neither am I, hon," Bruce said calmly, telling her a white lie. He was deeply concerned.

Chapter Thirteen

October 28. Lewis was sporting his new eyeglasses and seemed to relish his world of sight. It took a few days for him to get used to the feeling of having a foreign object resting on his nose. He was uncomfortable with them and kept knocking them off at first. An elastic strap resolved that issue. He continually pointed out new objects and attempted to form words.

Bruce and Jen were in the kitchen rounding up some last-minute items for their trip to Dr. Field's office in Hyannis.

"Where's Lewis's hat?" Jen said as if scolding Bruce.

"How the heck should I know? You took him over to your mother's yesterday, didn't you?"

"Oh, crap! I bet I left it there. She was being a real pain, and Lewis started to fuss. It's not windy, is it?"

"Nope, there's hardly a ripple on the bay. You can see the fish jumping a hundred yards offshore. I might throw my fishing rod in the back of the truck."

"Never you mind, Mr. Duncan! We need all the money we can get right now. Heating oil skyrocketed to almost sixty cents a gallon last January, remember?"

"Yeah, I suppose. Just wishful thinking. It'd be such a nice day to pack lunch with Lewis and you. Hit the shoals for some bluefish. It may be one of the last good runs."

"Bruce! Start the truck!"

Bruce shrugged his shoulders and left the kitchen. He picked up Lewis's diaper bag and put them in the truck.

"And don't forget your ham sandwich I made for lunch!" Jen reminded him.

"Oh, boy! I can't wait for that ham sandwich!" Bruce mocked her. Jen shook her head at Bruce and struggled to put Lewis in his bassinet for the ride to the doctor's office.

"Your legs don't even fit in this thing anymore! What are we going to put you in next?" Jen ribbed Lewis. He just looked up at her and smiled. Bruce marched in through the kitchen door.

"Ready when you are, Captain! Launching orders confirmed!" he stated loudly to Jen.

"Bruce, you know I don't like that military mumbo jumbo. Let's go."

"Yes, dear."

"And I don't like that 'yes dear' bit, either!" Bruce snickered to himself and closed the door behind them. Rex was not invited on today's trip.

It took the usual half-hour ride on Route Six into Hyannis. Bruce always liked taking the shore road on a nice sunny day but figured he better not press his luck.

"Save your back," he said to Jen. "I'll get him." Bruce picked Lewis up from the bassinet.

"We'll need a backhoe to get you out of this thing by next week!"

Jen held the door for Bruce as they entered the office. They got some curious stares from a few patients waiting for their appointments. A woman placed her hand over her mouth to hide a whisper but spoke loud enough for everyone to hear.

"I've never seen a baby with glasses. Have you, Billy?" Jen gave both of them a scowl.

"Hi, we're here to see Dr. Fields at eleven o'clock," Bruce said quietly.

"He'll be right with you. Please have a seat," the receptionist told them.

Jen put a small bag on the floor and took a seat as far away from the curious onlookers as she could. Bruce followed her and put Lewis in the middle between them. Lewis smartly maneuvered himself and stood. He looked around at the office surroundings, moving his eyes and head around the room like a secondhand ticking away on a clock. He knew he was there before, but now he could see pictures on three walls and toys in a basket in the corner of the room.

"Oh, my! Look at how big that boy is!" one of the mothers remarked loudly. "How old is he, if you don't mind me asking?"

"I certainly do mind!" Jen snapped.

"Lewis is eight months old tomorrow," Bruce interrupted.

"*Eight months*?" She giggled with two other women. "What are you feeding him, spinach? Is he Popeye?" All three women fell into hysterical laughter. "And what's with the glasses?"

Jen was tearing mad and started to get up from her chair to confront them. Bruce tugged on the rear of her blouse and pulled her down.

Lewis pointed his hand toward the ladies and started to mouth, "Ba, ba, bad," he muttered.

"That's right, Lewis!" Jen affirmed. "*Bad!*"

"Dr. Fields will see you both now, Mr. Duncan." Bruce took Lewis by his pointer finger and led him toward the exam room door. Jen picked up their belongings and stomped into the room behind Bruce and Lewis.

"I'm going to kick their ass!"

"Relax, Jen. Not many people here in the sticks see eyeglasses on a toddler. You know that." Dr. Fields walked into the room just in time to calm Jen down.

"Something wrong, Jen?" Dr. Fields asked.

"No, Dr. Fields. I'm a little wound up today."

"I see Lewis has new eyeglasses. How is he adapting?"

"We think he's doing great, Dr. Fields, but other people certainly have their opinion. It seems a whole new world has opened up for him. He doesn't stop talking and pointing all day."

"All day? No more naps?" Dr. Fields inquired.

"Lewis hasn't been napping since he got his glasses. I think he doesn't want to miss anything!" Jen broke her lousy mood and laughed at herself. "I know he looks pretty corny with them, but it's the best thing for him, isn't it?" Jen asked warily.

"It certainly is Jen. Let's put him on the scale." Dr. Fields fumbled through a folder and started mumbling to himself. "Six weeks ago," he paused. "Here it is, twenty-four pounds." He looked at the dial as the pointer stopped at twenty-seven pounds. Raising his eyebrows, he wrote down the figure.

"Is Lewis still couch cruising, Bruce? As you both called it?" Dr. Fields asked.

"Oh no, Dr. Fields. He pretty much walks wherever he wants to. We try to keep him off the stairs, and we put up a gate," Jen said.

"Stairs? At eight months?" Dr. Fields made another note.

"Bruce, can you walk to the end of the room with Lewis? When you get to the wall, both of you turn and face me, okay?" Dr. Fields requested.

"Come on, Lewis, this way. Look at the big doggy picture on the wall." Bruce took Lewis by his pinky and started walking. Lewis quickly pulled his finger away and stumbled along by himself. "Good boy!" Bruce praised him as they both turned around and faced Dr. Fields. He studied Lewis for a moment and made another note in his folder.

"Okay, Bruce. Walk back toward me. Lewis should follow you."

Bruce took him by a finger again and pointed Lewis in the doctor's direction. He walked with a few missteps, falling right onto Dr. Field's leg.

"Gotcha, Lewis!" Everyone laughed, even Lewis. "He feels like he weighs fifty pounds!" Dr. Fields commented.

"My back sure feels like he does, Dr. Fields," Jen remarked.

"That's what concerns me, Jen." Dr. Fields opened his folder to the first page. Before speaking again, he read his previous notes for a minute and looked at Jen and Bruce. "I believe we may have to do some baseline testing for Lewis."

"What do you mean, baseline testing?" Jen asked.

"His growth rate may be related to an over-active pituitary gland or a thyroid problem."

"Over-active what?" Bruce asked.

"Well, we don't know, Bruce. Do you remember the last time you were here? I mentioned we don't want his bones outgrowing his muscles. I'm just pulling strings at this point, but we have to get a handle on his growth."

"I agree, Dr. Fields," Jen replied.

"Well, I believe that is starting to happen. Lewis can walk fine, but if he continues to gain weight without proper support, his legs and shin bones won't be able to support him and may deform."

"Well, we can't stop him from walking, Dr. Fields," Bruce asserted.

"I know, Bruce. I know. We may have to outfit Lewis with special braces to ensure his legs grow straight."

"Leg braces? Grow straight?" Jen stood up. "Oh, great! What's next?"

"Jen, please sit down. These are only speculative theories that need to be confirmed," Dr. Fields informed them.

"Confirmed. How?" Bruce asked.

"Unfortunately, the only way to get an accurate diagnosis of what's going on inside Lewis is to have his blood drawn."

"He needs blood drawn? That will hurt him, won't it?" Jen quizzed Dr. Fields.

"Yes, it may be very uncomfortable for him."

"Can't you put him under?" Bruce asked.

"The risks of anesthesia for an infant far outweigh having some blood drawn. We would administer a local numbing agent before taking blood."

"Bruce, I can't handle this anymore. Poor Lewis, I can't do it!" Jen cried out.

Bruce put his arm around Jen and Lewis. "Shh. We have to, dear."

A moment of silence followed before Jen wiped away tears and looked up at Dr. Fields. "We don't have to go back to Boston, do we?" she sniffled.

"Not at all, Jen. Bloodwork can be done right here at Cape Cod General. We have pediatric specialists here." Another moment of uneasy silence followed before Bruce spoke.

"How soon can we get the testing done?"

"I'll put a priority on this, Bruce. We can have blood drawn today and have results within forty-eight hours. The lab is one floor up. I'll leave you two alone to discuss it. Please come to my office when you have made a decision."

Dr. Fields folded Lewis's chart and exited the exam room. Bruce let out a heavy sigh as he stood and looked out the window. Lewis picked a stuffed teddy bear from a basket and threw it across the room at Bruce, hitting him square in the back of his head.

"What the?" Bruce called out. Jen laughed along with Lewis at his antics. "I guess those glasses do work!" Bruce admitted with a smile as he rubbed the back of his head.

"Bruce, we don't have any choice. First, it's glasses for Lewis, maybe leg braces now. What's next?"

"I know, hon. I know. I just hate the thought of it." Bruce paused and looked at Lewis as if he were listening to every word. "I'll go tell Dr. Fields and get on with it."

"Okay, Bruce." Jen squeezed Lewis, gave him a big hug, and rocked him.

Bruce returned to the room five minutes later with a nurse. "Is this the little tiger I've heard so much about?"

"Is it good or bad?" Jen asked.

"Oh, it's all good, Mrs. Duncan, I can assure you." She leaned over and put an I.D. band on Lewis's arm.

It perplexed him, and he tugged and bit it. He didn't know what it was but knew he didn't like it there, not one bit. "Please follow me to the third floor. We can take the elevator."

The nurse tried to have a short conversation with Jen and Bruce, but they were preoccupied with thoughts of Lewis and didn't answer any of her routine questions. It didn't take the nurse long to figure this out.

"Here we go. You can have a seat while a lab tech prepares for Lewis." The nurse pointed to a set of chairs in the waiting room. Bruce and Jen nervously sat and fidgeted while waiting.

A small woman approached Bruce and Jen through a set of swinging doors. She was holding a clipboard with three pages attached.

"You must be the Duncans, correct?"

"Yes, that's us. This is Lewis," Bruce replied. Lewis was scrutinizing every feature of her face.

"I need you to sign here, here, and here to consent to this procedure," she told them while pointing to three different pages. Bruce obliged and scribbled his name.

"Only one of you may be present while the procedure's being done."

"Yeah, I know," Bruce said. "It makes it easier on the patient, right?"

"Sounds like you've been through this before." The nurse laughed.

"Yes, just last week. I'll wait here, Jen." Bruce gave Lewis a rub on his arm. "Go get them, Lewis!"

Lewis looked terrified as his floundering arms reached for Daddy.

Jen followed the nurse into a lab and sat Lewis on her lap in a chair with padded armrests.

Another nurse approached Jen and asked her, "How's your little boy with needles?"

"Excuse me? He's only eight months old! He's never had anything done like this before!"

"I'm sure you're more scared than he is. Don't worry, ma'am. I'll put this gel on and let it soak in for a minute. He'll feel a little pinch, but hopefully, it won't be that bad," she tried to assure Jen.

"What do you mean, hopefully?"

"I'll strap his arm to this pad. Try to keep him still, okay?" She attempted to push Lewis's arm down and strap it, but he resisted. "My, he is a strong one, isn't he?" the nurse remarked. She finally got his arm immobilized. "I'm practically out of breath! What do you feed him?"

Lewis was cautiously happy as the nurses praised him. The nurse had a short needle in one hand and four empty vials in her other.

"Are those for Lewis?"

"Yes, I'm afraid so. Try to distract him while I put the needle in, okay? Have him look at you."

Jen made playful noises to get Lewis's attention. He was grinning as the needle went into his chubby arm. Lewis didn't budge. He looked at the blood as it filled a vial. "*Red!*" He squirmed a little and knew he wanted out.

"It's okay, Lewis. Mommy's right here," Jen whispered to Lewis as she held him tight.

"He has good blood pressure, ma'am, so this should only take a minute." The nurse tried to ease Jen's concerns. Lewis stopped squirming and looked at the needle in his arm while trying to wiggle from Jen. "There we go. We're all done, Lewis. What a good boy you were!" the nurse commended him. She reached for a band-aid from her coat pocket and found one covered with stars and balloons.

After the nurse put it on, Jen held a little pressure on the band-aid.

"Is that it? Anything we should do for him?" Jen asked.

"He seems to have calmed down rather quickly," the nurse remarked. "Maybe give him a favorite treat?"

"He has many favorite treats!" Jen and the nurse laughed.

"As Dr. Fields said, we'll have the results within forty-eight hours. Why don't you make an appointment at the front desk for Friday, say around three o'clock?" the nurse recommended.

"Thank you. I'm sorry for how I acted earlier," Jen apologized to the nurse. "We've been through so much the past couple of months."

"No problem at all, Ms. Duncan. We understand what you're dealing with, but poor Lewis doesn't!"

"Oh, I don't know about that," Jen laughed as she looked at him, whose attention was consumed by the pretty band-aid on his arm.

Bruce took Lewis from Jen's arms and hugged him.

"How's my big boy? I heard you were very good!" Lewis paid no attention to Bruce and scratched at his band-aid. "How'd he do, Jen?"

"I was scared to death at first. I thought I would pass out when they put that needle in him, but it didn't faze him."

"I guess he gets it from me then. You can't stand needles. Let's get Lewis some ice cream. He deserves a big bowl!"

"I think we all do, Bruce! Dairy Queen is closing next weekend, so let's get our last fix of summer."

Jen smiled and agreed. Lewis looked up at Bruce and smiled, too. He knew what lay in store for him.

Chapter Fourteen

Jen spoiled Lewis for the next two days until his doctor's appointment. They went for long walks on the beach, taking advantage of the Indian summer weather. Jen bought him some new toys, too. Bruce had fallen behind at work, and a state audit due the following Monday was haunting him. He couldn't attend the conference with Dr. Fields on Friday. Jen had to drop Bruce off at work as usual.

"Call me as soon as you're done, alright?" Bruce said.

"Don't worry. There's a payphone in the lobby. I might call you collect, okay?"

"Put it on the state's dime. They can afford it." Bruce kissed Lewis on his forehead and went to Jen's window. "He'll be fine, dear. Don't worry."

"Easy for you to say." She started the truck and slowly pulled from the parking lot as Bruce watched them leave.

Jen took extra precautions to stay focused while driving. She was aware that her bad habit of speeding was dangerous. She gave herself plenty of time to arrive at the appointment a half hour before the scheduled time. Jen even made an effort to be courteous to the other patients and mothers in the waiting room when she got there. She approached the desk in Dr. Fields' office nervously.

"Hi, I'm Jen Duncan with Lewis for a three o'clock with Dr. Fields."

"Let's see. Here you are!" the perky receptionist said while looking at her calendar. "He'll be with you in a moment. We're ahead of schedule for a change."

Jen returned a smile, sat in a chair, and put Lewis next to three other toddlers on the carpet. Lewis picked up a toy and attempted to give it to one of them, but they stared at him with odd curiosity. One of the mothers addressed Jen.

"He sure is a handsome boy! Is he here for a checkup?"

Jen tried to keep her patience.

"Well, sort of. He's had some tests lately. We're trying to see what's going on. He's a little big for his age."

"What is he, about eighteen or twenty months old?" the woman inquired.

Jen looked at Lewis, happily chatting away with the other three toddlers, and smiled at the woman.

Jen hesitated. "Yes, he's nineteen months old."

"Good luck. My daughter is sixteen months old and hasn't uttered one word. We're here for some testing, too. We were in the other day. I remember you." The woman quietly told Jen. "Tasha looks at everyone and smiles but never makes a sound."

"Oh, my! Our son doesn't stop talking from the minute he wakes up!"

The girl extended her hand toward Jen. "I'm Veda."

"I'm Jen." She hesitated but returned a hand to shake.

"Testing, testing, testing, that's all we've been doing," Veda commented.

"Have you had to go to Boston yet?"

"Twice! Isn't the parking horrible?"

They both laughed and continued to enjoy light conversation for a few moments, exchanging tales of strained motherhood.

"Ms. Duncan? Dr. Fields will see you now," the receptionist interrupted their chat.

Jen tried to grab Lewis, but he had other ideas. He stood up, grabbed a chair, and cruised toward the exit door until Jen put the brakes on him.

"He's pretty fast!" Veda remarked.

"Lewis is like this all day! Maybe we could get together sometime for a coffee. I live in Yarmouth."

"Well, howdy, neighbor! I live in Dennis right over the Bass River Bridge."

Jen had an impatient Lewis in her arms and tried to control him. "The front desk has my phone number. Please give me a call anytime."

"I'll leave my number there, too. That'd be great! Good luck!" Veda gave her phone number to the receptionist, looking at Jen with admiration. *I'd do anything for just one peep from Tasha.*

Jen entered the office and sat waiting for Dr. Fields, feeling slightly strange. She finally met someone with a child who had issues, too, and suddenly realized she had made a big mistake by covering for Lewis. He wasn't nineteen months old. It came out so easy! Jen felt guilty about lying to her new friend.

"Good afternoon, Jen." Dr. Fields startled her.

"Pardon me. I must have been daydreaming. I'm sorry."

"It must be this fantastic weather! In thirty years, I've never seen a fall like this on Cape Cod. Any plans for the weekend, maybe some fishing? I heard there's a big run of stripers off Monomoy. Bruce fishes there, doesn't he?"

Jen was ready to stuff the apple sitting on Dr. Field's desk down his throat. Enough of this idle banter! How's Lewis? That's all she wanted to know!

"Yes, Bruce is an avid fisherman. He drives me crazy," she forced herself to reply politely. "He's been talking about the striper run, too."

Dr. Fields put a folder on his desk and leaned forward in his chair.

"Jen, we have results on the blood work done on Lewis. We sent samples to Lahey Clinic in Boston for double confirmation also." He paused.

"That doesn't sound good. Well, what's the verdict?" Jen asked warily.

Dr. Fields put his hands on the table and opened a folder.

"Jen, there is absolutely nothing wrong with Lewis. His pituitary and thyroid glands are perfectly normal. Red and white blood cells, iron counts are perfect."

Jen started crying uncontrollably. She couldn't believe what he said. It took a moment to regain her composure.

"Are you sure? They didn't mix up the results, did they?"

"Positive. That's why we took so much blood the other day. The samples were verified at Lahey. The data on premature babies isn't very reliable. I've never seen an infant recover so fast from early delivery. You have an extraordinary child on your hands."

"Oh, I know that, Dr. Fields. I know that."

"Jen. That doesn't mean Lewis is out of the woods yet," Dr. Fields told her somberly.

"What do you mean?"

"When you were in my office last, do you remember I told you Lewis might need leg braces if he keeps growing?"

"Yes, unfortunately, I do."

"I recommend you see Dr. Fleming in Orthopedics next week."

"Is it another trip to Boston?" Jen asked cautiously.

"Oh no, he's right here on our staff."

"Leg braces?"

"Jen, have you ever heard of the term 'bow-legged'?"

"Why, of course. I don't know what it is, but I've heard of it."

"Simply, Lewis is growing at such a fast rate his bones are not strong enough to hold him up, and they may deflect under the weight of his own body. He's off and running at an earlier stage of development. We want to prevent this condition from worsening as he ages. Another cause of bow-legs is rickets, but we certainly have been keeping track of Lewis and can rule that out."

Jen thought for a moment. "I'm not sure how I feel. I'm so happy there's nothing wrong with Lewis, but now you say he'll need leg braces. He already stands out, having to wear those eyeglasses. How long will he have to wear braces?"

"It's hard to say, Jen. That will depend upon whether he continues to grow at an alarming rate. His growth rate may taper off as his leg muscles strengthen. We'll leave that for Dr. Fleming to decide. I asked him to see Lewis ASAP."

"Well," Jen paused and picked Lewis up. "It is for the better, right?"

"Everything will be fine, Jen. Lewis is doing great. There are many other children on Cape Cod with problems much worse than his. I hope you can go fishing this weekend. It'll probably be the last good run."

"Yes. Thank you, Dr. Fields."

Jen wanted to feel good but didn't. Now Lewis would need leg braces. How many toddlers on Cape Cod wore eyeglasses and leg braces? None! She tried to feel good and realized nothing was seriously wrong with Lewis. His eyeglasses and leg braces were temporary, and he would grow to have a normal childhood. Jen tried reminding herself of meeting

Veda in the office today. Her daughter hasn't spoken a word or made a sound!

Jen walked past the payphone and forgot to call Bruce. It never dawned on her. She strapped Lewis into the bassinet and gave him a new dolphin toy.

*****

Since Jen was almost at the armory, she stopped to pick up Bruce. He saw their truck pull into the yard and became agitated when he saw Jen. He picked up a rag, wiped his hands, and then threw it on the floor as she rolled to a stop next to the open garage door.

"I thought you were going to call me!" Bruce yelled. "How's Lewis?"

"Please, Bruce. Can we just go home? I'm wiped out, and Lewis is fussing."

"Well, okay. I have to clean up my mess. That audit Monday is at 6 a.m. Just give me five minutes."

"Sure. We'll be fine waiting here."

"Oh, c'mon, the guys haven't seen Lewis in weeks. Bring him in, okay?"

"*Bruce*. I'm warning you!" Jen shook her finger at him.

"Okay, okay," he grumbled.

"I don't want to talk about it until we get home, and you're going to stop at Cliff's and buy me the biggest bottle of Merlot you can find, got it?"

"Yes, ma'am!" he replied smartly. "Boy, I guess it didn't go so good today, did it?"

Bruce cleaned his area and washed up. He walked to the driver's side door to relieve Jen. "I'm driving!" she yelled at him. "Get in before I run you over!"

Bruce couldn't figure out what was going on. He gave a friendly departing wave to his co-workers, who heard every word between Jen and him. Bruce made a quick stop at Cliff's for some much-needed refreshments. They were driving home on the ocean-view road in minutes.

Bruce gazed out the truck window toward the orange and yellow horizon dotted with fishing boats and trawlers. He wanted to mention one last fishing outing this weekend but didn't dare. A warm, southwest wind drove heavy salt air in the passenger window, ruffling his hair. Brilliant sunshine and flat seas were predicted for the weekend, and he knew stripers were hitting jigs hard.

What Jen said next surprised the heck out of Bruce. "What do you say we pack the Boston Whaler tomorrow with fishing rods and head out to Monomoy?"

Bruce almost jumped from his seat with excitement but tried to stay calm and said, "Maybe, we'll have to check the forecast."

Chapter Fifteen

Bruce unpacked the truck with Lewis in tow. Jen opened the kitchen door as Rex scurried onto the side lawn to water the garden fence, every foot of it. Jen went directly inside and uncorked the bottle of wine. Bruce came through the door with Lewis on one arm and a case of beer in the other.

"I figured I might as well join you," Bruce told Jen.

"I just called Meg. She's coming over to get Lewis for a night at Mom's house. He'll love all the attention. I hope you don't mind."

"Well, I'm kind of lost here, Jen. I can't figure you out. I don't know what's going on, but I'm sure Lewis will love being with Meg and your mother. I'll pack his bag if you can scrounge some grub for him."

"We're pretty low on food, but he'll eat anything, as you know."

Bruce went upstairs and packed some fresh clothes, a few toys, and Lewis's favorite 'blanky.' Jen had filled half of a grocery bag of food by the time he returned downstairs.

"Isn't he going for just one night?"

"Yeah, but you never know. We should leave all this food at Mom's, so she has some on hand anyhow."

"Why, are you going somewhere?" Bruce asked in a high voice.

"No, no. Here's Meg. Why don't you bring everything out to her car?"

"All right, I can only do one thing at a time, dear."

Uh oh! I called her 'dear' again.

He brought three bags of supplies to Meg's car. Jen was right behind him with Lewis on her hip.

"You'll be a good little boy, Lewis," Jen ordered and gave him a big kiss on his fat cheek. "Thanks, Meg. Why don't you and Brad meet us tomorrow at High Banks Landing around nine? We're going fishing, probably for the last time this year."

"That sounds great, guys. Should I bring Lewis, too?"

"He wouldn't want to miss it. I put some heavy clothes in the bag for him. I'd ask Mom to come, but she gets seasick just looking at the waves!"

"I know. I've never figured out why she lives on Cape Cod. See you tomorrow!"

Bruce, Jen, and Rex watched in silence as Meg drove away. Bruce turned to Jen.

"So, how is he? What the heck is going on?"

"Let's go inside and sit down, Bruce." Jen led the way, placed the bottle of wine on the table, and popped a beer for him.

"I hope those are victory drinks," Bruce said.

"Just listen to me, okay? Lewis's tests came back," she paused. "Fine, Bruce. Absolutely fine!"

Bruce screamed so loud it could be heard a block away. "You gotta be kidding me, right? So, what's with the big mystery? I thought he had some fatal disease!"

"All his organs, glands, and blood work were perfect! There's no explanation for his growth rate."

"But I'm confused. Isn't that a good thing? Aren't you relieved?"

"I am relieved. I'm happy! But there's something else."

"What. *What*?"

"We have *another* appointment next week with an orthopedic specialist. They want Lewis to wear leg braces."

"That's not so bad, Jen. He'll get used to them! He's been behind the eight-ball since he was born. I'm sure the doctor knows what he's doing. This Leap Year thing has been haunting us since the day he was born!"

"I know, I know. I just feel so sorry for him. Everyone looks at him funny already because he wears glasses, never mind wearing clunky leg braces."

"Jen, it's not as if he can't walk. He's already walking and talking more than a two-year-old! He'll be doing pull-ups on my bar soon if I let him!"

Jen started to laugh. "I do realize how lucky we are. Bruce, I met a woman today, Veda. Her daughter has never uttered a word, not even a sound! She's over sixteen months old!"

"See? I told you how fortunate we are, Jen."

"That's not all, Bruce."

"What do you mean, Jen?"

"I covered for Lewis. I said he was nineteen months old. I lied to her. I feel horrible deceiving someone like that."

"Come off it, Jen. You're under so much pressure. It's just a little fib, you know? Don't crack on me now."

"It's Lewis I'm worried about. Maybe the doctor next week won't recommend leg braces for him. You're right, Bruce. I should feel good about the test results, and I do. I just wish there was an explanation for everything."

"Someday, we'll look back on this and laugh about it, right?" Bruce tried to convince Jen.

"Yeah, someday, maybe someday."

*****

It was a beautiful weekend on the ocean, considering it was the last one in October. Harbor seals were basking in the late fall sunshine before their annual migration into waters infested with great white sharks looking for an easy meal. They enjoyed a seaside picnic and clambake on the refuge at Monomoy.

Lewis took in the sights of nature. Rex chased his ball endlessly on the beach. Meg's new boyfriend, Brad, got seasick from the boat ride and bent over the side rail, losing his dinner. Bruce and Jen put all their worries about Lewis on hold for a couple of days, relishing the entire weekend without being consumed by concern or fear.

On Wednesday, Bruce accompanied Jen and Lewis to the orthopedic specialist at Cape Cod General. Doctor Fleming took X-rays to confirm Lewis's condition. The tibia and fibula on one of his legs were deforming. Lewis was prescribed braces for both legs, which were very uncomfortable and noisy when he attempted to walk. He walked with much confidence before and occasionally would bolt into a trot. It seemed he'd been robbed of his confidence. He needed much prodding to walk alongside the furniture or venture across the floor. He loved it when they were taken off at night so he could sleep. It didn't take him long to figure out how to scale his crib and run down the hall without braces. He cherished those wild moments of freedom before being nabbed by Mom or Dad.

Jen's shopping trips and doctor appointments were as torturous as she thought. Children stared, pointed, and laughed at Lewis while he simply and innocently waved at them. It bothered Jen, even more when adults would stare and comment softly to one another as she passed by with Lewis.

A steady regiment of doctor's appointments at the new orthopedic office and Lewis's regular physician kept Jen on the move twice each month. Time passed quickly. Before she knew it, Lewis was in for his twenty-month checkup at Dr. Fields. She led him into the office by his hand.

"Here he is!" exclaimed Dr. Fields. "How's our linebacker doing today, Jen?"

"Oh, I think it'll be quite a while before he's a linebacker. He's taken to throwing things everywhere!"

"Does he seem frustrated with having to wear the braces?"

"When I try to put them on in the morning, he shouts "No!" very clearly. And he repeats a few other nasty words, too!"

"That's quite normal, Jen. He will certainly demonstrate some frustration and rebellious behavior from time to time. It's best not to make a big deal about it and move on to another task if possible. Does it bother you too?"

"Of course, it does. I don't want Lewis to grow up with everyone looking at him like he's the ringmaster of a circus act!"

"Jen, the more you assimilate him with other children, the better. It's not the Stone Age anymore, and this isn't a permanent handicap."

"What's going to happen when he starts school?"

"You're right, Jen. Schoolchildren can be cruel to anyone different. Just like jealousy, children learn pack mentality at a very young age. It makes you wonder if it's hereditary. I guess it's something all special-needs parents have to sort out. You'll have many mixed feelings, ups and downs. With any luck, Lewis will shed his braces by kindergarten or first grade. Let's take those braces off and get a weight on him, okay?"

"I'm sure he'd love that."

Lewis stretched on his back while the doctor removed his braces and measured his overall length.

Dr. Fields hid his astonishment quite well as he wrote Lewis's length in a folder. "Thirty inches long." Dr. Fields remarked quietly. He rubbed Lewis's legs, checking for muscle development. Lewis started laughing as if he was being tickled.

"I bet that feels pretty good, doesn't it?" Dr. Fields joked with Lewis. "Jen, muscle stimulation and massage are essential for him. Try and do this a couple of times a week. Get Bruce involved, too."

"Are you kidding? Bruce won't even rub my legs after I've been chasing that little monster all day!" Lewis giggled and flung his arms.

"Let's get a weight on him. Stand Lewis on the scale, and don't put your foot on it like last time!" Dr. Fields said jokingly. "Hmm, okay." He walked over to his desk and whispered as he made a note. "Thirty pounds."

"Well, Jen, I'm sure it's no surprise that Lewis is still growing, but not at quite an alarming rate as before. By the time he's two years old, he'll be the size of a four-year-old. He's in fine shape, but his leg muscles need a little catching up. I'm sure Dr. Fleming will agree. We've ruled out any abnormalities, so keep him on the same diet. I don't have any need to see him until his two-year checkup. His vaccinations are up to speed, so we'll see you both then."

"We have an appointment with Dr. Fleming in one month to see if any brace adjustments need to be made," Jen informed Dr. Fields.

"Thanks, Jen. I'll make a note of it on my chart. See you in six months."

"It'll be spring by then. Hooray! I can't stand winters here on the Cape."

*****

One month later, Lewis and Jen visited Dr. Fleming. He lengthened the braces supporting Lewis's legs, which was not uncommon. Given his remarkable growth rate, Dr. Fleming wanted to see him every three months for the following year.

Chapter Sixteen

Lewis's second birthday passed with a small celebration on February 28. There was hardly any celebrating at all.

Jen had documented every day of Lewis's life for the past year—everything she fed him, every new word he said, his emotions, physical activities, and habits. She recorded them in a journal. It became her mission to help him blend in with other children. She joined a support group with parents of special needs children. They shared the same concern. "Will my child ever be accepted?"

Lewis's second birthday brought his twentieth trip to a doctor's office; Jen kept track of that, too. Once again, Dr. Fields was not surprised at his size. He weighed almost forty pounds and was thirty-eight inches tall, perfect measurements for a four-year-old child, not a two-year-old. Lewis was in excellent health. His motor skills and reflexes did not coordinate. He was very thoughtful, hardly whined, and had an extensive vocabulary and a complete set of teeth.

*****

On a cool morning, Jen wanted a cup of tea to chase away the aches and pains of living in a damp environment. She put a kettle of water on the stove's rear burner as she always did so exploring little hands couldn't reach it.

While making a quick call to her sister, she heard the kettle whistling away. She cut her conversation short and returned to the kitchen. As she stepped back with the teapot in her grasp, she didn't notice Lewis was directly behind her. She stepped on his foot and emptied half of the boiling water onto his hand. She screamed in terror.

"Lewis! I didn't see you! Oh my gosh!"

Lewis looked at his hand and said nothing.

"You must be in shock!" Jen yelled at him. Lewis's hand quickly turned red and blistered, but he didn't cry. He asked Mommy why she was crying and screaming.

Jen ran to the phone and frantically dialed Dr. Field's office. They told her to get in immediately. Lewis still had not complained about the severe burn. She wrapped his hand in a cold towel and sped to Dr. Fields' office. They took him in right away.

Dr. Fields looked at it. It was a moderate burn. He told her to expect some blistering.

"He didn't even cry! I've put up more of a fuss than he has!"

Dr. Fields asked Lewis, "Does your boo-boo hurt?"

"No. Am I going to get a lollipop today?" Jen and Dr. Fields laughed, finally breaking the tense situation.

Dr. Fields opened his thick folder on Lewis and made some more notes.

"I'll be back in a moment, Jen," he told her. Lewis was happy just bouncing on her lap.

He brought a small pinwheel-type device and asked Lewis to raise his foot. Dr. Fields ran the pinwheel down Lewis's leg. He laughed. "That tickles!" Lewis said.

Dr. Fields also had a tiny, sharp needle in his other hand and asked Jen to divert Lewis's attention toward the window. Dr. Fields stuck it in Lewis's foot the minutest amount. Lewis said nothing. It should have at least startled Lewis, but there was no reaction. A familiar look of concern came across Dr. Fields' face.

"Jen, I've never encountered this condition where a child cannot feel pain. I believe some more testing may be needed."

"What?" she voiced in displeasure.

"I've only read about it, but I've never seen it. You've told me Lewis doesn't cry much, right? He may have a case of CIP, or what is known as congenital insensitivity to pain."

"He never fusses, even if he falls."

"There can be varying degrees of this condition. It is certainly something we have to keep an eye on."

"Something else? What's next?" Jen tried not to raise her voice.

"Jen, pain is a reaction that our bodies use to tell us when something is wrong. Lewis's interceptors and nerves may be confused."

"*I'm* confused!" Jen exclaimed. "Is *this* something he'll outgrow?"

"He might, or he may have it his whole life. It's something to be wary of," Dr. Fields admitted. "He may not be able to feel cold or heat either. He may get frostbite in winter or overheat in summer by not sweating. Both of those scenarios could lead to serious consequences."

"That's great. Something else to worry about!"

"Let air heal the wound, and don't pop the blisters. That could lead to infection. See me in a week while I do some more research on this condition. It may be nothing to worry about, Jen."

"Okay, Dr. Fields. I'll make another appointment."

Lewis was happy and talked to himself the whole time.

What am I going to tell Bruce this time?

That evening Jen told Bruce about the accident and burn Lewis received, but she decided not to say anything about the other possible condition Lewis may have. They've been through enough!

Jen decided to start a support group in their home. She invited parents and their children to her home for coffee and donuts once a week. Jen looked after many kids allowing their parents time off during the day for work, doctor's appointments, or plain old fun with their spouses. Bruce could finally afford a second car to shuttle friends around town. She found a purpose in her life and realized Lewis had opened the door.

Lewis made frequent visits to the doctor's office every couple of months. Each trip took a little more convincing. Dr. Fields asked Jen to note any injuries

Lewis might sustain and document if any pain was evident.

As Lewis approached three years of age, he understood that he wasn't like other boys who could run fast or play baseball. He always stayed on the outskirts looking in. He admired other children. Lewis often dreamt of running down the middle of a street, chasing other boys after a kickball, and what it would be like to go on a thrilling ride at the Elk's carnival.

Before he went to bed, he rubbed his calf muscles and talked to them. "Please grow, legs, grow!" he would say as he quietly sobbed himself to sleep. "I want to run and play. I hope I can someday."

Jen and Bruce made sure Lewis had every comfort available to him. They put a TV in his bedroom with remote control, so he didn't have to get up and change the channels, but there were strict rules about how much he could watch. One of his favorite shows was Willie Whistle. It was about a clown who could communicate only by whistling. Funny thing, Lewis felt sorry for him.

Lewis's physical strength continued to increase, and so did his size. Bruce and Jen allowed him to walk without his leg braces every Sunday. The doctor agreed that two hours every week would be an excellent place to start rehab. Lewis was so excited on Saturday night that he couldn't sleep. He would wait until noon on Sunday to remove them for a few precious hours of freedom.

Jen connected with Veda, whom she had met at the doctor's office. Her daughter still did not speak, but testing discovered that Tasha's hearing was fine. Rumors persisted throughout Cape Cod of higher-than-normal cancer rates and birth deformities. Everyone tried to link these high incidences of illness to Otis Air Force Base, located just over the Sagamore Bridge.

As Lewis approached his third birthday, Jen thought Dr. Fields wanted to do more blood testing to see if all was well. Lewis was walking very sturdily on his braces and seemed proud of them. He knew he was different and liked to have Tasha as a companion when Jen did their weekly food shopping. They seemed to develop a secret method of communication, including hand gestures as he mouthed words to her.

March 1, 1975, Jen brought Lewis into Dr. Fields' office for his third birthday checkup.

Dr. Fields compiled four binders dedicated to Lewis's growth records and progress. Dr. Fleming had a similar file of his own.

"Hi, Lewis. How are you today?" Dr. Fields directed a question clearly to Lewis.

"Good."

"Boy, he's pretty quiet today, Jen. Is there anything wrong?"

"He thinks you want to take more blood. He hasn't slept all night," Jen answered Dr. Fields.

"There's nothing to be afraid of, Lewis. You've had blood drawn before, but you probably can't remember, right?"

"I member, it didn't hurt me." Lewis calmly replied.

"Jen, Lewis thinks he recalls when he had blood taken at eight months of age!" Dr. Fields remarked.

"He does remember! He even told me what he was wearing that day. Blood got on his favorite shirt, and he recalled the band-aid with balloons and stars," Jen said.

"That's impossible, Jen," Dr. Fields replied. He shook his head and made another note in his chart.

"I'm going to need a new bookcase to keep up with Lewis here, Jen," he joked. "Okay, it's time for the usual height and weight."

When the doctor looked at Lewis, he was already on the table waiting to be measured.

"You're too much, kid!" Dr. Fields and Jen laughed. Lewis did too. "Forty-four inches." He noted.

Lewis sat up and unstrapped the braces from his legs. He knew the routine well.

"Lewis, easy does it. And no jumping from the table," Jen warned him.

He carefully slid from the table and slowly walked to the scale. Dr. Fields followed him and looked at the dial.

"Forty-eight pounds, not bad." Dr. Fields jotted the number down and took a seat on the corner of his exam table. He tucked a pen behind his ear.

"Jen, I went over Lewis's complete history last night at home."

"Well?" Jen asked.

"I think Lewis's growth rate is stabilizing. He's still way above the norm, but not as dramatically."

"You're kidding me, right? Did you hear that, Lewis?" Jen belted loud enough for the whole waiting room to hear. She got up and hugged Lewis, who had no idea what was happening. She hugged Dr. Fields.

"Easy, Jen, easy," he told her. "I don't feel any real need at this time for any blood work unless some unusual event happens in the future. I don't need to see Lewis for six months, okay?"

"Oh, my! I don't know what to say. I know Lewis has an appointment with Dr. Fleming next month. I hope he has some good news, too!"

"Let's not jump the gun, as they say, Jen."

Lewis was sitting on the table, trying to take it all in, when he looked at Dr. Fields and unassumingly asked, "No band-aid?"

Everyone laughed, and Dr. Fields said, "No, Lewis. No band-aid!"

Chapter Seventeen

Bruce was elated with the good news from Lewis's physical. Maybe things were looking up for him, and he wouldn't be six feet tall by first grade. The local clam shack had just opened for spring, and a fresh seafood dinner was just the ticket for Bruce and Jen. Lewis stuck with a hot dog.

The following week Lewis had an appointment with Dr. Fleming to check the progress of his legs. Unfortunately, it was recommended Lewis keep the braces on for another six months. Doctor Fleming said he could go without them all day Sunday if he promised not to run and climb the stairs. He was allowed to walk with someone if they watched him closely. Lewis didn't mind at all.

Veda continued to bring Tasha over twice a week. Three mothers dropped their disabled children at Jen's at least once a week for some respite. Joey had cerebral palsy and was confined to a wheelchair. He loved the attention from Rex. Patsy was born with no hands but could use her arms quite well. She didn't have a problem walloping anybody, anytime. Ripley fell off his father's station wagon tailgate while going to the dump one day and suffered a head injury. He was very slow and could only communicate by grunting. It was quite a group when all were present at the same time.

Lewis and Tasha would help serve lunch but forgot about cleaning up; it was playtime then. They thought it would be funny to cover Joey in shaving cream one day. Bruce always kept a few extra cans on hand. Jen hid her laughter when she saw the results and took a picture for posterity. Luckily, Joey's mother thought it was funny, too. Joey's fresh change of clothes did the trick, and he smelled nice too.

Lewis's development through his third year of life mirrored any other child. His speech and motor skills were fine, if not above average. He favored using his left arm for throwing and developed quite an aim for his target, usually Bruce. Bruce realized he would be the only southpaw in both families for generations.

If the leg braces held Lewis back, you really wouldn't know it. Lewis came into the house at the end of every day, covered in dirt, mud, and tree bark.

By summer, he was trying to run as fast as possible, with his braces rattling the whole way. Rex would come running from behind and tackle him. *What'll he be like when those braces come off?* Jen thought.

Lewis had eye exams for the next two years to see if he could distinguish between a dog, cat, apple, banana, etc. His eyesight did not regress, and by the time he was almost four, Lewis was slated for an exam to see if his prescription could be decreased from his present "coke bottle glasses."

This would be the first exam where Lewis could tell the doctor if the images he was looking at through the binoculars looked 'more or less fuzzy.' Jen hoped he wouldn't be burdened with those heavy, thick lenses for many more years.

Unfortunately, after the exam, the eye doctor determined his vision was worsening and prescribed thicker lenses. His glasses were so thick his eyes could hardly be seen. Lewis didn't mind, but Jen and Bruce did. They were given a set of eye exercises for Lewis to try and turn his regression around. Every night for one hour, they would remove his glasses and perform specific tasks to make his eyes focus better at short and medium distances.

*****

It was only one week until his fourth birthday. Since he was a leap-year baby, it was his first actual birthday! Lewis's past three birthdays were small celebrations. One on February 28th and the other two on March 1st.

Jen couldn't wait, but Bruce was apprehensive as another February 29th approached. He started to feel a sense of impending doom, remembering what they went through four years ago. Jen tried to brush off any dark thoughts and conversation. She told Bruce to knock it off.

Jen and Bruce decided to have a large party for Lewis's fourth birthday. She invited her parents and Bruce's mother. Veda and Tasha were also invited. Joey attended in his wheelchair, along with Ripley and their parents. Jen decorated the house to the max.

"Bruce, did you put those streamers up in the dining room?" Jen asked him.

"All set, hon. And don't fill the balloons yet. Rex keeps popping them!"

"I was wondering what the commotion was about!" Jen replied, laughing. "Did you pick up the cake at the bakery?"

"Yep, it's in the fridge." Jen ordered 'one present only' for Lewis from all attending the party, but she knew certain people wouldn't abide by her request.

Sure enough, Kay, Clint, and Fran arrived at the house with grocery bags full of presents. Bruce and Jen couldn't believe the number of gifts for Lewis, but what the heck? The past few years were filled with tension, appointments, and testing. Everyone needed an enjoyable day.

The eight-foot-long dining room table was packed with sixteen relatives and friends as Lewis opened his presents. There were so many gifts; he didn't know which one to open. He knelt on a chair and screamed when he opened each present. Everyone wore birthday hats, even Rex, seated in Lewis's old highchair at the end of the table with him.

Lewis knew what his favorite part of the whole day would be: cake and ice cream! Bruce went into the kitchen and removed the cake from the refrigerator. He put five candles on it. Kay asked, "Why five candles?"

"Well, Kay," he explained. "One is for each of his years, and in his case, the extra one is for good luck. I don't think he needs one to grow on!"

There was such a feverish pitch coming from the dining room that Bruce could barely think. He lit the candles and dimmed the lights as he walked in. Instantly, everyone stopped talking and broke into a harmonious "Happy Birthday."

Lewis wore such a giant smile; you could see his tonsils. He even broke out singing to himself along with everyone else. Halfway through the song, Lewis got a serious look and stopped singing. He looked toward the end of the table and pointed. One by one, everyone turned their head and stopped singing. By the time Bruce realized it, one beautiful little voice was singing. *It was Tasha!* She kept singing as her mother broke out into screams of joy.

Veda started crying and hugged everyone. Lewis jumped from his seat at the other end and ran across the tabletop. He smashed into the cake and slid head-first into Tasha. Everyone got covered in a shower of cake and icing.

".I hope you got that on film, Clint!" Bruce yelled out. Clint never went anywhere without his hand-held VCR motion camera.

It was absolute pandemonium. Veda and Jen were so happy they were bawling their eyes out. Tasha kept singing while everyone was on the floor, laughing and crying so hard.

Lewis was covered head-to-toe with cake smeared over him. He got up from the floor, saying, "Mom, Tasha! Mom, Tasha!" He was so excited he could hardly talk.

"C'mon, buddy, let's go into the kitchen and get cleaned up!" Bruce told Lewis, trying not to laugh.

"Dad, Tasha! Dad, Tasha!" Lewis blurted out.

"I know, I know! Come with me."

The excitement simmered as everyone wiped tears from their eyes. Rex jumped out of his seat and cleaned up the floor.

"This is unbelievable! Thank you, God!" Veda dropped to her knees. Tasha walked over and put her hand on her mother's shoulder.

"Mommy, I'm here, Mommy."

"I know you are, sweetie. I know you are," Veda said as she pulled a big piece of cake from Tasha's hair. Veda looked at Jen. "I don't know how to thank you!"

Jen thought for a moment. "Thank Lewis, not me. How about some ice cream and cookies for everyone? I think that's about all we have left!" Jen said, laughing, trying to break the silence.

Everyone chipped in to clean the table and regrouped for some refreshments. Fran and Kay made some coffee while Bruce and Clint headed to the fridge for a cold beer.

After a quick clean-up and recess from laughing and crying, Bruce gathered everyone around the table and proposed a toast.

"We came here today to celebrate our son, Lewis. Something very magical and special has happened before our very eyes. It appears another life has blossomed from a seed into a flower. I'm not a religious man, but we have truly seen a miracle here today."

"Amen!" Veda shouted and hugged Tasha.

It wasn't just a birthday party anymore. There was an intense conversation between everyone. Many emotional outpourings of happiness, newfound revelations, and hugging continued for hours. Lewis and Tasha quietly disappeared into the sanctuary of an empty living room. They sat on a couch with their tiny feet dangling, covertly whispering to each other with hands and fingers covering their mouths. They had a lot to catch up on.

Chapter Eighteen

The following week at work, Bruce took inventory in the supply room. It was a tedious task neglected for years. Lewis had one appointment with his orthopedist every four months to adjust his braces. He was relieved Leap Year had passed without incident.

Jen kept Lewis busy three to four days a week with his friends from "The Club." Jen proposed using a name for the program that she and Veda ran. She made t-shirts that read, "I'm in The Club!" Eight disabled children in the Yarmouth and Dennis area enjoyed afternoons at Jen's house on various days. She got irritated when people referred to her group of children as 'special, handicapped, or mentally retarded.' Jen and Veda never accepted one cent for their efforts and years of support for these children.

Jen's house was filled with constant commotion and confusion. Both of them loved it. Veda's only complaint was since Tasha started talking, she never stopped.

*****

Lewis's growth slowed down during his fourth year, but he still towered over six-year-olds. He was four feet tall and weighed fifty pounds. As he neared five, he knew there would be a complete round of physical checkups and wasn't happy about it.

Jen put Lewis in a spring kindergarten class when he was five. He would be starting first grade in the fall. She hoped the change of scenery and opportunity to meet some new faces might be good for him, but she was dead wrong. Although the morning session lasted only five hours, it was stressful for Lewis. He was rarely included in games because he couldn't run like the other kids. He also needed one-on-one attention at the chalkboard because he was a little slower than most children.

Summer couldn't come quickly enough for everyone in the Duncan family. Bruce accumulated one month's vacation time and planned to take it from July 1 through August 1. The weather was spectacular, and they spent most of their vacation on the beach or boat. By this time, Jen thought she might like to have another child, but a recent exam showed abnormalities in her abdomen. Ultra-sound revealed another tumor attached to her only good ovary. It wasn't cancerous but was removed along with the ovary. She was devastated and didn't like the idea of Lewis growing up as an only child. The thought consumed Jen. *Maybe I should have tried to conceive sooner.* Those guilty feelings would haunt her forever.

Lewis signed up for first grade in August when he was five. He could have been held back another year because he just made the cut-off in age. He towered over third graders, and Jen didn't want to wait another year. Lewis scored average on preschool testing but wasn't applying himself. Jen and Lewis went to the elementary school in West Yarmouth to register him.

As they entered the doors through the foyer, conversations between adults and children ceased when Lewis lumbered in with his noisy braces. He strode toward the sign-up desk with Jen, eyeing everyone.

"Good morning, ma'am," a suited gentleman addressed Jen. "I believe sign-up for third and fourth grades are down the hall."

Jen hushed her feelings. "My son, Lewis, is here to sign up for the first grade. I realize he's a little big for his age," Jen said calmly.

"I'm so sorry! He'll be on the football team by the time he's in sixth grade! What's your last name?"

"Duncan."

"Okay, first table on the left. A through J is over there." He pointed the way for Jen and Lewis.

"Thank you very much, Sir," Jen replied kindly. Lewis gave him a confident nod as he walked to the table. Jen tried to take Lewis by the hand, but he insisted on walking alone.

"This way, Lewis," she firmly said as he attempted to join a conversation with other children.

Jen approached a table with two well-dressed ladies sitting between piles of paperwork.

"Well, good morning, Miss," one of the women addressed Jen. "And who do we have here today?"

"Hello, this is Lewis Duncan, and I'm Jen. Nice to meet you both."

"I've heard about you from a mother in town. You run that special program in your home, don't you?"

Jen was infuriated and hid her frustration once again. Lewis and his companions were *not* special!

"Well, yes, I did. Most of the children are starting school this year."

"Will your son need special attention this year, Mrs. Duncan?"

There was that word 'special' again. Jen was ready to tip the table over onto the pair of women. At her boiling point, she took a deep breath and answered politely.

"No, Lewis does not need 'special' attention." She used her hands and fingers to mock a set of quotation marks around 'special' as she spoke. "He will be in leg braces for another six months and wear eyeglasses for a few more years. He exercises his eyes every night."

"How tall is he, Mrs. Duncan? It's strictly for school records. We keep charts on all students."

"Lewis is fifty inches tall," Jen replied. "He's had quite a growth spurt."

"Spurt?" one woman commented. "More like an avalanche!" She tried to be humorous. Jen bit her tongue.

One of the women handed Jen a folder of paperwork to fill out and send back to school.

"Here you go, Mrs. Duncan." The woman paused. "And we'll see Lewis on the Wednesday following Labor Day, right? Enjoy the rest of your summer."

Both ladies extended a handshake, but Jen turned around quickly and marched out the door five steps ahead of Lewis. "Come on, Lewis!" she reprimanded him as he dilly-dallied his way through the lobby, sizing up other children registering for school.

Jen opened the passenger door of their car and practically threw him clear across the seat. "What's the matter, Mum?"

"Nothing is the matter, nothing at all, Lewis. Just put your seat belt on, and don't bother me!"

"But Mum, I didn't do anything!"

"I know you didn't. Someday, you'll understand."

Jen drove in silence while Lewis looked at pictures in a book about first grade. He couldn't wait to meet new friends. His neighborhood became a ghost town after Labor Day. Most year-round residents were retired, and many homes closed up after the last weekend of summer.

Jen filled Bruce in that night when he got home from work about the events at school. Bruce didn't read much into it. He figured Jen was overreacting to their comments, but Jen knew what she heard and didn't like it one bit.

*****

The summer passed away quickly as Lewis counted the days until school started. He crossed them off on a calendar in his room. He was also sad Tasha wouldn't be attending school with him. She lived *way* over the bridge in Dennis, the next town. Veda was also very concerned classmates would make fun of Tasha. She had developed a stutter before first grade. The family doctor attributed it to Tasha not talking for almost three years. He was right. Happily, once school started, Tasha dropped her stutter within two months.

Nolan planned a large cookout on Labor Day. Jen always felt out of place there. She was very tired of the same old place, people, and Lewis being the youngest of the children. The closest other kid in age was twelve, light years ahead of Lewis. He couldn't run the bases but could hit the softball in the family game. Everyone was so shocked he really could see through those thick eyeglasses and knock the ball over the fence with every pitch. He developed a few short-lived friendships with some kids at the cookout, but they didn't acknowledge him once school started. There was one day to recuperate from the long weekend.

It was then D-Day, his first day of school.

Chapter Nineteen

Bruce came into Lewis's bedroom with a glass of milk. It always helped him sleep through the night. He tucked him in and propped a pillow behind them.

"I bet you're excited about tomorrow, aren't you, Lewis?" Bruce asked him.

"Sort of. I wish Tasha and Joey were with me. I didn't see any other kids like me."

"What do you mean, *like me*?" Bruce asked softly.

"Everyone stares. Will they always stare at me, Dad?"

"No, Lewis. No. You'll be out of those leg braces in six months and kicking a soccer ball out of the schoolyard!" Bruce tried to bolster Lewis's confidence.

"That's a long time. Isn't it, Dad?"

"By the time you're six, they'll be gone, I promise."

"Really?"

"If you keep doing your exercises every weekend and drink lots of milk, the doctor said you'll be fine, remember?"

"I kind of member," Lewis said with his head down.

"Has Mummy been in to kiss you goodnight?"

"Yes, but I want another kiss!"

"Okay, I'll send her in. We'll have a nice breakfast ready for you in the morning. Rex will keep you company till then. See you in the morning, tiger."

"Night, Dad," Lewis replied as he snuck under his covers.

Bruce went into the living room, where Jen was nervously pacing. She had practically worn a path on the carpet.

"What the heck is the matter with you, Jen? I don't think I've ever seen you this uptight!"

"Since we signed Lewis up for school, I've hardly slept. I doubt I'll get any sleep tonight either!"

"Why? Do you think he's going to get crucified tomorrow or something?"

"Yes, I do! Those kids will laugh at him, and the parents, too!"

"C'mon, Jen, we've been through this already. There are lots more kids in school that have worse problems than Lewis does."

"I know, but when he's your kid, it's a different story."

"I know what you mean." Bruce thought for a moment. "He's waiting for another goodnight kiss from you."

"That little bugger!"

Jen snuck quietly into his room and saw he had one eye open, pretending to be asleep.

She leaned over the bed and gave him a soft kiss on his cheek.

"Goodnight, little man," she whispered to him and turned around to exit Lewis's room. He slyly opened his eyes to see her walk out his bedroom door.

"Night, Mummy," he barely whispered and fell fast asleep.

Jen didn't sleep at all that night. She was exhausted by morning and could barely keep her eyes open at the breakfast table. She tried napping in the recliner or watching TV to fall asleep. Nothing worked.

"Jen, you look like crap!" Bruce said as he removed the muffins from the oven. "I didn't hear you come to bed last night. Did you sleep?"

"Heck no, and thanks for the compliment. I'm so worried about today. I'll probably end up like Gunther with a heart attack!"

"Come off it, Jen. I know you're worried about Lewis. He's already bathed, dressed, spit-shined, and in his braces. He did it all by himself, too! He's wearing baggy pants to cover them up. Just the bottoms show. He can't wait to get to school. Whatever you do, don't let on to him. You know he has that crazy sixth sense."

"Oh, believe me, I know about his sixth sense. He never lets me get through a day without showing it off. He can see through anyone like a shower curtain!"

"Yeah, that's what I'm leery of when he gets in school. Remember, he's almost twice the size of his classmates, and so is his brain!" Bruce laughed, trying to cheer up Jen. "C'mon, hon, lighten up. He's going to have a ball!"

"If you say so, Bruce. I can hear Lewis jumping down the stairs. What happened to the no-jumping-down-the-stairs rule?"

"Jen, give him a big hug when he comes into the kitchen, okay? If anybody needs one, it's him."

"Got it," Jen replied as if taking orders from a drill sergeant.

"How did our big first-grader sleep last night?" Jen quizzed Lewis.

"Good. I had a nice dream."

"And what was that, Lewis?" Bruce asked.

"I didn't have my braces or glasses on, but I was still taller than everyone."

Jen knelt beside Lewis, put her hands on his elbows, and looked directly into him.

"Lewis. That was not a dream. Soon, you'll be running faster and seeing better than anyone. Your time will come."

Lewis had no clue what Jen meant but smiled and said, "I'm starving! What's that smell? What's in the oven, Dad?"

"It's your favorite breakfast!"

"Booberry muffins? All right!" Lewis shouted and scooted to his seat at the table.

"He's too much!" Jen happily complained.

Lewis downed two whole muffins and a glass of milk.

"Milk is going to make me strong someday!" he professed.

Bruce and Jen cried tears of joy and relief.

They couldn't believe Lewis was finally going to school. They knew he was against the odds, and a long road was ahead. Bruce tried to be the strong one for Lewis because Jen was ready to fold.

Bruce gathered his lunch box and hugged Lewis before heading to work. He remembered something he said when Lewis was born. *Look out, world. Lewis Clark Duncan is coming for you!* He laughed and backed out of the driveway.

Jen tried to fix Lewis's hair, but he had already combed it. She wanted him to put on a coat, but he said it was too hot outside. She tried to tuck his shirt in, but he fussed and pulled it out.

She remembered what a terror she was to her mother. *My dress is wrinkled, my hair is curly, I have freckles, I'm flat-chested, and I'm long in the crotch.* Every single day for twelve years of school, she complained. *My poor mother!*

Somehow, Jen got Lewis into her car, and they were off to school. Jen hadn't been out that early in months. She was surprised to see how many school buses passed her in every direction, filled with students. Traffic Police monitored every intersection, controlling the stoplights for bicyclists and walkers. Lewis found this hubbub very interesting. He'd never seen so much commotion before.

Jen pulled in front of the school, where other parents let children out of their cars. The school housed grades one through six, so there was quite a variation in age. Jen was nervous because she saw large groups of kids huddled together in boisterous conversation under the large roof in front of the entry doors. First-grade students could walk to their classroom for one day with a parent. Jen dreaded the thought of walking past those students, afraid someone might say something.

Jen walked around to the passenger door. Lewis was already standing there with a new package of pencils gripped tightly in his hand.

"You ready, Lewis?"

"Yup, let's go!" he eagerly replied.

As tempted as she was to take hold of his hand, she let him walk through the parting students. Some students gave him an odd look, but many offered him a warm hello or wave.

"Your classroom is this way, down the hall, Lewis," Jen reminded him as he broke into a noisy trot, his braces echoing off the empty metal lockers. He stopped about two feet short of the door.

"Come on, Mom!" Lewis blurted.

Jen and Lewis entered the classroom together. A feverish pitch of voices went utterly silent when Lewis entered the room. There was an awkward moment before the elderly teacher spoke up.

"Hello, Miss. I believe you may be looking for the third or fourth-grade classrooms on the other side of the school?"

Jen knew something like this might happen and confidently replied, "No, ma'am. This is my son, Lewis Duncan. He's here for first grade."

"I'm sorry, Mrs. Duncan. Please, please. Come right in."

Lewis maneuvered his way to the front desk with Jen at his side. The teacher checked her attendance chart and saw three students were missing.

"Nice to meet you, Lewis," the teacher addressed him.

"Same here! I'm almost six, six in February," Lewis said coolly.

"I'm Ms. Rounds. I'll be your teacher for the whole next year!" She tried to drum up some enthusiasm for Lewis. "Well, Mrs. Duncan, I'm sure we'll see you throughout the school year. We have many fun events scheduled. Maybe you could volunteer if you have any time?"

"Certainly, thank you. I should be going, though."

"I'll keep you posted with a calendar. Lewis can bring it home to you."

Ms. Rounds followed Jen to the doorway and stepped out of her classroom. "Does Lewis need a special seat close to the chalkboard?"

There was that word 'special' already. Jen covered her frustration and gritted her teeth.

"No, he can see fine!" Jen snapped. "And Lewis also wears leg braces. He won't run as fast as the other kids at recess, but he will certainly try. You don't have to stop him from trying either!"

"Well, thank you, Mrs. Duncan. I just want to know his limitations," Ms. Rounds said politely.

"Lewis has no limitations, Ms. Rounds; only the ones people put on him. Do you know what I mean?"

"Yes, I do. I've been teaching for thirty-five years and have seen it all. I'm sorry if I offended you or Lewis."

"He has bigger shoulders than you, and I put together. I'm sure we'll be meeting again, Ms. Rounds. Good day and good luck with your class."

Jen turned around sharply and forcefully walked down the hall. She made her way through a crowd outside the office and almost pushed some kids out of her way. She started her car and left some rubber on the pavement as she drove from school.

Chapter Twenty

Ms. Rounds returned to her desk and addressed the class. "Class, this is Lewis Duncan. Please give him a nice welcome."

The class half-heartedly moaned, "Hello."

"Lewis, you may take any seat. I see three near the window, or you can sit in front of my desk." Lewis looked around at a silent room and saw thirteen pairs of eyes glued onto him. He didn't dare make a move for fear of falling or his braces making noise.

"I'll sit near the window," Lewis said softly.

Lewis turned carefully and grabbed a desk for support. He was determined to walk straight and firm, as his doctor always told him. He chose a seat in the middle of a row. As he attempted to sit at an undersized desk, his knees lifted the desk six inches. The metal and hardwood top came crashing down on the hard tile floor with a thunderous clap as it flipped over on him.

The class broke into a fit of laughter, with fingers pointing at Lewis as he lay on the floor, tangled in his seat and desk.

"Class, class, quiet, please!" Ms. Rounds screamed as she ran to Lewis, who was on his hands and knees trying to get up. It took another reprimand from Ms. Rounds to return the class to order.

"Are you okay, Lewis? Do you need to go to the nurse?"

"No, I'm fine," he said, looking down. A few children were still laughing.

"You can sit beside me. We'll call the janitor and get a bigger desk for you, okay?"

"Yes, Ms. Rounds." Lewis addressed her with his eyes focused on the floor.

Lewis sat beside the teacher's desk at a separate table with a larger chair.

Ms. Rounds walked to the intercom beside the chalkboard and called the office.

"This is room 103 calling the office, room 103 calling the office."

"Yes, Ms. Rounds?"

"Could you please dispatch building maintenance to our room?"

"Any problems?"

"You could say that. Reggie, the janitor, would be fine," Ms. Rounds replied.

"He'll be right there."

"Thank you, Margie."

Ms. Rounds snapped her fingers, calling for attention as another student entered the room.

"Class. We have a new student." She turned to the boy. "And what is your name, young man?"

The little boy put his hands on his hips and crudely said, "Jerry, Jerry Alfonzo. What's yours?"

The class erupted into laughter again, taking some heat off Lewis. He raised his head from the desk.

"Class, *quiet*!" Ms. Rounds pleaded.

Jerry's mother interrupted and spoke in an annoying New Jersey accent.

"I'm Madeline Alfonzo. That Jerry, he's a handful! You gotta watch out for him. He likes to spit. We're new in town. I just moved here from Newark." By now, Jerry had his arms folded across his chest and scanned the class.

"Well, Mrs. Alfonzo, I certainly won't tolerate Jerry's spitting or any other bad habits he may have. I am Ms. Rounds and will be Jerry's teacher this year."

"Yeah, yeah," Ms. Alfonzo obnoxiously stated as she loudly chewed a piece of gum and blew a bubble. "Jerry made his kindergarten teacher quit last year. She couldn't put up with him."

"I've never had to send a first grader to the office, but that doesn't mean I won't if he's disruptive," Ms. Rounds informed her politely.

"Disruptive?" Madeline Alfonzo replied loudly. "What about that kid over there?" pointing at Lewis. "Is he in detention, already sitting at that table all by himself?"

Once again, the class got out of control, laughing. Meanwhile, Jerry had already found himself a seat in the first row and put his feet up on the desk to stretch out.

"Get your feet off that table and sit up straight! I will have none of that behavior in my class! What's going on here?"

"Looks like you can't even control first graders," Mrs. Alfonzo remarked snidely.

"Mrs. Alfonzo? I kindly ask that you be on your way so we may begin our lesson today."

"Yeah, yeah, thanks for watching my kid."

Madeline Alfonzo spun her fake leopard-skin pocketbook over her shoulder and almost took Ms. Round's face off. Ms. Rounds accompanied her to the door and made sure she made her way down the hall.

"We're not off to a very good start here, are we, children?" Ms. Rounds spoke to the class as they were quieting down. Lewis was seated beside her desk and felt very uncomfortable being the center of attention.

Ms. Rounds broke away from a short conversation with her class when she heard the janitor coming down the hall. She could tell it was Reggie from the sound of his squeaking mop bucket.

Reggie entered the room with a mop in hand. Once again, the class broke out in laughter.

"Class! You will remain silent! Class!" Ms. Rounds sharply yelled.

Reggie was an impish man. He stood around four-foot-six and was bald. The mop handle was taller than he was.

"I'm sorry, Reggie. I don't know what has gotten into this class!"

"No problem, Ms. Rounds. Did one of the little kids throw up?"

"Oh, no. We need a larger desk for one of our new students. Lewis, can you come over here, please?"

Lewis carefully put both hands on the chair, stood up, and walked toward Reggie.

Reggie smiled at Lewis and stood his mop against the wall.

"Looks like you need a bigger desk, don't you, Lewis?" Reggie said kindly.

"Yes, Sir," he replied quietly.

Pointing at Lewis, Jerry Alfonzo hollered, "Hey, is that a Four-eyed King Kong in our class?"

Once again, the children broke out into hysterical laughter. Ms. Rounds stormed over to Jerry, spun him around in his chair, and forcefully slid him into the corner.

"You will *never* say that again in my class! Do you hear me? Do you hear me?"

Jerry refused to make eye contact and sat looking at the wall, giggling.

"Looks like you've got another great class this year, Ms. Rounds," Reggie said sarcastically. "Lewis, would you like to help me?"

"Sure!" Lewis got a little upbeat. "Can I, Ms. Rounds? Can I?"

"Yes, Lewis. But hurry back, Reggie. We have a lot to cover today."

"Certainly, Ms. Rounds. We have to go to a storeroom on the other side of the school for a larger desk. Let's go, Lewis."

Lewis was delighted to get out of that classroom, even for a few minutes.

Once in the hall, Reggie remarked to Lewis, "What a crotchety old bat, huh, Lewis?"

"Do you mean the teacher, Ms. Rounds?"

"That's what I said, kid. Hey, you're almost as tall as me. What do you have on your legs there?"

"Oh, I have to wear these braces until I'm six. I hate them."

"Hate is a very powerful word, Lewis. Be careful how you use it."

"Well, I don't like them."

"You can walk real fine. I bet you're going to be a really strong boy someday. You'll teach all those spoiled brats a lesson."

"Why would I do that?"

"I used to be called half-pint by everyone. Now look, I'm just a janitor in a school filled with little people like me. I like little people."

"I'll be bigger than you soon," Lewis said.

"You sure will, Lewis."

Reggie removed a chain from his belt and fumbled for the correct key to the storeroom. He opened the door and peered into a large room filled with desks, chairs, and tables.

"I'm going to find you something comfortable, Lewis. Here we go, take this chair." Reggie handed Lewis a nicely padded chair that fit him perfectly. "Now, let's see if we can find a bigger desk. There's one stacked up against the wall. Hey, it's brand new! Nobody's even carved their initials into it yet. You're pretty lucky!"

Lewis stood there and watched as Reggie crawled across the heaping pile of furniture.

"Okay, that's it. Can you lift that chair onto the cart, Lewis?" Reggie asked.

"I'll try."

Lewis showed no effort lifting the heavy chair.

"Can you grab one end of your new desk and put it on the cart with me?"

"I'll try," Lewis said again.

Reggie and Lewis placed the desk alongside the chair. Reggie turned the light out and locked the door. Lewis started to walk down the hall. Reggie smiled at him and said, "Hey, Lewis, I'm going to need some help pushing this cart. How about it?"

"Sure!" Lewis got on one side of the handle to push it with Reggie.

"Wow!" Reggie smiled at Lewis. "You sure are strong! You can help me anytime! I heard what that kid called you. Stay away from him, Lewis. He's bad news. I can spot a rotten apple a mile away. You may have to deal with him for a long time. I know who you are."

"Well then, who am I, Reggie?"

"You're a rock, kid. Solid like granite, I can tell. I wish I were you. If you ever have a problem, come find me."

Lewis felt tall as a mountain pushing that cart down the hall with Reggie. They both entered a very quiet classroom as Ms. Rounds asked Reggie, "Where have you been?"

"We walked clear over to the fourth and fifth-grade side of the school, ma'am. Lewis was a great help."

Lewis smiled at Reggie.

"Why, thank you, Lewis. Where would you like to put your desk?" Mrs. Rounds asked him. There's an open spot beside Jerry at the end of the row."

"No, thank you, Ms. Rounds. I want to sit near the window. I like fresh air."

Reggie looked at Lewis and grinned. He unloaded the desk and chair from the cart and placed them in line with the chalkboard.

"Is that all, Ms. Rounds?" Reggie asked politely.

"Yes. Thank you, Reggie."

Reggie walked with his usual slow gate to the corner of the classroom for his mop. He turned and looked back at many curious children analyzing him. Lewis, the furthest away, stood out like a king on a chessboard.

"I'll be seeing you around, Lewis. Thank you kindly for your help."

Reggie shuffled out the door and dropped his mop into a brand-new galvanized wash bucket. Lewis looked in silence at Reggie. Lewis knew he would be in for a long haul getting through his first year of school. He made at least one friend out of everyone he met at school today, Ms. Rounds, sixteen classmates, and Reggie.

Chapter Twenty-One

September and October passed very slowly for Lewis. He spent much of his time looking out the window in the classroom. He daydreamed of running with other students and playing kickball and tag. Ms. Rounds moved Lewis's desk to the front of the aisle, just two rows away from Jerry Alfonzo. Although he could see the chalkboard clearly, there was a delay in processing information or questions from Ms. Rounds. Lewis's slow reaction to regular classroom activity quickly yielded him a nickname from Jerry.

One day, Ms. Rounds asked Lewis to hand out a new pencil and two pieces of paper to every student. He liked to be called upon for such tasks and tried to walk sturdily between the tight rows of desks.

As Lewis finished his assignment, Jerry yelled out. "Hey, Duncan, can't you count? You gave me two pencils!" The classroom started to laugh at the jokester. "What are you, a dunce? Dunce Duncan!" The class went into full-blown laughter at Lewis. He dropped his head and returned to his seat.

"Class! Boys, stop that!" Ms. Rounds demanded. "Jerry, report to the principal's office immediately! I've never had to send a first grader to the principal in my life, but there will be none of that talk in my class!"

Jerry proudly rose from his seat with a smirk as he passed Lewis. "See ya, Dunce," he whispered to Lewis.

The remainder of the school day dragged on painfully slow. Jerry spent the afternoon in the principal's office writing, "I will not call Lewis a dunce," one hundred times.

Lewis didn't know what a dunce was and asked his mother on the ride home.

"How was your day at school, Lewis?" Jen asked as he slid onto the car seat.

"I don't know, Mom. Everyone laughed at me again, and somebody called me a name."

"What name? What did they call you?"

"Jerry called me a dunce, Dunce Duncan."

"He called you that?" Jen fumed. "That little...."

"What does it mean, Mom?"

"Lewis, children can be ruthless." She paused. "A dunce is someone who may not be as smart as everyone else."

"I'm pretty smart, aren't I, Mom?"

"Of course, you are, honey. Sometimes, children who stand out like you get picked on. It's not fair. I'm turning around right now to talk with your teacher!"

"No, Mom. Please, let's go home. I just want to play with Rex."

"Then, I'm going to call that boy's mother."

"No, Mom. I don't want you to. I'll get picked on even more," Lewis pleaded as he looked out the car window toward the harbor. "I'm okay."

Lewis started school only five weeks ago, and this was the third incident with the class bully, Jerry. Jen was steaming and called Bruce at work when she got home. He didn't like to take personal calls at his job and got a little hot under the collar but quickly calmed down as she explained the infuriating situation.

"We have to put our foot down, Jen. I'm getting pretty tired of Lewis getting pushed around by that kid," Bruce yelled into the phone.

"I am too, dear, but Lewis doesn't want us to say anything."

"Are you kidding? Well, I'm not going to stand around and wait around forever while this kid keeps pestering Lewis."

"I know, Bruce. I know. Let's give it a little more time. There's only one first-grade class. Lewis can't change rooms," Jen reminded him. "There's a parent-teacher conference at the end of October. We'll discuss it with Ms. Rounds then. Let's keep our cool for now."

"I don't want to, but I guess so. I have to get back to work. I'll see you and Lewis later on."

"Bye, hon," Jen said, practically crying.

Jen didn't know it, but Lewis was right on the other side of the wall listening to every word she said. He didn't dare move, fearing his leg braces would squeak and give him away.

Jen got up from the table. "Come on, Rex. Let's go outside." She walked to the staircase and yelled, "Lewis, I'm taking Rex for a walk."

Lewis cleverly put his hands over his mouth and spoke into the coat closet.

"Okay, Mom. I'll be down in a minute."

Jen opened the kitchen door as Rex scurried onto the side lawn to relieve himself. Lewis warily peeked around the corner of the dining room. He walked to the refrigerator and poured himself a large glass of milk. Lewis peered out the window at Rex and raised his glass as if he were making a toast. The pupils in his eyes dilated like lightning bolts.

"Someday, Jerry Alfonzo, I will hurt you badly," Lewis stated calmly.

*****

The remainder of October and November slid by without any incidents at school. Jen and Bruce decided not to press any bullying issues at the parent-teacher meeting. Ms. Rounds highly complimented Lewis on his first-grade achievements. He was at the top of the class in penmanship and math but lagged behind everyone in English. She also remarked on his incredible patience in dealing with the class clown.

Jen didn't want to get on the subject of Jerry Alfonzo, but she couldn't help asking Ms. Rounds, "It's hard to believe a child can be that cruel, isn't it, Ms. Rounds?"

"I've seen a lot of problems with first graders. Some come to school with shoes on the wrong feet or untied, no coats in winter, and even a hamster shoved into a student's pocket one day." She laughed at herself. "There are many students who have underlying issues. It's usually at home where they learn this type of behavior. I'm not an expert, just an observer."

"We thank you for your input anytime, Ms. Rounds," Bruce said as he stood up from the desk. "Come on, Jen. There are a few people in line behind us. We'll see you at the Christmas concert, Ms. Rounds?"

"Yes, I can't wait! We're all practicing. See you then," she replied enthusiastically.

Jen courteously extended her hand and shook hands with Ms. Rounds. Conversation between parents waiting outside Ms. Round's office came to a halt abruptly as Jen and Bruce passed by. They made their way to Bruce's truck in the parking lot.

"Did you notice that, Bruce? Those people stopped talking when we walked by them?"

"I did. Yeah, that was pretty weird. Were my pants unzipped or something?"

"No!" Jen laughed out loud. "I think they were talking about us or maybe Lewis."

"Oh, come off it, Jen. Now *you're* getting a little paranoid."

"You saw it! And no, I'm not paranoid!"

"I'm dry as a mackerel. Let's get a beer at Studs. We don't have to pick Lewis up for another two hours."

"Sure, but just a couple. I'm parched, too. I always get nervous going back to school. I'll probably have 'hall locker' dreams tonight!"

"Yeah, me too," Bruce laughed.

*****

Tourists and summer residents on Cape Cod were long gone. Many houses and hotels were boarded up for the usually mild winters. A wisp of snow covered the dunes in front of Bruce and Jen's house. It was one week before Christmas, and Lewis was preparing for his role in the Christmas play at school. He was going to be a shepherd alongside the manger. He had to sing and walk with a large cross and kneel beside the crib while holding Baby Jesus. The entire play lasted about seven minutes, but Ms. Rounds was very nervous if the kids could pull it off.

The small auditorium filled up quickly as parents entered. Bruce and Jen took some empty seats in the middle row. Everyone was in good spirits greeting friends and neighbors. As the curtains came down and the lights dimmed, the school principal separated the curtains from backstage. He welcomed the crowd.

"Good evening and Merry Christmas to all!" Mr. Naples bellowed.

"Our first graders have a short presentation for you tonight. Ms. Rounds will be accompanying on piano." He paused as the spotlight moved to shine on her. A courteous round of applause followed.

"Mr. Sloan's second-grade and Mrs. Watson's third-grade class will follow. So, without any further ado, I present to you *Silent Night*."

The curtains opened slowly to reveal a beautifully constructed scene with a mountain sunset and a group of shepherds kneeling beside the manger. As

Ms. Rounds started her intro to *Silent Night*, more shepherds appeared, clearing the way for Lewis, who was holding a cross. They walked across the stage, singing in perfect unison. Lewis beamed ear to ear as he looked at the audience.

Jen and Bruce heard some commotion coming around them and turned to listen.

"Look at the size of that kid!" Bruce heard a man whisper.

"I thought these were only first graders, not fourth!" he heard another joke. Some giggling from surrounding parents accompanied these remarks. Bruce and Jen became uncomfortable and started to fidget in their seats.

A shepherd took Jesus from Lewis and placed him in a crib. The stage actors knelt beside the manger. Lewis knew to be careful with his leg braces as he dropped to one knee. He'd practiced this many times and used the cross as a crutch while carefully lowering himself. Even after he knelt, he was still taller than the few remaining shepherds who were standing. This brought another round of quiet snickering and remarks from the crowd.

"Boy, the Boston Celtics could use him in a few years!" Jen heard a woman remark.

"Is that kid on stilts?"

"Who's his father, Lurch from the Addams Family?"

Jen and Bruce were distracted by these rude people and did everything humanly possible not to blow up and ruin the show.

When the song ended, everyone stood and clapped with a standing ovation. Bruce and Jen connected the faces to those they overheard during the performance.

Jen looked toward the stage. She was concerned Lewis couldn't stand from his kneeling position. His classmates were at the stage front taking bows and didn't notice him having trouble. Sometimes this happened to him. His knees would lock if kept in one position too long.

Jen and Bruce could see a look of desperation and panic on his face. Luckily, as Ms. Rounds got on stage, she noticed Lewis's awkward predicament and helped him stand. This prompted another round of questions and comments from a few audience members.

"He must be handicapped," a woman whispered to her husband.

"Yes, too bad. I'm surprised he's in the play, not the special class."

That was it for Jen. She tapped the woman on her shoulder and politely stated, "If the two of you don't shut up, you'll both be handicapped and in the special class."

Here we go, Bruce thought. *All hell will break loose.*

The people around them were stunned and silent but still clapped for the performers.

Jen proudly yelled, "Way to go, Lewis!"

He adored the praise. While raising the heavy cross with one hand, he picked a girl up with his other arm and lifted her over his head. The crowd roared. Jen and Bruce started to cry, along with other audience members. Now, everyone around them knew Lewis was their son. Most were embarrassed, and a few shamefully left their seats.

The curtains closed. Behind the floor-to-ceiling of burgundy velvet, high-pitched screams of joy filled the auditorium. Bruce and Jen gathered their coats and went backstage to greet Lewis. He was wearing a huge smile as he took off his costume.

"Mom, Dad! Did you see me? Did you see me?" Lewis ran and hugged them.

"Of course, we did! You did great, Lewis!" Jen praised him.

Bruce mussed up Lewis's hair and said, "You'll be on the Broadway stage before you know it!"

"What do you mean?" Lewis paused. "Something happened. I couldn't stand up. My knees froze. I felt stupid."

"Don't ever say that, Lewis!" Jen scolded him. "You were probably scared stiff, that's all."

"Can we watch the second and third graders?" Lewis begged. "Can we?"

"Of course, honey. Let's get some seats during intermission and *not* where we were before, Bruce."

"I hear you, Jen. Let's go, Lewis."

As they left the stage, Bridget, the little girl who played Mary, approached Lewis with her parents, the ones with which Jen had lost her cool.

"I apologize for our behavior." The man extended his hand to Bruce. "Chet Davis."

"Bruce Duncan. This is my wife, the boss, Jen," Bruce said. They all laughed. Jen deliberated for a moment but managed a forced smile.

"I like you, Lewis," Bridget said, breaking some tension between everyone.

"Come on, Lewis. We'd better get those seats before they're taken," Jen said.

"Can Bridget sit with us?"

"That's up to Mr. and Mrs. Davis."

They looked at each other. Chet said, "Great! Come on, Bridget! And give the Jesus doll back. I think the next cast needs him."

Lewis was sore from kneeling so long and tried to hide a slight limp, which worried Jen and Bruce. They knew his sixth birthday checkup was right around the corner, and the doctor told Lewis he could shed his leg braces by then. Lewis was counting the days.

Chapter Twenty-Two

Lewis's sixth birthday was fast approaching. A small celebration was held on February 28, two days before his physical. Preoccupied with getting his braces off, Lewis told his parents that he wasn't in the mood for a big party,

Jen brought him to his orthopedist on Thursday, March 2nd. Lewis couldn't wait to go. "Are we almost there, Mom?"

"Lewis, if you ask me one more time, I'll go crazy!" Jen exploded.

"Sorry, Mum. I'll be running tomorrow at recess!"

"Hold your horses there, partner," Jen joked. "You haven't been in to see Dr. Fleming yet." Lewis had a puzzled look on his face.

They checked in at the front office as Dr. Fleming rounded the corner into the waiting room.

"Dr. Fleming, I get my braces off today! Don't I? Don't I?" Lewis quizzed him. "I've been doing my leg exercises in bed every night, just like you told me."

"That's great, Lewis! Let's go into my office and have a look at you, okay?"

"I'll beat you!" Lewis said happily.

"No running down the hall, Lewis!" Jen reminded him and got a 'no way!' look from Lewis as he bolted away.

"I said I'd beat you!" Lewis proudly informed Jen and Dr. Fleming when they caught up with him.

Lewis hopped onto the table and stretched out like he usually did without being asked.

Dr. Fleming removed the braces and carefully examined Lewis's calf and thigh muscles.

"You *have* been doing your exercises, haven't you, Lewis?" Lewis happily grinned in response. Dr. Fleming took out a tape measure and checked the length and diameter of each leg in four places. Tapping his pencil and scratching his head, he wrote the numbers down and examined his previous calculations for a few moments in silence. He slowly spun around in his chair. Lewis and Jen were looking right at him.

"Lewis, I believe you'll need your braces for another six months."

"But you promised!" Lewis whined. "I've been good!"

"I know you have. Your legs are still growing very fast. My chart shows you're taller than every third and fourth-grader in school. Your leg muscles are striving to keep up with you." Lewis started to cry. Jen moved over and held him.

"Isn't there anything we can do, Dr. Fleming?"

"Jen, he's doing great. He's going without the braces one day a week, right?"

"Yes, just on Sundays."

"He could suffer a relapse if we discontinue their use. I think we can safely expand his range of freedom to Saturday and Sunday."

Lewis perked up a little and stopped crying when he heard this.

"But there's still absolutely no running or jumping without them. Okay, Lewis?"

"Yes, Doctor Fleming," Lewis said, sniffling, barely managing an answer.

"Jen, we've never had a case like this on Cape Cod. Lewis's records are analyzed after every exam by the Lahey Clinic. He is a groundbreaker as modern medicine applies."

"I understand, Dr. Fleming. He got his hopes up. Me, too, I guess. Maybe things will change come springtime," Jen said optimistically.

"I believe we will see a drastic improvement by June. I will give Lewis a new exercise to do before he goes to bed. That's when he takes his braces off, right? He will need some help balancing, also."

"Certainly, Dr. Fleming, we'll do anything to help Lewis."

"I will, too!" Lewis sat up and joked.

Jen was worried Lewis might get depressed and sulk about his trip to the doctor. Bruce was surprised Lewis was still wearing his braces when he got home from work, but Lewis explained very carefully to his dad why he still had to wear them.

Lewis was more determined to shed those leg braces than ever. He did exercises on the stairs as Dr. Fleming recommended: two sets of heel raises, ten times each set. Exercise one leg each night and rest a day. Lewis ate everything on his plate at dinner. Bruce was finicky about his eating and wasn't much of a vegetable lover. Only meat and potatoes were for him. Lewis put his Dad's appetite to shame.

As spring approached, the schoolyards were busy with outside recess. The classrooms emptied in a wild frenzy of pent-up children. Lewis was the last one out the door at recess and milled around the swing set and monkey bars. The teacher was organizing a game of kickball when Jerry Alfonzo walked over to Lewis.

"Hey, Duncan, gonna play kickball?"

Lewis looked right at him and didn't say anything. He remembered what Reggie, the janitor said. "Stay away."

"When are you gonna get those things off? All they do is make you wobble. Hey, that's your new name, Wobble!" He laughed at himself and a few other kids who joined in harassing Lewis.

"Take it back, Jerry," Lewis said.

"Wobble, Wobble, how's your hobble!" Jerry egged him on.

"Don't call me that. Take it back."

"What are you going to do, tell Mommy?"

"Take it back, Jerry."

Jerry walked over to Lewis and tried to push him over. Lewis didn't budge, which surprised Jerry. Lewis made a fist and was holding it at his side. Jerry pushed him again.

Lewis swung hard and hit Jerry in the mouth, knocking him over and splitting his lip into a bloody mess. Jerry reeled and screamed like a baby in pain as he ran to a teacher. Jerry's friends tattle-tailed. While another teacher aided Jerry to the nurse's office, Ms. Rounds marched up to Lewis.

"Lewis! Did you hit Jerry in the face? Answer me!"

"Yes. He was calling me names."

"We don't hit people because they call you names."

"He pushed me."

"Well, what was it? Did he push you or call you names?"

"He pushed me twice."

"Come with me, young man. It looks like you've earned a trip to the principal's office this time!" Ms. Rounds grabbed Lewis by his shirt collar and took him directly to the principal's office. Now, it was Lewis's turn to write one hundred times, "I will not punch Jerry in the face."

Jen picked Lewis up at the principal's office. She got quite a lecture from Ms. Rounds and the principal. Lewis told them his side of the story.

Jen led him through the front door as a small man pushing a cart approached her on the way out of school. It was Reggie, the janitor. Lewis's eyes lit up.

"Reggie!" Lewis shouted.

"I thought Reggie was one of your classmate friends?" Jen was confused.

"He is, Mom. He's my only friend."

Reggie slowly walked toward Jen.

"I saw the whole thing from a window while mopping up a spill, ma'am. They were picking on him, three against one. What he told you is probably true. I apologize. I'm Reggie, just a janitor here."

"Why, thank you, Reggie. And you are not *just* a janitor here. I've heard many kind words from Lewis about you."

"Why, thank you. You know, I've never had much courage, ma'am, like your son has. I got picked on my whole life. Look at me now. What do you see?" Reggie asked in a somber tone.

"I see a brave man, Reggie. I see a very brave man."

"Your son has a lot of courage but also has a long road ahead. His resolve will be tested many times."

"I know," Jen admitted. "My husband and I have been tested for six years as well. Would you like to come for dinner sometime?"

"No, thank you, ma'am. I'm just a janitor here at the school and have two dogs at home for company."

"That doesn't matter to us. You have an open invitation – with your dogs, anytime!" Jen tried to cheer him up.

"Thank you kindly, but I'll be on my way." Reggie held the door open for Jen and Lewis. When Lewis got to the curb, Reggie yelled, "Hey, Lewis, nice left hook!"

Jen shook her head in agreement with Reggie and patted Lewis's back.

Chapter Twenty-Three

The school year ended on a happy note. Lewis had perfect attendance and a satisfactory on his progress reports. After getting whacked, Jerry Alfonzo stayed clear of Lewis for the rest of the year. Luckily, it was only his pride that got hurt. It was clear to Jen that Lewis would never be friends with Jerry. She never told Bruce what happened; it was her and Lewis's little secret.

Lewis never made any friends that summer. Jen felt guilty about his situation. Bruce was so busy at work he didn't have any vacation time until July. Lewis knew August was coming. It was his next appointment with Dr. Fleming, and he couldn't wait.

Jen revived her relationship with Veda. Lewis loved seeing Tasha again. Although it was unusual for a boy and a girl of six to become best friends, they did. They would spend hours playing in the sand at the water's edge while Veda and Jen gossiped, keeping a close eye on the pair. Childish laughter could be heard up and down the beach.

Tasha and Lewis always had fun romping through the chilly Cape waves. Lewis's leg braces did not deter him from wading in the bay up to his waist, Jen's rule. He found this to be a good exercise for his leg muscles.

August 1, 1978. The appointment with Dr. Fleming marked the first day of the family vacation. Jen had a folder filled with records from Dr. Fields and Dr. Fleming. She had been reading them for a week and wanted to be ready for any questions or suggestions from Dr. Fleming. Bruce and Jen packed the truck and headed to the doctor's office again.

"Come on in, folks!" Dr. Fleming greeted everyone at the office door.

"It looks like this week will be a beauty here on the sandbar."

"Yes, Dr. Fleming, we have the next two weeks off!" Bruce happily added.

"Lucky you! Think of me while you're out on the bay. Do you still have your boat?"

"It wouldn't be worth living on the Cape without one!" Bruce boasted again.

Dr. Fleming turned and addressed Jen while they were making their way down the hall into his office.

Lewis sat at the end of the exam table.

"I haven't seen Lewis since February," Dr. Flemming said. "How did he do in school this year, Jen?"

"Lewis did great. His grades were wonderful, except one, and we'll work on that next year, right, Lewis?" Lewis wasn't paying any attention to his mom. He was studying the periodic table of elements on the wall.

"Lewis did have some issues with a few classmates, but he got through," Jen informed Dr. Fleming.

"Issues? What kind of issues did he have?"

"Truthfully, Bruce and I would rather discuss that some other time, if possible," Jen asked.

"Certainly, I didn't mean to pry." Dr. Fleming glanced at his folder of their previous meeting and turned toward the exam table. Lewis had his braces off already, lying on his back with his hands folded behind his head.

"Don't fall asleep, Lewis!" Dr. Fleming joked. "Let's get some measurements with my trusty old tape," Fleming instructed himself. He made a few notes at his desk and walked over to the scale.

"Okay, Lewis, jump up on the scale. Well, don't jump. I just meant...."

"I know, I know," Lewis replied.

Dr. Fleming took a height and weight on Lewis and returned to his desk again.

"Let's see here, according to my records; Lewis was forty-eight inches tall and fifty pounds one year ago. He has grown two inches and gained only five pounds. I believe he's falling into a much more..." he thought for a moment for the right words. "A much more normal growth curve."

"Oh, my God! Are you kidding me, Dr. Fleming?" Jen asked as tears started flowing. Lewis just stood there on the scale, not processing what was said. He was still focused on the table of elements.

"Bruce, did you hear that?"

"Yes, Jen, I did. So, what does that mean, Dr. Fleming?"

He leaned forward from his chair and smiled.

"Lewis doesn't need his braces anymore." That, Lewis heard!

He ran over and gave Dr. Fleming a big hug.

"Did you hear that, Mom? Dad! Did you hear that?"

"We did, Lewis! We did!" Bruce jumped in for a hug too.

"Calm down, Bruce, Jen. There are a few simple guidelines for Lewis to follow for the next six months. I'll print a chart of new exercises for him. These have to be strictly followed, understand?"

"I don't doubt Lewis will follow every one of them. He's been exercising more than me and Bruce combined in the last six months!" Jen laughed. "Thank you so much, Dr. Fleming."

As Lewis was leaving the room with Jen and Bruce, Dr. Fleming pointed to the leg braces still on the exam table.

"Hey, Lewis, what are we going to do with these?"

Lewis looked up at his parents and then at the doctor.

"Maybe give them to another little boy like me. I don't need them anymore!"

Dr. Fleming nodded to Lewis, closed the folder, and put it on his desk. He pulled a handkerchief from the pocket of his scrubs. He, too, felt a tear rising from deep within.

Bruce and Jen left the office on a cloud – well, you know. The new guidelines for Lewis to follow were straightforward: 1) Don't run fast – not likely. 2) No swimming over his chest – improbable. 3) No jumping from trees – highly impossible.

Jen and Bruce were so happy for Lewis. He could now play and roughhouse with any of the kids at school, run fast with Rex and kick the waves with Tasha.

Bruce hoped and prayed that Lewis could begin a somewhat 'normal' life. Bruce would get his wish, almost.

Chapter Twenty-Four

Second grade flew by for the Duncan Family. Lewis had his eye prescription decreased. He faithfully performed eye and leg exercises every day. He no longer needed the 'coke bottle' lenses by the time second grade ended. Lewis did very well in school and took quite a liking to art. He loved drawing pictures of birds and fish.

Jerry Alfonzo was still a painful bully, but Lewis shrugged off weekly rituals of teasing and taunting. It was clear that Lewis and Jerry despised each other, and a showdown loomed in their future.

Jen and Bruce were surprised that Lewis had no friends in school when summer vacation arrived. Third grade was around the corner, and he had no one to play with except Tasha. One day during early summer, Jen heard some music coming from Lewis's bedroom. She tip-toed up the staircase to his closed bedroom door and put her ear to it. Listening for a moment, she scratched her head and then knocked.

"Come in, Mom."

"What type of music is that? It sounds like a dentist's office!" Jen teased Lewis.

"It's Piano Concerto 21, by Mozart. Mom, did you know he was only five when he wrote his first song?" he asked, standing by his radio.

"He did what?" Jen said, totally flabbergasted.

"He wrote,"

"I heard you. I never knew you liked classical music."

"Classical? Is that what it is? Yeah, I like it." Lewis surprised the heck out of Jen.

She turned toward the door. "Do you have a fever?"

"Nope, I feel great! I'm going to take Rex to the beach for a walk. Wanna come?" Lewis posed near the window, pointing to the water. "I'm going to bring my crayons and paper, too."

"Sure, Veda and Tasha are coming over too. We can meet them, okay?"

Lewis's eyes lit up. "Oh, boy! I haven't seen Tasha all summer!" he grinned.

"You saw her just last week, you big joker!" Lewis and Jen shared a laugh as they made their way downstairs.

What's next? Algebra at age eight?

*****

Third grade started with no big huff for Lewis. He was the biggest kid in their class. He was the biggest kid in fourth grade as well. Lewis still needed a much larger desk than the other students in his class.

Fourth grade was the first year for changing classrooms. Lewis wasn't looking forward to it. Only two boys in fourth grade were taller than Lewis—the feared Gallagher brothers. They were mean as cornered rattlesnakes and nasty to everyone, even the teachers. He knew he might have to face them next year when they were in middle school together.

*****

December 1979. Winter set in fast on the Cape. Bruce's job was demanding more time from him. He was working ten-hour days, six days a week.

Rex came down with a mysterious ailment. The vet couldn't find anything wrong with him, but Rex passed away on February 28, just one day before Lewis's birthday party. He told Bruce and Jen he didn't want any presents if it meant Rex could come back.

It was Lewis's first look at death. He would never forget Rex sleeping under his bed at night and running down the hall, taking a flying leap into his arms. The day Rex died, Lewis went to the beach and drew a picture of himself and Rex looking at the ocean together. He pinned it on his closet door. The image would stay there until Lewis moved out.

Lewis was tracked by Dr. Fields every six months. He couldn't explain Lewis's growth spurt, but the worst seemed to be over. He was growing at an average rate for eight and ten-year-olds.

In the third grade, a new boy moved into the class. Everyone stared at him. He was a different color than everyone in his class. He was black. Not many black families lived in Yarmouth at the time. There were only four blacks in the whole school system.

Lewis noticed him one day at school on the playground and went over to him. "Hi, I'm Lewis. Are you in the third grade, too?"

The wary child-sized Lewis up. "Yes, I am. Are you? You're huge! I'm Philondrious."

"Phil, what?"

"Philondrious, but everybody calls me Phil. I was named after my great-great-grandfather. He was a slave."

"A slave? What's that?"

"Oh, never mind. Where do you live?" Phil asked. Phil and Lewis talked until recess ended.

Jerry Alfonzo wasted no time drumming up his troops for verbal and physical assaults on Phil. It wasn't long before Lewis took him in as a close friend and protector. Lewis had built quite a reputation himself, so Jerry didn't bully him for a while. Jerry still remembered getting flattened by Lewis but was always scheming.

*****

Jen and Veda's friendship dwindled in the summer of 1980, just before Lewis started the fourth grade. Veda's husband got transferred to Boston, a move that she and Tasha despised. Lewis would never see Tasha again.

Lewis and Phil became best of friends that summer. Phil accompanied the family on a one-week camping trip to Truro. Bruce trailered the family boat to Provincetown and kept it at the docks for the whole week. Daily sightseeing and fishing trips to Stellwagen Bank were a nature lesson for Lewis and Phil. Both had never seen whales before, which visit in summer while feeding their young. Phil grew up in Worcester and never went to the ocean.

A few months into fourth grade, Jen thought Lewis was anxious about being mixed with older kids. She was right. He suffered a new round of teasing about his height and odd demeanor. Jerry Alfonzo teamed up with the dreaded Gallagher brothers on the second day of class. They taunted Lewis and Phil weekly. It just depended on what day it was who got picked on.

Lewis was an excellent student, and Phil leaned on him for help. They met at the fish scales on the town docks every day after school and helped unload boats for some spare change.

As Lewis approached his eighth birthday, Jen secretly planned a large party. He hadn't had a big celebration on his actual birthday for the past three years. Jen tried to shrug off any bad feelings about Leap Year. After all, nothing happened during the previous Leap Year.

*****

February 29, 1980, was Lewis's birthday. Another ice storm was moving in from the Gulf of Maine. The armory became headquarters for relief efforts from a crew of eighteen reservists. Bruce was in charge of maintenance on the fleet and dispatching the entire

Cape. He was scrambling to get an outdated ten-wheeled dump truck back on the road.

"C'mon, Smitty, let's get moving!" Bruce yelled across the garage. "We have six hours to get a new rear end in that old girl!"

"Lay off, Bruce! Have you ever tried to find parts for a 1958 Mack? I'll just go to K-Mart and take them off the shelf!" Smitty joked.

"Remember, Smitty? I have a party later on for Lewis. Nolan, get that payloader staged to be brought in. You know, the one with the transmission problem?"

"Yeah, yeah, I know which one it is. I wish we were still playing horseshoes at my house on a nice seventy-degree day, cold beer in my hand, a bottle of...."

Bruce interrupted Nolan. "I know! Quit your daydreaming and get that loader in here, now!"

"I liked you better when you weren't the boss!" Nolan ribbed Bruce.

Bruce walked next to the ten-wheeler.

"Need some help under there, Smit?"

"Yeah, we need some heat on these bolts. Grab a torch, will you?"

"Sure! Greg, bring those acetylene and oxygen tanks here and step on it!"

Greg wheeled the tanks next to the aging heap of iron, lit a torch, and handed it to Bruce. He slid on a creeper next to Smitty and started to heat the rusty nut and bolt assembly.

Nolan meandered into the yard and fired up the payloader. It was starting to spit ice and sleet. He let it warm up for a few minutes and departed the cab to open the behemoth oak garage door that was twenty feet wide and eighteen feet tall. Nolan went around the building first to take a leak behind the dumpster. He wasn't done relieving himself when he heard strange noises from the loader, a revving, then a loud squeal. He turned around and saw the loader going in reverse, idling toward the garage door by itself. He scrambled toward the driverless machine, slipping on his hands and knees. It was too late to stop it. Nolan violated the number one safety rule of the shop. Never leave a vehicle running without an operator.

The loader crashed into the ancient building and brought the five-ton door down on the old Mack truck. The jack stands kicked out, crushing Bruce and Smitty. They were killed instantly.

A small fire spread from the burning torch but was quickly extinguished. Pure chaos ensued, trying to get the men out from under the collapsed truck. The only jack capable of lifting the truck was under it, destroyed. Nolan went into an immediate panic-shock attack, screaming and rolling around on the floor. He had to be tranquilized and brought to the hospital.

Bruce's old friend and retired firefighter, Murph, heard the distress call on a police scanner while sitting at his kitchen table. He knocked his wife over as he rushed out the door.

It took six smaller jacks and half an hour to retrieve Bruce and Smitty. Neither could be recognized except by their clothing. The fire and police departments arrived and combed through the heaping pile of smoldering debris to sort out the cause.

Most co-workers sat on a bench while the head lieutenant of the armory questioned them. The rescue team, who grew up with Bruce and Smitty, were crying.

Murph was looking around the garage floor of the truck and spotted an envelope. It rattled and had something in it. It was addressed to Lewis. Curiosity got the best of Murph. He sat down and opened it. It was a birthday card for Lewis with a silver chain and a Celtic cross.

Bruce had written, "To Lewis. Today is a special day for everyone, your Mom and I use your strength to guide us each day. This cross belonged to my father and his father before that. It comes with a blessing to keep you safe. Wear it proudly, and no harm will ever come to you. Happy Birthday, Your Dad."

Murph couldn't believe it. Bruce probably put that cross in the envelope today, and now he's gone? Murph never saw Bruce without wearing that cross, and now he had the unpleasant task of going to Bruce's house to inform Jen of the tragedy.

Murph put the envelope in his pocket and walked to the bench for moral assistance. He looked up at the wall. In Bruce's handwriting, February 29th was marked off the calendar; "Lewis, Happy Leap Year!" Murph tore the calendar from the wall and threw it into the closest garbage can.

Chapter Twenty-Five

Murph arrived at Jen's home about an hour after the accident. A fireman and policeman accompanied him. It was only three o'clock, but a few cars were already in the driveway for the birthday party. He recognized Jen's sister's car, Fran's, and Kate's too. He didn't know what to say but knocked on the door.

In a flash of excitement, Jen quickly opened the door, eager to get the party rolling. She looked at Murph and the other two men in confusion.

"Murph, are you here for the party?" she asked inquisitively.

He said nothing but broke down crying and hugged Jen. "There's been an accident at the armory."

"Bruce?"

"Yes," Murph said quietly.

Family members started to gather at the door, wondering what was happening. "Please, step back!" Murph asked everyone.

"Murph, please, what happened?" Jen begged.

"Bruce. It was Bruce and Smitty, a freak accident. They were – crushed." That was all he could gather his voice to say.

Jen dropped backward as she passed out. Meg caught her before she hit the carpet. "Get her some water!" she yelled.

Jen was placed on the couch, and a cool washcloth was put on her forehead. Her cries could be heard by the neighbors from two doors down. Murph looked up and saw Lewis standing in the doorway to the second floor, confused by all this commotion. Murph walked over to him.

"Dad's – gone?" Lewis asked in a shaky voice.

"I'm so sorry." Lewis looked at the ceiling as tears ran down his face. "Let's go upstairs. Okay, buddy?" Murph asked him.

Lewis turned around and said nothing. He slowly and precisely made each step going up the stairs. He went into his room and sat on the edge of his bed. Murph followed.

"I have something from your father for you. Here, open it."

Lewis took the envelope and carefully opened it. He read the card and shook the envelope to spill its contents. He smiled when he saw the cross. "He should have worn it one more day," Lewis said. He wiped tears as he stretched the intricate braided chain around his neck.

"Do you think it will protect me, Murph?"

"It did for your father. He was an exceptional man. You're already on your way to fill his shoes."

"What do you mean by that, Murph?" Lewis sniffled.

"You'll find out soon enough, Lewis. You'll find out soon enough. Let's go downstairs and take care of your mom, okay?"

Lewis walked to the mirror and looked at himself. He adjusted the chain perfectly and straightened his shirt collar.

"Murph?" Lewis asked him.

"What, pal?"

"I think today is the last day I'll ever be able to cry. Let's go see Mom."

When Lewis saw his mother, she had regained consciousness, and he sat on the couch. Lewis asked as he hugged her, "Mom, why have so many bad things happened to us since I was born?"

"I don't know, dear, I just don't know. I don't think I can take anymore." Lewis held her in a long embrace, probably the longest in his life.

Murph gave Lewis a tap on his shoulder and motioned him to come outside. Shocked and disbelieving, party-goers gathered around Jen on the couch, trying to console her. Murph brought Lewis for a walk to the beach, neither saying anything.

There wasn't any funeral service for Bruce, per his will. There weren't any priests or sermons—only meaningful words shared between family and friends. A small ceremony of life was held on a beautiful spring day at Scrappy's Landing. Over fifty boats formed a semi-circle in the bay. A wreath was placed on the still water as a lone fireman played haunting bagpipes at the end of the breakwater.

*****

The summer of 1980 breezed by and warmed up for only one week. In the first week of August, temperatures soared into the nineties. Bruce usually took his vacation then. Jen tried not to think about the past vacations they shared. Jen's mother, Kate, started showing up unannounced to comfort her but was a pain in the neck as usual. Kate tried to schedule appointments with grief counselors and get Jen to join a support group. Jen thought she should mind her own business, driving a wedge between them.

Lewis started fifth grade. He was still good friends with Phil. Lewis continued his interest in music. He wanted to play the violin, but the music instructors didn't know how to play the instrument. Jen hired a private teacher for Lewis three afternoons a week. Phil joined in and took flute lessons. The continual harassment from Jerry Alfonzo and the Gallagher brothers never stopped, especially after they found out Lewis and Phil had joined the school band. That was definitely for sissies.

Lewis mastered the violin in no time. His interest in playing many instruments was apparent. He soon learned to play the stand-up bass, guitar, and harmonica. He wasn't interested in any brass instruments.

In January of 1982, Jen received her insurance settlement from Massachusetts. She received a $250,000 check and a monthly social security check for her and Lewis of $1200. Lewis could not inherit any money until he turned twenty-one. She continued to live meagerly and squirreled away the entire settlement for Lewis.

As February 28th approached, life at the National Guard maintenance depot dragged on. A charred spot on the concrete was a constant reminder of what had happened.

Something was missing. Everyone's jovial, carefree attitudes were long gone. Commander Briggs died of a heart attack in his chair just one week before retiring. Nolan was on leave for depression and sadly did a swan dive from the Sagamore Bridge on March 1st. His body was never found in the icy canal, only his idling truck at the highest point of the span. No one came to Jen's house the day he jumped to tell her. She read about it in the newspaper and didn't shed a tear.

*****

Lewis excelled through sixth and seventh grades. He tutored failing students after class, and even the math teacher started consulting Lewis on complex math equations. It was clear that something was going on inside Lewis's head, and his homeroom teacher wanted to find out.

When Lewis turned thirteen in eighth grade, Miss Morris suggested Lewis have an IQ test at year's end. Although such tests weren't usually administered to children before they were sixteen, she felt the test might prove valuable in steering Lewis's future. Jen agreed to a meeting in her home.

Miss Derosa came on an afternoon when Lewis tutored a student until 4:00. She arrived promptly at 2:30.

"Good afternoon, Ms. Duncan." She politely introduced herself.

"Oh, please! Call me Jen. You must be younger than me!"

"Just turned thirty-six, but don't tell anyone. I'm an old maid. Not many good pickings here on the Cape, if you know what I mean. I'm Leah."

"Pleased to meet you, Leah. Take a seat. Would you like a coffee, tea, or a beer?"

"I'd love a beer, but just one."

"Glass?"

"No thanks, a bottle or can is fine. I grew up in Wellfleet next to the sandpit where everyone partied."

"I've been there, too!" Jen replied. "We were probably there at the same time."

"I hate to bring back any sad memories for you, but Lewis lost his father, didn't he?" Leah cautiously asked.

"Yes, back in 1980. An accident at work."

"How's Lewis coping?"

"Okay, I guess. We don't talk about it anymore."

"As I mentioned on the phone, I would like to administer an IQ test for Lewis. He is extremely bright and very helpful to other students, also."

"He got his patience from his dad, not me!" Jen snorted and laughed. "I've heard of an IQ test but don't know what it is."

"There are different kinds. An IQ test measures a person's mental strength and weakness against people of the same age. I can administer the test this Saturday morning here if Lewis agrees. All he will need is a pencil and some quiet time."

"It's been quiet as a church around here. I'll ask him tonight."

"I have a few more questions about Lewis, if you don't mind, Jen."

"Go right ahead."

"Is Lewis spiritual? I mean, does he go to church?"

"No, we've never gone to church. Weddings and funerals, that's about it."

"Me, too," Leah said. "I know he's in the school band. Does he have any hobbies? Writing or art, maybe?"

"Art? Are you kidding? Follow me."

Jen led the way up the steep staircase to Lewis's room. The door was closed and had a large peace sign painted on it.

"Are you sure he won't mind?" Leah asked.

"He won't mind at all. Lewis shows his room off to everyone. Come on in."

Leah's mouth dropped. Beautiful paintings adorned three walls from the ceiling to the floor. Boats, birds, dunes, and fish came to life in a splash of colors bathed in afternoon sunlight from the salt-sprayed window.

"Lewis did these?" Leah asked. "I've never...."

"Yes, everyone."

"Now I really want to give him that test! Lewis has been tutoring a student in another class. Who taught him sign language?"

"Sign language? Are you for real? Lewis never told me he knew sign language!" Jen paused and thought a moment. "Wait a minute. When he was younger, he had a friend who didn't talk. We all joked and thought they used secret hand gestures."

Leah raised her eyebrows. "Well, thank you for your time, Jen. I must be going. Please let me know Lewis's decision. Here's my card."

"Thank you. I'll be in touch either way."

*****

Jen filled Lewis in that night about the IQ test. He was eager to take it, knowing he was different from other kids at school. He got a good night's rest before taking the test Saturday morning.

Leah showed up promptly at nine a.m. the next morning. She told him the test would take about two hours at a leisurely pace and left him alone in the kitchen. After about forty-five minutes, he walked into the living room, where Ms. Derosa read a newspaper.

"Yes, Lewis? Any problems?"

"I'm all done."

Leah looked at him in shock. She took the exam from him and thumbed through it. "I guess you *are* done. And for some reason, that doesn't surprise me."

He looked at her and grinned. "Can I go now? Me and Phil are going fishing at the pier today."

"Yes, you can, Lewis. Thank you for having me in your home. I feel truly privileged. I'll have the results by Monday afternoon. Do you want your mom to sit in on the discussion?"

"Sure, whatever. I'll see you on Monday." Lewis slung his backpack over one shoulder and departed. Leah replied with a smile but didn't say anything. She wasn't sure if she was ready to look at his test, so she continued shuffling through the newspaper.

Lewis walked to Phil's house a block from the Bass River and found his mother sitting on the porch with his father. Lewis approached cautiously. He could tell they were in deep conversation as Phil's father stood and threw his hands up in the air.

"Hi, Mr. Kingsley. Hello, Mrs. Kingsley. Is Phil ready to go fishing?"

"I don't think he is going anywhere today, Lewis," Mr. Kingsley said.

"Is he sick?" Lewis asked. He then noticed some tears in Mrs. Kingsley's eyes.

"Is Phil okay?"

Mr. Kingsley leaned against the porch wall.

"Phil got beat up on the way home from school yesterday. That Jerry kid and the Gallagher brothers gave him a good work-over – told him to go back to Worcester where he belongs and left him on the sidewalk bleeding. They said blacks couldn't live here anymore. Look at the side of my house."

Lewis walked around the corner of the house. He looked at the wall where someone sprayed racist graffiti. Even though he couldn't understand what it said, Lewis became enraged. It wasn't the first time he had these uncontrollable feelings. It took a few moments for his rage to subside before he could speak.

"Do you have any paint, Mr. Kingsley?"

"Paint? Do you mean for the house?"

"Yes, house paint, the white?"

"I think there's some in the cellar."

"Why don't you get it and also a brush, please?"

"Lewis, you don't have to," Mrs. Kingsley said.

"Yes," Lewis looked them in the eye. "Yes, I have to."

It took two coats of white paint to cover the black spray-painted words of hate. Phil watched from his upstairs window as Lewis carefully dipped the brush into the paint and applied it to the house. Phil struggled to open the fussy window.

"You still feel like going fishing, Lewis?" he yelled down.

Lewis couldn't help noticing a large patch of hair on his head that was shaved, revealing some fresh stitches.

"I'm going to get them someday, Phil, real bad. What they've done to you and me isn't right." He looked up at Phil with one hand blocking the bright sun from his tender blue eyes.

Phil watched his only friend from above in silence. He had never heard such threats come from him before.

"I'll be down in a minute," Phil said. He gathered a light coat from his closet and skipped down the stairs. He went out the front door and passed his parents without saying a word.

"Philondrious, you're not going anywhere!" his mother reprimanded him.

He put two hands on the porch rail and kicked his legs like a gymnast over a set of parallel bars. He landed precisely on two feet and darted across the lawn.

"I'll be home before dark," Phil yelled, looking back at his confused parents. He grabbed his fishing rod and tackle box by the garage, meeting Lewis by the curb.

Lewis took a deep breath and put his arm around Phil's shoulder. He led the way toward the ocean.

"I bet they're biting good today. Don't you think, Phil? Do you have any suntan lotion for that goofy bald spot on your head? Do blacks have to use suntan lotion?" Lewis razzed him.

Phil gave Lewis a fake punch to the gut as he replied, "Funny, Lewis. Real funny, you big jerk!"

Chapter Twenty-Six

Jen met Leah in the guidance office after school on Monday. Lewis forgot he was tutoring a student in math, so he missed the appointment with them. Leah held a stack of papers in her hand.

"Hi, Jen, come on in and please take a seat," she greeted Jen.

Jen sat down nervously and crossed her legs.

"So, is there any encouraging news from the test?"

Leah looked at her with a straight face, and it concerned Jen.

"I don't think *encouraging* is the correct word."

Jen didn't know what to say.

"Jen, I think *astonishing* is more like it! He scored over one-sixty."

"Is that good?"

"Good? Jen, that's unbelievable! He might as well be in a class with Einstein and Alexander Graham Bell! He falls into the genius category!"

"I don't know what to say. Should I be happy?"

"Lewis can call the shots through high school and college if he applies himself!"

"I think he's doing pretty good now, don't you? I don't want to push him. He's pretty sensitive, you know."

"I have another battery of tests to give Lewis."

"Hold it right there, Leah. We've been put through hell this past year, and I don't want Lewis becoming some circus sideshow just because he's smart. Lewis has been on the ropes since he was born, and I think he's just starting to come out of his shell."

"I know, Jen, but this is a once-in-a-lifetime opportunity for Lewis to get out of school in Yarmouth and attend one of the finest academies in Boston."

"I don't want him to attend an academy in Boston, and I don't want him to leave Yarmouth!" Jen found herself getting irritated.

"Please think about it, Jen. My door is always open for you and Lewis."

Leah stood up and opened the office door for Jen, who turned around and politely replied, "Thank you for all your hard work throughout the school year, but I think Lewis will be staying put. He finally has a real friend in town."

Jen extended a courteous handshake. Walking down the hall, she peered into a classroom and saw Lewis writing on a chalkboard. Two students analyzed a long math equation as he feverishly scribbled a solution for them. Jen looked at him through a small window in the door. *Who would have thought, another Einstein?*

Lewis returned home late in the afternoon. Jen was sitting at the kitchen table.

"How did I do?" he said to Jen.

"On what?" Jen said coyly.

"The test, the IQ test, Mom!"

"Oh, I'm sorry, honey. I was on another planet, I guess. Good, you did very well on the test." Jen paused for a moment. "You did excellent, Lewis. The teacher said you shouldn't have any problems getting through high school and college if you apply yourself."

"That's it? That's all?"

"Yes, dear. Why?"

"Nothing." He laughed. "I guess it's good to know that I'm not some kind of freak!"

"Not at all, honey." Jen looked at the folder containing the test results on the table and put it under her arm. "I saw you today teaching those students after school. You're a natural."

"I knew you were watching me. I was just showing off."

"You were not, and I know it! Have you ever thought about being a teacher, Lewis?"

"No, Mom. I have to make it through high school first, don't I?" he laughed. "I don't think I'm college material anyhow."

"Lewis, I've never seen you bring any schoolbooks home. Do you ever study?"

"No, I guess not. It just comes naturally."

"See? See what I mean?"

"I guess so." He looked at the floor.

Jen was thinking of any possible way to lighten the moment. "Lewis, why don't you call Phil and see if he wants to go to the spring opening at Chill's Grill? Invite his parents, too. I heard the clams and scallops are out of this world."

"Can we use your money?"

"Yes, Lewis. That's what I mean. Treat them with *our* money. When your father died, he set up a fund for you and me at the armory. I haven't spent a dime of it. I'd better start spending it before the government takes it all!" she joked. "You be sure and tell Mr. Kingsley that dinner is on Mr. Bruce Duncan, okay?"

"Gotcha, Mom."

*****

The Kingsley family was very humbled by Jen's invitation and accepted. Wade Kingsley was a little skeptical at first, but they met two other black families at the restaurant and hit it off with them. They even joked about how awkward it was to live in an all-white town and feel so out of place. At the end of dinner, Wade made a toast and thanked Lewis and Jen for welcoming them into their family.

Lewis saw beyond people's color and disabilities. He was embarrassed when several nearby patrons clapped as Wade finished his speech. Jen never saw his face turn so red. She knew Lewis and Phil's friendship bond would be tested when they started high school the following year. Unbeknownst to everyone, the series of events that were destined to happen would alter the lives of both families forever.

Chapter Twenty-Seven

Phil took an interest in football. He was very small but could run like the dickens. Nobody could catch him on an open field. He made the J.V. team as a receiver and was the fastest runner in the league.

Lewis dropped out of Band and joined the track team. He faithfully did his weekly leg exercises after dumping his leg braces five years ago. His unusual style of galloping down the track made him look more like an ostrich than an athlete. The basketball coach pestered Lewis to try out for the team. No one matched his 6'7" height in a five-town radius. However, Lewis's clumsiness and coordination quickly ended the coach's ambitions after one practice session.

Phil and Lewis walked to school together every morning. After school, they spent their time fishing.

The daily teasing and bullying from Jerry Alfonzo and the Gallagher brothers were rolling strong.

Jerry was in another class, so neither Phil nor Lewis saw him much, but he continued to harass them.

"We got something for you and your friend real soon, Lewis!" Jerry threatened.

The Gallagher brothers would be seniors next year, and Lewis counted the days until he wouldn't have to see them again.

Lewis and Phil's friendship dwindled to an occasional fishing outing by late spring. Phil's new girlfriend occupied his time, something he didn't mind for a change. Lewis had yet to meet anyone.

One day, Lewis and Phil accidentally met up while walking home. It was like old times for the two. They stopped for a pizza and chatted away the hours. It was starting to get dark when Lewis suggested they'd better get home.

On a deserted shortcut, Lewis heard a car pull up from behind. He cautiously turned around. It was Jeff and Simon Gallagher, along with Jerry Alfonzo.

"Hey, what are you two lovers doing on this street? Making out?" Alfonzo yelled, getting a roar from the Gallagher brothers.

"Just keep walking, Phil. Don't even turn around," Lewis said.

Simon Gallagher wheeled the car around in front of them and blocked their escape. They got out of the car.

"I asked you, Dunce. What're you doing out here? Are you causing some trouble?" Alfonzo pried.

"Going home," Lewis muttered as he turned away.

"Hold on there, you two nerds!" Simon Gallagher yelled.

"Mind your own business, Simon," Lewis said. "What we're doing is no business of yours and you, Alfonso."

"Well, it's about time you started showing some gumption here, Dunce," Jerry addressed Lewis. "And didn't you get our message spray-painted on your house, little boy?" Jerry asked Phil.

Phil was shaking uncontrollably. He was so nervous.

"You can go on home to your Mommy and Daddy. Tell them they better be getting out of town. You hear me, boy?"

"Yeah, I hear you. You're not running anyone out of town!" Phil said, sticking up for himself. "It's going to take a lot more than of the three of you to tangle with my father, but you don't have the guts to face anyone head-on, do you?"

"Look, little boy, our beef today is with Lewis. Didn't you learn your lesson? It's about time he started showing us some respect. We'll deal with you later, pipsqueak."

Lewis told Phil, "Get a move on. I can handle these three losers."

Phil looked at his three foes intently, then at Lewis. "I'm not going anywhere, Lewis. Two against three is fine for me. I've got a score to settle myself."

"It's your move, Jerry. We don't have all day. Your babysitter is waiting for you anyhow," Lewis said, making two fists held at his side. "Every time I see you, Jerry, the Gallaghers are by your side. Do you need them for protection?"

Jerry looked at the Gallagher brothers and smirked.

"C'mon, let's go. We'll settle this later with you, Lewis!" Jerry said as the three started walking away slowly. They got back in the car, and Simon showered them with a cloud of dust as he peeled out.

"They're chickens, just chickens. Not one of them has the balls to face us!"

"Oh, I know, Lewis. I know. Easy for you to say. You're six-foot-seven, two hundred-twenty pounds. I'm five-foot-six, one-forty. I'm dead meat."

"Why did your parents move from the city to the Cape, anyway?"

"There were too many drugs and gangs forming. Our neighborhood wasn't safe anymore."

"Yeah, it looks like you're a lot better off here, aren't you? Drugs are plentiful in our school, too. I heard Jerry and the brothers are dealing," Lewis said. "How do you think they can afford that nice car? They don't even have jobs."

"I've never thought about that, Lewis. Those guys are going to get real bad, aren't they?" Phil said as they rounded the corner to his house.

"I think it's just starting. Alfonso's been after me since first grade. I can't take it anymore, but my dad always wanted me to settle things peacefully, with words, not fists."

"Well, you certainly got us out of that pickle with your words!" Phil said, laughing.

"You didn't do so bad yourself! But I don't think words are going to satisfy them much longer. Hey, there's your Mom on the porch. Hello, Mrs. Kingsley," Lewis addressed her.

"Lovely day, boys, isn't it?" she noted. "And only one more week of school! I bet both of you are looking forward to summer vacation!"

"Oh, if you only knew, Mrs. Kingsley, if you only knew! Hey, I'll see you tomorrow, Phil." Lewis tried to lighten it up a bit.

"Yeah, hopefully, it'll be trouble-free, and I won't crap my pants like I almost did back there!"

"Better get used to it, and you should start working out. Put some muscle on those skinny pencil arms!" Lewis joked.

"Yeah, yeah. We can't all be Popeye like you. See you tomorrow."

Lewis turned around and walked toward his house, just five minutes away. He didn't get far when he heard the familiar sound of a car pulling up from behind again. It was Jerry. This time he exited the vehicle and walked directly to Lewis. He had a gun and pointed it at Lewis's head.

"Get in the car and don't say a fuckin' word."

Lewis got in the open front door and sat next to Simon. Jerry slammed the door and barked, "Let's go!"

Jerry reached from the back seat and put a blindfold on Lewis. He thought they were going to take him somewhere and kill him. They drove for about twenty minutes on a paved street and then took a hard turn onto a bumpy dirt road. Lewis was convinced he'd be dead soon. His fingers searched for a door handle, but he couldn't find anything except a small nub. The handle was removed.

Minutes seemed like an eternity. The car abruptly halted as Simon jammed the shifter into park. Someone opened the door and yelled, "Get out, *now!*"

Lewis obliged and stepped out with his hands over his head. He heard a gun chamber spin as the barrel jammed against his back.

"What are you gonna do now, Dunce? Huh?" He knew it was one of the Gallaghers but couldn't tell which one. His mouth was so dry from fear that he couldn't even swallow.

"Take off your shirt!" one of them ordered Lewis.

"What? Take off my shirt?"

"Take it off! Then your shoes and pants, nice and slow."

"No tricks! And there is no little boy to help you this time, Lewis," Jerry said.

Lewis reached slowly, removed his shoes, and then his pants down to his underwear.

"Off with those tighty-whities, Lewis!" one of the Gallaghers yelled.

"Oh, come on, hasn't this gone far enough?" Lewis pleaded.

"Do it!"

He removed his underwear and stood there.

"My, he's one fine specimen, isn't he, boys?" Jerry laughed. "Open the trunk, Simon."

Lewis could hear the trunk open, then a rustling of some type.

"Don't move, Lewis!"

He felt a warm liquid being poured from his head to toe. At first, he thought it might be gasoline, but it didn't smell like gas. It was sweet and smelled like candy. Some dripped onto his lips. Syrup! Maple syrup! That's what it was!

Lewis felt something dropping over him, kind of like leaves but lighter. All three were laughing hysterically at Lewis.

"He looks like a big damn chicken!" Jerry boasted. "Cluck, cluck!"

Lewis didn't move.

"Don't take that blindfold off until we're gone. You got a long walk home, and we're taking your clothes, too!" They broke out laughing again.

Lewis heard the car doors open and close. The car started and drove off.

He didn't remove the blindfold until he couldn't hear the car anymore. Pulling it off, he looked at his body. Feathers! They covered him completely in tiny feathers, sticking to him everywhere. He could hardly move as the syrup dried.

Lewis looked around and tried to get a bearing on where he was. He could see the sun over his shoulder, probably west, he thought, this time of day. His only choice was to start walking on the dirt road and see where it led him. He came to a paved road in five minutes but still had no idea where he was.

"Should I go left or right?" he wondered. It didn't matter. He was screwed either way. He felt like such an idiot and was totally embarrassed.

Lewis was walking for another five minutes when a car approached him and slowed. He tried to wave it down, but the vehicle sped quickly by him as he heard children screaming from the back seat.

"Great!" he shouted. "Who in their right mind would pick me up looking like this?" He was worried about his mother at this point. He was sure it was well near dinner time, and Jen was always on time with it.

He must be out in the boonies because only one car passed him in the last twenty minutes. Lewis could hear another vehicle approaching around a corner. He thought about jumping into the woods so as not to scare anyone again. He didn't. The car barreled around the turn and slammed on its brakes. It was the police! That other car must have called them! Lewis was relieved but quite nervous as well.

The car door opened, and a female officer stepped toward Lewis.

"What the heck? I have never seen anything like this before! Are you okay?"

"Yes," he said, cringing with embarrassment.

"What's your name?"

"Lewis Duncan. I live in Yarmouth."

"Yarmouth? How the hell did you get here? You're at least thirty miles from there. We're in Wellfleet! I'll get a blanket from my trunk and cover you up! You look like a big chicken!"

"Thanks, officer. I might have scared the last car that went by, right?"

"You sure did. That lady stopped at the first gas station and called it in. She thought you were a monster or something!"

The officer wrapped a blanket around Lewis.

"Get in the back seat. If the feathers start flying off, I don't want to breathe them in. Never in my life have I ever!" She cut herself off, shaking her head, trying to hold her laughter. "Where do you live in Yarmouth?"

"I live off Wood Road near the ocean and state police barracks. If you get me close, I'll walk home the rest of the way."

"You *are* crazy! You're getting a ride right to your front door. I'll have to call this one in. I'm going to be out of my area for a while. Who did this to you, anyway?"

Lewis looked out the window as they were driving along. He thought long and hard for a moment.

"Hey, kid, are you awake back there?"

"Sorry, ma'am. Just wondering how I'm going to get this stuff off me, that's all. It was an initiation, an initiation to my track team. It happens to everyone."

"That's the cruelest initiation I've ever seen! I may have to report this to your school."

"Oh, no, please, ma'am. I'll be kicked off the team!"

The officer tapped her fingers on the steering wheel.

"Okay, but if any more of your track buddies get dumped off, there will be a big problem. Comprende?"

"Yes, ma'am. Thank you so much, thank you. What's your name, anyhow?" Lewis asked graciously.

The officer adjusted her rear-view mirror on Lewis.

"Damn! That's the funniest thing I've ever seen, kid!" The officer laughed again as she picked up her microphone from the dash.

"Car 156 to dispatch, car 156 to dispatch, over."

"Go ahead, 156."

"Requesting early dinner break at 1700 hours, returning at 1800."

A moment of silence ensued.

"Dinner break approved, returning 1800. Dispatch out."

"See, kid, I'm even giving up my dinner for you!" she joked.

"I feel so horrible, ma'am. You'll never know how much I appreciate this. I don't even know your name." Lewis asked her again.

"Ransom, Patrol Officer Pat Ransom. I'm taking the detective test next month in Hyannis. I'm hoping to get a promotion out of Peyton Place here. And look, I'll keep this quiet between you and me. No one would believe me anyhow!"

"Good luck on your test, Officer Ransom. I truly hope we never meet again unless I have clothes on!" Lewis joked with her.

Lewis tried to relax in the back seat. His mind was going a million miles an hour. What was he going to tell his mother? Was he going to tell Phil? He pondered the demise of Jerry and the Gallagher brothers and swore to get even with Jerry and the Gallaghers.

Little did he know it wouldn't be his first run-in with the law. It also wouldn't be his last encounter with Officer Ransom.

Chapter Twenty-Eight

Lewis snuck in through the back door of his house. He saw Jen on the phone and scrambled up the stairs into his bathroom. He turned the shower on and jumped in. The feathers and dried syrup made a gooey mess and clogged the drain. He heard a knock on the door.

"Lewis, is that you in there?" Jen asked warily.

"Yeah, Mom. Who else would it be? You were on the phone, so I didn't want to bug you." Lewis emptied the shower drain again into a basket beside the tub.

"Okay, dear. Dinner will be ready in fifteen minutes."

"That sounds great, Mom. I'll be down in a bit."

Lewis knew he had averted a disaster. He leaned on the sink and looked at himself in the steamy, cracked mirror.

How much longer can I put up with this? "I'm going to snap!"

He gathered his emotions and got dressed. Jen was noticeably silent during dinner and didn't have any appetite. She was going out with some friends she had just met. Harmless, he thought.

After dinner, Lewis looked at the phone and was tempted to call Phil but reconsidered. He didn't want to burden him with his misfortune.

Jen left immediately after dinner, not saying where she was going. Very unusual, he thought. He enjoyed a relaxing evening on the couch, watching the Red Sox destroy the Orioles. He fell asleep at the game's end and dreamt of days spent fishing with his father on the ocean.

All night long, he was with Bruce: in the truck, on the beach with Rex, laughing with Nolan and Briggs at the clambakes playing horseshoes. He woke up in a cold sweat, shaking. He realized they were dead, all of them! Did they come to see him? Was this some type of weird message?

*****

Lewis sat up and rubbed his eyes after many hours of sleep. He looked over and saw his mother passed out in the recliner. He got up and walked over to her.

"Mom? Mom, are you okay?"

There was no response.

Lewis looked in her hand. There was something in it. He opened her fingers to reveal a large bag of a white powdery substance.

"What the hell is this, Mom?" he screamed at her.

Still no response, but he knew she was breathing. She took up heavy drinking the past few months and suspected she was smoking marijuana, but this took things to a whole new level. He saw her get onto some guy's motorcycle several times but didn't think anything of it. It was time to start paying attention to her whereabouts.

Lewis went to the kitchen and soaked a facecloth in cold water. He drew it over her face, awakening her slightly. Jen managed to crack her eyes open and smile.

"I love you, Lewis," she slurred.

"I love you too, Mom."

He looked at the clock. Seven a.m.! "Holy crap, I have to get ready for school!" It was the last day before much-needed summer vacation.

Lewis took the bag of powder, walked over to the sink, and turned the water on. He emptied the contents through a strainer and down the drain.

The telephone rang, startling and waking Jen like she was stone-cold sober.

"Oh, hello, Mrs. Kingsley," Jen paused and listened intently for a moment. Lewis was trying to hear what was being said also.

"Oh, no! Oh my God! He what? *No!*" She screamed.

"What, Mom, what?" He knew this wasn't good.

"Lewis will be...."

"I'll be what, Mom?"

"I just don't know what to say. Lewis will be devastated."

"Devastated? What the hell is going on?"

"We'll be here for you. Our thoughts and prayers are with everyone." She hung up the phone.

"Mom, did something happen to Mr. Kingsley? Phil said he was sick."

"Sit down, Lewis," Jen said as she took his hand, looking at him with tears. "Lewis, I've never had to tell anyone something like this my entire life." She paused and took a deep breath. "Phil tried to kill himself last night," she said quietly.

"*Nooo!*" Lewis screamed in agony.

"He hung himself in their garage with the dog's chain. Luckily, his father found him moments before he may have died. He was – naked. It seems he was tarred and feathered earlier in the evening by some other boys in town. Mrs. Kingsley helped clean him up and saw him to bed. He must have snuck into the garage at some point. The ambulance is still there."

"I know who did it! I know who tarred him. It was Jerry and the fuckin' Gallagher brothers! I'm going to kill all of them!"

"That's a horrible thing to say! And how do you know this, Lewis?"

Lewis looked out the window at the peaceful harbor, trying to regain his composure.

"We had a run-in with them yesterday. They must have gotten to Phil after they got me." He said lowly.

"What do you mean after they got you?"

"I got tarred and feathered yesterday, too, after school. That's why I was in the shower before dinner!" Lewis admitted to his mother.

"Why didn't you tell me? We could have done something and have had them arrested!"

"Yeah, right, Mom. The police officer who brought me home naked was laughing her ass off! I lied. I told her it was an initiation to the track team."

"A police officer brought you home? You lied to her and covered up for those boys?" Jen was fuming. "I didn't see any police car pull up here yesterday!"

"You were on the phone, and I went up the back staircase. Mom, I was dumped off in a sandpit in Wellfleet. They had a gun and said they'd kill Phil and me if I squealed."

"You have to go talk to the police right now! They are still at the Kingsleys. It's the least you can do!"

"The least I can do? I'm feeling guilty about leaving him yesterday after they threatened us! He must have gone somewhere when I left him. I made a vow to myself. This ups the stakes!"

"I don't like the way you're talking, Lewis! Remember what your father said about getting back at people? Violence never solves anything. It doesn't make it right to hurt someone deliberately."

"Oh, I'm not going to hurt them. The crabs will be feeding off them!"

"Lewis, just calm down! Remember, it's the last day of school, and you have to get your report card."

"School? Report card? Are you kidding?" Lewis slammed his fist against a door. "Mom, I've been picked on in school for eleven years, stared at, and bullied. How much more can I take? Is the rest of my life going to be like this? I'm trying to be strong. Everyone I've loved has died – Dad, Rex, and Nolan. This morning I came downstairs and found a bag of white powder in your hand while you were passed out. What was that? What was it?" He demanded to know.

"You found a bag of powder?" Jen asked. "Oh, my God! Where is it? Did you hide it?" Jen frantically screamed at Lewis, grabbed his arms, and shook him.

"It's down the drain, Mom! Probably on Route 28 by now, and I hope it is!"

"There may be hell to pay for what you did, Lewis!"

"For what *I* did? That's right, Mom. There will be hell to pay when I get done in this town!"

*****

Lewis stormed from the kitchen and slammed the door behind him. He started walking. He didn't know where he was going but knew it wasn't to school. He could hear Jen's voice calling him from afar, but he kept walking. By habit, he found himself walking toward Phil's house. He needed to see him. A police cruiser slowly drove by as two other officers intently eyed him standing outside Phil's home. He stopped at the driveway and looked in through the living room door. A large figure approached from the hall shadows. It was Mr. Kingsley.

"Lewis," he said quietly. "Lewis, please come in."

Lewis nodded and walked up the driveway, his head and shoulders slumped. Once again, he felt two feet tall. Lewis saw Mrs. Kingsley in a rocking chair in the living room.

"Please come and sit with us, Lewis. Here, beside Ma."

Lewis obliged and put his hand on Mrs. Kingsley's knee as she sobbed.

"I don't know what to say, Mr. and Mrs. Kingsley."

"Philondrious is a fine young man like you. He's been pushed around ever since we moved here years ago. He didn't deserve to try to kill himself!" Mr. Kingsley told Lewis in a rising tone. "He was just going for a bike ride to get an ice cream."

"Dear, calm down. Your heart, remember?" Mrs. Kingsley blurted out.

"I don't give a damn about my heart! It was my stupid decision to leave the city and start somewhere new. Our son was almost bullied to death, and the house was egged and sprayed with racist slurs. Why do we even stay here?" He started to tear up. "It's my entire fault!"

"It's not your fault, dear. Now get that out of your head!"

"I'm going to find and kill those boys involved with this. You know the police aren't going to help. They're all white!" He stated firmly. "Do you know who may have done this, Lewis?"

"I won't have you talk like that in my house or any other house we live in, Wade!" Mrs. Kingsley yelled at her husband.

Lewis was stuck in the middle of this argument and started to think. Jen had the same conversation with him not a half-hour ago. Both men want to hunt the boys for revenge and kill them. Is this an instinct for men only? What were they thinking? Lewis went into a fog and ignored the ensuing feud and questioning from the Kingsleys. He looked at the floor and waited a few moments before interrupting their heated battle.

"Pardon me, Mr. and Mrs. Kingsley, but I must attempt to attend the last day of school. I'll stop over later. I realize there's nothing I can do for you at this time. Please tell Phil I'll see him after school. We all have to sort this out."

"You've been so kind and always there for Philondrious. Please excuse our squabbling," Mrs. Kingsley asked him.

I wasn't there for the most important day of his life. How can I live with this? Should I tell them?

*****

Lewis walked in the opposite direction of the school. Instead of going to his classes, he went to the ocean, where he felt safe. He ran as far as he could on the beach between the Bass and Parker Rivers. He skipped stones and quahog shells across the water, studying the arrival of summer birds and their graceful mating dances while sitting on a dune. He observed a high and low tide as time passed in a blink. There was nothing like the smell of low tide – it was always so peaceful here. Why step into the reality of a cruel and vicious world?

Lewis didn't eat or drink anything all day, and the effects took a toll on him. Pangs of hunger brought him to his senses. He started the two-mile trek back to his house. Honking horns and car exhaust at rush hour made him nauseous.

Lewis approached his house and stopped in the driveway. Three motorcycles were parked on the grass. He never saw them before but noticed they were very shiny and had skulls and crossbones painted on the gas tanks. He knew if you flew that flag on a boat, you were declaring yourself an outlaw pirate. He cautiously walked through the door into the kitchen, where the riders were seated. His mother was nowhere in sight.

"Well, well," the largest man said in a deep, booming voice. "Isn't this nice? The little schoolboy is finally home from special education!" Two smaller men stood up, approached Lewis, and grabbed his arms. Lewis had fifty pounds on each man and tossed them across the floor.

"Who are you fuckin' guys? Get out of my house now!" Lewis yelled at the seated man.

"Take it easy, boy. Meet the new man of the household. I'm Honch, short for Honcho. I say what's going on. You'll listen to me, or you'll have a real problem. I've been getting it on with your mother. She does what I tell her to with no backtalk. You'll do as I say, and we won't have a problem." The two smaller men got up from the floor and dusted their pants off, itching for another shot at Lewis.

"If you ever come back in this house by yourself again, you're gonna have a big problem, asshole!" Lewis assured him.

"Your mother did say you were feisty! I could use you in my club, boy. But we do have one rather large matter to discuss. Your mom said you emptied something down the sink today that belonged to me. Is that true, or did she snort it herself?"

"You're right. I emptied it down the sink! Don't ever bring that crap into this house again!"

"Well, that crap just happened to be $2000 worth of Cape Cod's finest cocaine. I'll be takin' it out of your hide or your mother's — either's fine by me. Here's the address of our clubhouse. You bring that money to me anytime, and we'll be square. I might even make you one of my prospects. They'll do anything for me, too. You're a lot tougher than your Mommy said!" They all broke out laughing.

Lewis's brain was spinning out of control. He never had such an insane, crazy day.

"Jen is upstairs in bed. We've already had our way with her today. You got one month to give me the money, kid. Remember that."

Lewis stepped aside as they departed the kitchen. They started their motorcycles with a furious sound, spraying the house with grass and dirt as it shot up from their spinning tires. The windows rattled as they sped off. Lewis vowed revenge on these men if it was the last thing he ever did.

Lewis crept up the staircase, not knowing what he would find. He could hear Jen throwing up in the bathroom. The door was wide open, and her hands were clutching the wall. She was bent over the toilet.

"Oh, Lewis, I'm so sorry for what I've done!" Jen apologized profoundly.

"Here, Mom. Let's get some hot water and clean you up."

Lewis wet a facecloth and wiped her mouth.

"That feels so good, Lewis." Jen put the toilet cover down and took a seat. "I promise you, Lewis, I'm done with all the drinking, the smoking, and the drugs. I've been so depressed since your dad died. I just couldn't handle it anymore. Those men downstairs just happened to be in the right place at – well, you know."

"I know, Mom. I know," Lewis interrupted her. "Never mind the burden I've put on you the past seventeen years. Eyeglasses at one year of age, leg braces, the countless doctor visits."

"Lewis! You have never been a burden on us. Don't ever think that! Our mettle has certainly been tested – and I don't think it's over."

"That guy, Honch, said I have one month to pay him $2000, or he's coming after you or me."

"I haven't touched your father's life insurance or settlement money. I'll pay him with part of that."

"Like heck, you will, Mom. I'm not afraid of him or any of his puny sidekicks. Just stay away from them, okay?"

"I will, Lewis. They can be nice but are also very dangerous. I've seen them in action."

"Well, Mom. I think this can be remembered as one of the worst last days of school I've ever experienced. How about you?"

"You're right about that, kid. I'm sure the Kingsleys could use a shoulder to lean on. Let's go downstairs and make them some hot muffins."

"Sounds great. I'll turn on the oven."

"See? You can always cheer me up. You have such a kind heart, and you're just starting to do good things. Remember that, Lewis."

"I've been taking one step forward and two steps back my whole life, Mom. From now on, it's going be three steps forward and maybe one step back, okay?"

"Me, too," Jen said, smiling as he left the bathroom.

Lewis charged down the stairs, skipping steps like he bravely did as a child.

Jen examined the dark circles under her bloodshot eyes and wrinkled face in the mirror.

"I have to turn my life around before I'm dead," she whispered. "I hope I can."

Chapter Twenty-Nine

Jen came downstairs in the morning, lured by the smell of bacon cooking on the stove and freshly brewed coffee. She was surprised when she walked into the kitchen. Lewis had set the table for breakfast and was reading the *Cape Cod Times* newspaper.

"Catching up on Wall Street, Lewis?" Jen asked sarcastically. "Are we getting the paper now?"

"I ran uptown to Moe's Store and got one. I ran back, too. I'm getting ready for the fall track season this year. I want to be in good shape."

"I decided I'm going to start walking again too. I have let myself go to pot – literally." They both smiled and laughed.

"I'm going to look for a summer job, Mom. It'll be good for me to earn my own money."

"You don't have to get a job if you don't want to. You're on both bank accounts and the house deed, remember? You've never withdrawn a cent from either account."

"I know, but maybe I can meet some new friends or interesting people."

"Did you ever think about going down to the boatyard? They're always plenty of interesting people there."

"Nah, I'm tired of those fishermen smelling rotten all the time, you know? Hey, here's one. Sounds pretty cool. Part-time helper/driver wanted, Meals for Seniors. Three hours a day, three days a week, car provided." Lewis's wheels were spinning. "That would allow me plenty of time for training."

"You'd probably meet some nice people there, too. I think you'd be great at it. But you walk everywhere, and your driving skills might be a little rusty. You've had your license for almost a year, haven't you? Did you ever get your picture taken?"

"I have my paper license and have never gone to the registry to finalize it with a picture. I don't want to be seen in the 'brown bomb,' you know? It's the ugliest Impala on Cape Cod!"

"Well, you're right about that. It's a good grocery-getter, and who cares if someone dings it up, right?"

"I have to agree with you on that, Mom. I don't think too many girls my age would like to be seen in it, either."

"I've never even seen you with a girl!"

"I have my eye on one, but she's a year older and hasn't talked to me yet. A bunch of seniors from last year were after her, but I think she's just waiting to meet me."

"My, you certainly are full of yourself today! Well, good luck with your job hunt, honey. I'll be doing some errands in the 'brown bomb."

Jen and Lewis had an excellent breakfast together, something they hadn't done in months. She mentioned how nice it was and wished to have more meals together at the table instead of fast food on the couch.

Jen made a concerted effort to reel her life back in. Lewis was hopeful, but he knew what she had been put through the past seventeen years. The impending deadline at month's end weighed heavily on both of them.

*****

Lewis passed Meals for Seniors headquarters hundreds of times during his daily walk to school. People were loading vans with coolers and small lunch bags. Odd, he thought, now he was trying to get a job there. Was his life all planned out?

He met an elderly man inside who gave him a job application, something he'd never seen before. Hmmm, he thought as he read the questions to himself. Birthday – easy: every four years! Previous experience – easy: none! Previous jobs – easy: none! Education – yes: still in school. References – easy: most of my family's dead. He got halfway through the application and decided to give up. This was ridiculous.

Lewis walked to the man behind the counter and neatly placed the application in front of him.

"Are you done? That was quick!" the man commented.

"I'm sorry, Sir. I don't want to waste your time. I don't have any background to qualify for this position. I'm just a high school kid looking to meet some new people and help the elderly if I can." Lewis took a deep breath to calm his nerves.

As the man on the other side of the counter looked at the application, he rolled his fingers on the desk a few times. He adjusted his reading glasses and stared at Lewis.

"Is this the first job you've ever applied for?"

"Yes, Sir."

"Do you have a license?"

"Oh, yes, Sir! I've had it for almost a year. It's just a paper one, but I passed my test. I've never been back for a picture at the DMV. I don't drive my mother's car too much. It is the ugliest thing in town!"

The old man smirked.

"Are you in good physical shape? My gosh, you must be six-five!"

"Six-seven, Sir. I'm in fairly good shape. I was born with a few issues, but I've concentrated and am determined to overcome them. It can be a daily struggle for me. It's a long story. Know what I mean, Sir?"

The man looked hard at Lewis, crinkled his job application, and threw it in a trash can.

"Come with me. Do you have time?"

"Time?" Lewis replied. "That's all I have!"

The gentlemen opened a pair of swinging doors and pointed toward an assembly line of workers. They were in various stages of putting meals together for delivery. Lewis was amazed at the team of employees. Some were cutting meat and buttering bread, and others were wrapping sandwiches. The man looked at Lewis.

"I'm sorry. I've forgotten to introduce myself. I'm Ben." He reached to shake Lewis's hand. "All of these workers, Lewis, have what you may call issues. Some may not speak, a few cannot hear, and that woman packing lunches is blind. We are non-profit and can't pay much, but I have to go with my gut instinct on this one. Let's go back to my desk."

Lewis followed Ben around the corner and through the double doors.

"Have a seat," Ben said as he brought out some paperwork. "I never liked job applications myself, Lewis. How about if I start you with one of our drivers as an assistant, kind of like training."

"Are you kidding me? Really? I thought you were going to boot me out the door!" Lewis and Ben both laughed.

"We have some pre-employment paperwork that's required, but you can take it home and fill it out."

"I appreciate your giving me a chance, Ben. I won't let you down. When would you like me to start?"

"If tomorrow's fine with you, it's good for me," Ben replied. "The drivers meet at the loading dock at eleven a.m. sharp. I'll team you with Millie. She's retiring in two weeks, and you can take her route if all goes well."

"I'll have a route already?"

"Don't worry. It's not that glamorous. See you at eleven. Oh, I forgot to tell you the starting pay!" Ben yelled to Lewis as he walked away.

"It doesn't matter, Ben! Thank you very much!"

Lewis was elated while walking home and decided to stop at Phil's house. Phil dropped a bomb on him. His family was moving back to Worcester.

Once again, a moment of happiness for Lewis was cut short. He didn't take the news well and left immediately. He started brooding about Honch, never mind his fragile mother.

Lewis tried to turn it around and be positive for a few moments. It was the beginning of summer vacation, and he had just gotten a new job. He didn't have to see Jerry Alfonso until September in school, and the Gallagher brothers graduated. Lewis knew they were all driving new sports cars because they were getting rich selling drugs on the Cape. He tried not to let it bother him, but it did. Lewis knew to avoid Jerry until he could devise a plan to punish all of them. They were bad seeds and needed to be dealt with thoughtfully. Lewis thought, "One minute, I'm happy. The next second I'm seeking revenge and thinking crazy! What's wrong with me? Bad thoughts outweigh my good ones!" Those up-and-down thoughts plagued him the entire walk home.

Lewis pumped himself up and enthusiastically told Jen about his new job. She was very proud that her little boy made such an impression on Ben, even though he didn't complete the application. Maybe things were starting to come around for them, but Jen also knew someone would be coming to their door soon, and she tried not to show her anxiety to Lewis.

Lewis showed up at 10:45 for his new job the next day. He didn't want to take any chance of being late. He met Millie at the rear of the building.

"You must be my new helper Ben told me about!" she cheerfully greeted Lewis.

"Yes, ma'am. I'm Lewis Duncan. How did you pick me out?"

"Ben told me you were about seven feet tall! There aren't many Paul Bunyan's on the Cape, you know!"

Millie was a frail, tiny woman who weighed barely a hundred pounds. She had a weathered face and was pushing eighty.

"I'm only six-foot-seven," Lewis returned jokingly. "It's nice to meet you. That's a lot of food for you to be lifting every day, isn't it?" he said, noticing her small frame.

"Keeps me on the topside of the grass and out of the grave, know what I mean? I retired from Barnstable schools twenty years ago, been doing this ever since. It's a great organization, the people who work here and the ones we serve. Let's get this truck loaded and hit the road. We have a light day, only fifteen stops, and about two hours to do it! I can't forget to pick up Ms. Paulson's cat litter along the way, neither!"

"And this is a light day, you said?"

"Yep, a heavy day is twenty-five stops on Fridays. You can't spend much time gabbing. These lonely souls are energy vampires. You're a food provider and a psychiatrist. C'mon, let's haul some ass!"

Millie ran her route most efficiently. Lewis wondered how he could absorb everyone's name, address, and habits. Millie even knew the dogs' and cats' names. She was in and out of each stop in six minutes flat.

Lewis found himself one step behind Millie on her route the whole morning. He could barely keep up with her. He was whipped in two hours and wondered how she could do twenty stops in one day. "This certainly keeps you in shape, Millie! I've been doing this for a couple of hours, and I'm huffing and puffing!"

Millie laughed. "Oh, don't worry. You'll catch on in no time. We'll go on training rides two more times before I retire and hit the road in our camper."

"Camper? You have a camper?" Lewis craned his head as she was driving.

"Sure do! Me and my hubby are hitting the open road next month, heading cross country!"

"Wow! That is so cool. I haven't been off this sandbar except after I was born, but I can't remember that. It was when I was a baby, I guess. I had so many ailments; my parents took me to Boston hospitals to get fixed."

"Fixed?" Millie laughed. "It sounds like you were a machine or something."

"I guess you could say I *was* a broken machine. Things have gone wrong my whole life, but I'm trying to turn it around," Lewis thought pensively, then smiled at Millie. "You've left a mark on this world, Millie. That's all I ever want to do."

A tear fell on her rosy cheek. "Awww, c'mon, Lewis. You're gonna get me bawling here! I think you're a remarkable young man, and I have no doubt you'll find your place. You'll leave a very big mark someday, somewhere. But you're right. If you're different, you'll get labeled. I was picked on by everybody in school when I was a child."

"You're kidding me, right?" Lewis shot out.

"Nope, I talked with a lisp and was known as Hillbilly Millie."

"What the heck is a lisp?"

"It is the way you say the letter 's.' An example would be; that it sounds like you're saying 'lithp,' instead of lisp. Every time I said a word with an 's' in it, kids would laugh at me."

"And you got made fun of because of that? How did it go away?"

"After high school, I took a year off. My parents couldn't afford speech lessons for me, so I went to the library every week. I would bring a book to the beach and read it aloud. I think the sound of the waves breaking on the sand, the birds, and the distant ringing of buoy bells did something for me. After six months of doing that, the lisp went away. It was a miracle, and I realized I should help others and become a teacher. I enrolled in college that fall." Millie spoke quietly, drifting away in time.

"I know what you mean!" Lewis belted. "I love the beach. After my father died years ago, it was the only place I found comfort."

"Your father passed away?"

"Well, I guess he didn't pass away. He got killed at work in the armory. He was crushed by a truck when a big loader broke through the garage door."

"Oh my, God, Lewis!" Millie gasped. "I don't believe this." Millie pulled the truck over into a sandy parking lot by the beach. She shut the engine off. Lewis was baffled.

"Let's get out of the truck," Millie said to Lewis. She walked to the rear van doors, opened them, and took a seat. Lewis was perplexed.

"What's going on, Millie?"

"I think it was fate that we meet again, Lewis."

"Meet again? What the heck are you talking about?"

"Lewis, it brings back sad memories for me. I remember you from the service at the harbor. My nephew, Nolan, was operating the loader that day when your father died."

Lewis felt his knees weaken as Millie continued. "I felt so much sorrow afterward. Then, after he jumped off the bridge, nobody in our families spoke to my sister because she was so depressed. She overdosed on pills six months later."

Lewis shook his head in disbelief. "I guess I don't know what to say. It might be fate that we've met, and you told me this, Millie. It seems like a lifetime ago when it happened. I've had so many challenges, and I'm still trying to overcome them every day, as you can see. Let's get this truck back, and I'll buy us milkshakes on the way home, okay?"

Millie smirked. "As I thought before, Lewis, you *are* a remarkable man. Now I'm convinced the world will hear from you very soon!"

Lewis chuckled to himself. If she only knew what he'd been through the past week, it would put her in a grave.

Chapter Thirty

Lewis's two training rides with Millie went fine. After she retired, Lewis took the route over and built a rapport with customers rather quickly. He found it hard to limit his time and often joked about his awkward size and gangly movements. He felt at ease with his co-workers. Many of them had intellectual disabilities and impaired thinking. Lewis thought he had found a place he fit in for once in his life. He knew a deadline with Honch was pending but wasn't nervous about it. He figured it would pass.

Lewis would break into a sprint to test his muscular legs and flat feet after an enjoyable day on the road. This would become a habit he looked forward to, and he wondered why it took him so long to discover that he loved to run. His strides were almost as long as a sheet of plywood, and he didn't have any bad thoughts, only good ones.

One afternoon while jogging home from work, Lewis heard the familiar sound of some vehicles pulling up beside him. Jerry and his new girlfriend, the cheerleading team captain, were in a brand-new red Corvette. The Gallagher brothers were in a fancy GTO. A couple of motorcycles were tagging along as well. Lewis recognized one of the bikes from his yard. He was starting to put it together.

"When will you trade those legs for some real horsepower, Lewis?" Jerry yelled at him.

"I'm just getting in shape to settle a score with you and the Gallaghers. Did drug money buy you that glitter and the girl too?"

"You wouldn't know what a hundred-dollar bill looked like if it bit you in the ass!" one of the Gallaghers joked.

"Don't worry, all the money in the world you bums are making isn't going to save *your* asses. I make that promise to you," Lewis threatened them and thought of Phil and his parents. He had no idea how to make good on his threat, but he knew it would happen. His father always condemned any violence Lewis might take out on anyone. As a child, he got weekly lectures about avoiding conflict and revenge.

"Use your brains to defeat the bullies," his dad would say over and over. "It'll come to you someday." Easy for his dad to say, right?

Both cars peeled out, showering Lewis with bits of hot rubber and smoke as Lewis choked on the rancid fumes. Lewis said out loud, "How about a little help now, Dad?"

Lewis got back into his running groove and made it home quickly. As he entered his yard, he heard music from the living room. He entered through the kitchen door. Jen had passed out in the recliner.

It didn't surprise him that she'd fallen off the wagon again. There was an empty bottle of booze next to her, half of a smoked joint, and this time there was something new – a two-inch square piece of folded paper with the letter 'H' stamped on it. Next to it was a needle with remnants of a transparent liquid. She had a red dot on her forearm. He knew about the drinking and the pot but shooting up drugs was in a new league. This crossed the line for Lewis.

He knew she needed medical help right away and called 911. Lewis gave them the needle and paper for analysis when the medics arrived. He knew that hard drugs like heroin and cocaine were abundant on the Cape, and maybe what she took could be traced. Really? Lewis knew it came from Honch and his band of outlaw peddlers.

Lewis rode in the ambulance with Jen. The EMT told him it didn't look good for her. She had a slow heartbeat and hardly any blood pressure. The EMTs were met at the hospital by a team of doctors. They worked on her for over an hour. Lewis was in the waiting room pacing nervously when a door opened. A woman in a white coat approached him.

"*No*, you're not going to tell me that!" Lewis guessed as he screamed at the doctor.

"Lewis, we are sorry, but we couldn't save her. It was too much. She's the third one this week. We've also seen that paper envelope with an 'H' embossed on it. We'd love to find out who's selling it."

"It was the third death from that crap? How long does this have to go on? Don't the police know who sells it?" Lewis cried.

"Is there anyone you should call, maybe your father or a relative?" The doctor changed the subject.

"Father? My father? He's been dead for years, and my best friend moved away! Now, my mother? No, there's no one to call."

"Any grandparents?" the doctor asked as she put her arm on his shoulder.

"No. They all died and left me, one after another."

"Do you need help in making arrangements?"

"Arrangements? Do you mean for a funeral? My mother handled that when my father died. There's not much sense in having a wake or funeral. Nobody'll come. Her sister moved to California years ago, but I'll call her — if she even cares. They haven't spoken in years."

Lewis's mind was spinning. Why was his whole life a test? How much can one person take before they blow?

"You rode in the ambulance, didn't you? Do you need a lift home?" The doctor asked kindly.

"Thank you, ma'am. I'll walk. It'll do me good."

"Here's my direct number, Lewis. You can have the funeral home call me, and I'll make arrangements."

"Thank you, that's very kind. I guess I'll put her ashes beside my father. She'd like that, in the harbor out in the ocean."

Lewis turned and walked through the automatic doors into the pitch dark of night. It was a five-mile walk home. He had plenty of time to think about a burial at sea and to get steamed up about Honch again.

Lewis knew he was a dangerous man and had a lot of protection around him. He didn't know where their clubhouse was or what to do if he found it. He suspected that Jerry Alfonso and the Gallagher brothers were on Honch's bootheels. It would take some time before they would lead him to Honch. Lewis hoped Honch would show up alone to make good on his threat to reimburse the $2000. He would kill him on the spot.

Lewis was growing cold as a stone with each passing minute. He didn't own a gun and never shot one, but he knew his dad had a closet full of rifles and shotguns. That closet hadn't been opened since Bruce died. There was one thing for sure: when Lewis got home, he planned to check out that closet.

Chapter Thirty-One

This was supposed to have been a joyous summer for Lewis before entering his high school senior year. Halfway through summer, his mother and best friend were gone. His job was going well, and only one person knew of Jen's passing. Lewis told Ben what happened and requested that it remain between them. The only saving grace for Lewis was Jen put him on every bank account and the deed to their home.

Although he could access the insurance money worth hundreds of thousands from his father's death, he never withdrew a penny. The house was paid for, but he quickly learned to pay an electric bill and real estate taxes. Jen's car got him around if he needed four wheels. His meager salary at Meals for Seniors barely covered his food bill. He knew after high school, he would have to get a good-paying job to stay afloat and figured he could withdraw minimal funds each month.

Honch's threat to make good on a beating for Lewis came and went. Lewis still ran daily, increasing his leg strength and stamina. He would stop at the beach and whip off two sets of fifty pushups. He always remembered what his mother told him about avoiding heat exhaustion since he may not sweat. Although Lewis wasn't religious, he felt someone was looking out for him and had a better plan than his, which was none at all.

Most of Lewis's clients were pleasant along his route. Only a few were grouchy. One man, in particular, was always nasty and a complainer. He had no close family and lived in a rundown house on a small tidal creek. A few camps were around him, but it was a long drive down a dirt road to his shack.

Lewis pulled into Mr. Webb's driveway and exited the truck robustly. He opened the rear doors.

Hmmm, "Mr. Webb, Mr. Webb, where are you in this mess back here? There you are. How'd you get way up there?"

He grabbed a black cherry soda for his thirst and knocked on the door.

"Hello? Hello, Mr. Webb. Are you home?" With that, the interior door flew open.

"Of course, I'm home. Where the hell ya think I'm gonna go, Provincetown in my car? Oh, that's right! My daughter took it away!" Mr. Webb growled.

"Well, Sir. Better days ahead, right?" Lewis tried to spark his mood.

"Better days ahead? Are you kidding me? The squirrels and chipmunks around here eat better than I do!" Mr. Webb exclaimed. "Did you bring me the same old sandwich today, kid? Baloney and butter with only one side buttered, right?"

"Well, I don't make the sandwiches, Sir. I just deliver them. Every other day, we come here, right? I have time today if you'd like. I can play a game of checkers with you when you're done eating. I only have two more stops."

"Okay, go set them up in the living room while I wolf this down. And don't bug me while I'm eating!"

"Yes, Sir. I'll be waiting for you," Lewis replied as if addressing a drill sergeant.

Lewis heard the kitchen chair drag across the floor as Mr. Webb got seated. He cursed and swore as he opened his sandwich.

"Get in here, kid!" he demanded. "What the hell is in this sandwich?"

"Looks like baloney to me, Sir."

"Baloney and butter, baloney and butter, butter on one slice, that's all I ever get! This is baloney and mustard on both slices!"

"Well, Mr. Webb, as I said earlier, I don't make the sandwiches; I deliver them. That sandwich may have gotten mixed up during the sort this morning. I'm sorry."

"Sorry? You're sorry? What the hell am I going to eat?"

"I'll take a look in your fridge if you'd like. I can make you something, okay?"

"You'll make me something? I just want a baloney sandwich with butter on one slice! There's nothing in the damn fridge!" Mr. Webb yelled at Lewis.

"Is there any food in these cabinets?" Lewis said.

Mr. Webb hurled the baloney sandwich at him, and he ducked. The sandwich separated, flew past his head, and stuck to the wall.

"Come on now, Mr. Webb. Let's not get too upset about this. It's only a sandwich." Lewis tried to settle him down. He walked to the sink and grabbed a towel to clean the mess up.

While Lewis turned his back, Mr. Webb snuck behind him. He jumped onto Lewis's back and wrapped his arm around his neck, putting him in a chokehold. Webb's whole body was on him from behind.

"You big oaf, I told you I wanted baloney and butter, baloney and butter! I never liked you from the first day I met you!" Webb shouted with stale whiskey breath. His grip around Lewis's neck tightened even more. Mr. Webb prided himself as an ex-Marine, and his strength certainly showed it.

Lewis spun around a few times, trying to knock Mr. Webb off but to no avail. *This is it! I'm going to be killed by an eighty-five-year-old man and end up in the creek as crab bait.* He could feel himself blacking out. Falling to his knees, he gasped and almost threw up.

Webb was still yelling, but his iron-strength hands loosened, and he dropped to the floor.

Lewis rolled over and looked at Mr. Webb, who was clutching his chest and gurgling. His eyes and mouth were wide open as he grabbed his shirt over his heart.

"What the hell just happened?" Lewis yelled as he leaned back against the kitchen wall. "This guy tried to friggin' kill me! I'm getting it from all ends! What the heck am I gonna do now?"

Lewis got up and paced around the kitchen for a few minutes thinking Mr. Webb might come to, but no – he was dead. *What am I going to tell the police?*

Lewis walked to the phone. His hand went to dial, but he froze. The EMTs and police had just interrogated him about the death of his mother. *I could tell them I had found him like this. What, am I crazy? Who will believe he almost killed me? Nobody! I could go to jail for the rest of my life!*

Lewis picked the sandwich up from the floor and put it on the table. He neatened the chairs from the scuffle and left Mr. Webb on the floor where he lay. He looked around, still not believing what had happened.

Lewis had two more deliveries to go. His hands were shaking. He moved toward the phone and looked at it intently, wondering what he would say if he called the police. His mind went blank.

Lewis turned around and peeked outside through the curtain on the door. Nothing in sight except his van. He grabbed his soda, opened the door slowly, and left Mr. Webb on the floor.

Chapter Thirty-Two

Lewis finished his route and went home. His heart weighed heavy as he wondered if he had made the right decision. The only good thing was he had the next day off. He planned on trying out for the track team but was unsure.

Screw it! He kept to his plan and signed up for the team in the morning. Tryouts were held, and he decided to give a shot at long-distance running. Heck, for him to cover a hundred yards at a comfortable speed was nothing. After one of the time trials, a coach was very impressed and spoke with him.

"What's your name, son?" the coach asked.

"Lewis Duncan, Sir. I realize I'm new at this, but I enjoy running."

"I can honestly say I've never seen anyone run in such an unorthodox manner. You can certainly cover a lot of ground quickly!"

"I don't know if that's a good or bad thing, Sir."

"Well, you just smoked five of our seven returning seniors in the six hundred meter. *That's* pretty good. Do you want to join our squad? It's a lot of work and requires practice four afternoons a week," the coach said.

"I have a part-time job three afternoons a week. I enjoy it, and I'd have to give it up." Lewis told the coach. *What am I, crazy? I just had some guy try to kill me yesterday. And I want to keep working there?*

"Yes, Sir," Lewis said to the coach. "I'm in and looking forward to it. I'll give my notice tomorrow. When's the next practice?"

"All practices now are voluntary. The real stuff starts one week before school's in session." The coach extended a handshake. "I'm Coach Belmont, but everybody calls me Tank."

"I can see why! You're built like a brick, you-know-what!"

"Yeah, I get that all the time. See you in a week, kid. The practice schedule's in the boy's locker room." Tank shook his hand firmly.

"See you then!" Lewis said enthusiastically.

Lewis felt great. He liked being part of a team with his needy co-workers or a bunch of guys he had never even met before. He wasn't a joiner in school except for the band. He never saw anyone from the track team in school, either. Maybe they tried to keep a low profile, like him.

*****

While Lewis was leaving the track field, he noticed a girl fall while walking the oval. She was holding her ankle.

He ran over to her. "I saw you fall. Are you okay?"

"I think I sprained my ankle bad in that stupid pothole," she said as she moaned in pain.

I don't believe this! It was the older girl he had a crush on. He was so nervous his hands shook.

She held her foot up. "I can't put any weight on it. Can you help me stand?"

"Certainly, just go easy."

Lewis extended his arm around her waist. He couldn't help but notice a perfectly shaped pair of breasts under her V-neck t-shirt. She got up very slowly, stalling long enough for him to get a splendid view. She looked at him and smiled.

Lewis's heart was pounding, and something else became very alert. This had never happened to him before in the presence of a beautiful girl. Her eyes were a stunning shade of green, almost like a perfectly flat ocean at sunset.

"I can help you to that bench if you'd like," Lewis offered. It was thirty feet away.

"That'd be great," she said.

Lewis was tongue-tied. He didn't know what to say.

"I'm Lewis, Lewis Duncan."

"Hi, I'm Elizabeth, but everybody calls me Emmie. My mom started calling me that when I was two because of my emerald green eyes," she said as she winced in pain again.

"That's a beautiful name! I've never seen eyes prettier than yours." Lewis didn't mean to say that; it just came out. "Are you trying out for track?"

"Well, not really," she answered politely. "I guess you could call me the team mascot or water girl."

"What?" Lewis seemed baffled. "I don't want to be nosey, but weren't you a senior last year?"

"Yeah, but I had to stay back a year because I skipped too much school. My family was messed up, and I didn't have my head on straight. My friends graduated last year, and now hardly anyone will talk to me because I'm a year older than them. I have some very concerning health issues also. How did you notice me?"

"Oh, I passed you in the halls between periods and thought you were always talking with your friends, so I never said hi. I know what you mean about your family being messed up. Mine was too."

"Honestly? I noticed you too. I thought you were a college kid or teacher."

"I know," Lewis said. "I stick out like a sore thumb, right? It's been that way my whole life."

"No, no, it's not that at all!" Lewis sat her on the bench.

Lewis noticed two vehicles parked on the knoll overlooking the track. One was a Corvette, and the other a GTO. The three occupants were leaning on the GTO hood eyeballing him.

Great! he thought. *If they come near us, I'll kill them right now!* He tried to ignore their presence. Lewis knew this was his only opportunity to ask Emmie for a date. He was afraid his voice would crack if he spoke.

"Would you like to go out for a pizza or take a ride in my boat sometime?" Lewis asked her shyly, fully expecting "no" for a response.

"Hey, Lewis! Get over here! Come on!" Coach Belmont motioned for him to come to the other side of the track, interrupting his conversation with Emmie. "Come on, Romeo. Let's move it!" Tank yelled again.

"Well, it looks like I have to go." He asked again. "So, what do you think?"

Emmie stared at Lewis for a moment. "I'd love to! See you tomorrow, okay? Hey, wait a minute. I probably won't be here on the field with this sore foot. How's Mario's Pizza on Route 28? I'll meet you there at six!"

"That'd be *great!*" Lewis said. He couldn't believe it! She said yes! He turned to run and almost stumbled. Charging across the field, he did a fist pump as he jumped in the air.

Emmie's teammates came to the bench and assisted her toward the girl's locker room. She looked at Lewis as he flew through the air. "What am I getting myself into this time?"

Lewis bent over and put his hands on his knees to catch his wind. "Yes, Coach, you wanted me?"

"Lewis, this is Assistant Coach Walter Gibbs. He trains long-distance runners. We feel it would be a good place for you to start training."

Lewis straightened up. "It's nice to meet you, Sir. As I told Coach Belmont, I have a summer job, but I'll give my notice tomorrow. I work only three days a week so that I can come to practices any morning."

"That'd be great, Lewis." Coach Gibbs replied. "And by the way, a couple of your future teammates want a rematch in the six hundred."

Lewis looked at a group of four cocky teammates who were trash-talking him. "C'mon, dork! C'mon, geek! Scared?" they taunted.

Lewis looked at them, grinning. "Sure, let's go, boys!"

They approached the starting line and got in a runner's crouch, except Lewis. He stood relaxed with his hands resting on his hips.

Tank raised his hand with the pistol and said, "Six hundred meters again, one and a half laps. Ready? On your mark, set." The pistol fired.

The four teammates got off to an incredible start and were fifteen yards ahead of Lewis when he covered five. They rounded the first corner twenty yards ahead of him.

"I told you that goofball was a fluke! Long-distance runner, my ass!" Gibbs remarked to Tank.

Lewis was getting into his groove as he approached the second straight. He looked up the track seventy yards or so. Jerry Alfonso and the Gallagher brothers were cheering him on. "Come on, Dunce! Come on, Lewy! You can do it!" they were screaming and laughing. Lewis knew this was very odd and out of place for them.

The runners went around the track once. He closed the gap to ten yards by the final corner into the home stretch. Lewis took the corner wide and turned it on to catch everyone. Lewis was at full power.

"I can't believe this kid, Tank! You were right! He looks like a gazelle outrunning a cheetah!" Gibbs admitted while looking at his stopwatch. "He's on pace to tie the school record!"

Lewis was ten yards ahead of everyone as he approached the finish line. He noticed the Gallagher brothers were jumping up and down for him, but Jerry was sitting on a bench. What was that about?

With twenty yards to go, he approached the finish line. Lewis saw something shiny reflecting in the sunlight. It was stretched across the track at knee level. It was an almost invisible fishing line! Jerry had strung it after their first pass!

Lewis jumped over it with ease as a runner does a hurdle in track. He tried to slow down as he crossed the finish line and turned to warn his teammates, but it was too late. They hit the fishing line at full speed and were in a twisted mess on the ground. Jerry and the Gallagher brothers scrambled up the knoll to their cars and split.

"Who the hell were those guys?" Tank yelled in anger across the field.

Lewis helped everyone up. They suffered some good abrasions from the gravel track but didn't have any broken bones.

The boys were breathing heavily and cursed at the departing pranksters. Tank and Gibbs ran from the other side of the track.

"What's with the big pile-up?" Gibbs asked feverishly.

"It was my fault, Sir, my fault," Lewis said, still winded.

"What're you talking about? You were at least ten yards ahead of everyone!" Tank exclaimed.

Lewis walked to the finish line and bent over. He picked up the broken fishing line. "Look, Tank. This was meant for me, just me." Lewis threw the line on the ground. "Tank, can I talk to you in private over there?" Lewis pointed. They walked a short distance out of earshot from Gibbs, assisting the other runners.

"Tank, those guys have been after me since first grade. They've pushed me too far, and I know I'm going to do something about it. I can't take it anymore."

"Have you told your parents?"

"My parents? Are you kidding? They're both gone, dead. My dad was killed at the armory, and my mom died last month from drugs."

"And you're out here trying to run track? Where are you living? Who are you living with? How do you get enough money?" Tank demanded to know.

"Hold on, Tank. Let me catch my breath."

"I was in Nam with your dad, you little squirt! We all joined at the same time."

"I wish I could answer your questions, Tank. It would probably suck up the rest of your day. I guess I'm not cut out for this track stuff anyhow," Lewis said with his head down.

"Like hell, you're quitting! You're going to give your notice tomorrow and be here Friday at nine a.m., *right*? Even though you're bigger than me, I'll twist you like a pretzel if you're not here. And those three guys, when you're ready, just let me know. I haven't been in a good scrum for years!"

"That's not all, Tank. I have the president of that bike gang in town coming for my hide someday," Lewis confessed.

"What the heck did you do, steal one of their bikes?"

"Nothing like that. He was dating my mother. Months ago, we got into it pretty good at my house, and I tossed two of his prospects around. I know the drugs they sell killed my mother."

"Boy, for someone barely eighteen, you certainly have something to look out for. There are some bad dudes in that gang. The prospects are the ones you have to look out for. They're always trying to impress the senior patch holders. Me and a few of my buddies have fought them in some bars around town. They have a lot of strength in numbers."

"Well, thanks for the advice. I want to go talk to the guys before I leave and apologize," Lewis told Tank.

"You don't have to apologize to anybody, and I'll help you when that president comes looking for you. Two against eight sounds fair to me. How about you?"

"I'd rather take him on myself, one on one. That's fair to me. I have a score to settle; you don't. See you on Friday." Lewis walked over to his new teammates and shook their hands. He spent a moment with each runner and departed after giving pats on the back.

Gibbs came over to Tank and asked, "What the heck was that about? You guys were talking for fifteen minutes! Do you think he's going to drop off the team in a few weeks, Tank? Is it worth me trying to train this kid?"

"Quite frankly, Walter, I don't think he'll be alive in a few weeks," Tank said somberly.

Chapter Thirty-Three

Lewis didn't sleep well the previous night. He thought about the events leading up to Mr. Webb's assault on him a hundred times. Did he make the right decision not to call the police? He was angry over the prank by Jerry and the Gallaghers. On top of everything else, he would give notice at a job he truly loved until two days ago. He liked his co-workers, the clients, and being on the road. He finally felt like he was doing good. He knew he would be on the road today, and Mr. Webb would have a meal packed and ready to deliver. Do any other 17-year-olds have such a catastrophic life as this, he wondered? Is this normal? Is this a test for easier times to come? He was hoping to catch a break before hell came for a visit.

Lewis went to see Ben. He understood Lewis's desire to join a sports team in high school but was truly saddened. Good employees were hard to keep at a minimum wage job.

Ben had to let Lewis go after his route that day. It was a new company policy because an employee faked an injury after giving notice last month. It was quite a relief for Lewis.

Ben would ride with Lewis on his last day. *What? Is Ben going to ride with me to Mr. Webb's house?* Was this a good or bad thing? He probably would be on the kitchen floor still. Maybe it was a good thing. Ben could say they found Webb on the floor. Yes! Perhaps this would work out. Lewis felt a little relief.

The first eight stops went fine. One by one, Lewis said goodbye to his newly acquired friends. He took the long dirt road over the creek and approached the corner to Mr. Webb's house. He was so nervous he thought he might have diarrhea.

As Lewis turned the bend into Webb's house, his heart sank. An ambulance and two police cruisers were parked in front of the shack. An officer who was standing outside approached their truck slowly. Lewis nervously rolled his window down.

"What the heck is going on, officer?" Ben asked.

"It seems Mr. Webb had a heart attack, probably yesterday or the night before. His neighbor down the road found him this morning. Yeah, she noticed Webb hadn't picked up his newspapers from the front porch, got curious, and went in. She found him dead on the floor, still holding his chest."

"That's horrible!" Lewis said, trying to act surprised.

"What's your business here, men?" the officer asked, looking directly at Ben.

"We deliver Mr. Webb a baloney sandwich a couple of times a week. Today is one of his delivery days."

"Well, I guess Mr. Webb won't need any more sandwiches, will he, boys?" The officer started to chuckle at himself. "You might as well take him off your list, too! Have a nice day, gents!"

Lewis cautiously backed the van out of the driveway and onto the road. He proceeded over the creek bridge and onto the paved road.

"Wow," Ben remarked, "That was the weirdest thing that's ever happened to me in twenty years of delivering sandwiches. Was that cop for real?"

Lewis was stunned as well and a little relieved. Was he in the clear? Had the smoke blown over?

"I don't know, Ben. You got me on that one. I've been doing this for only six weeks, but that was pretty strange." Lewis agreed. "I'm glad you were with me, Ben."

"After we finish our route, I'll remove Mr. Webb from our delivery schedule and make some notes," Ben said. "This isn't the first time we've had a client pass away, and our driver found them deceased, Lewis. Don't let it ruin your night's sleep."

If he only knew he hadn't slept in two nights. Have other drivers found clients dead when they showed up with a delivery? Millie never told him that! Maybe there was some solace for him. What kind of notes was Ben going to record? He tried not to think about it. It was going to be positive thoughts from here on for Lewis.

Chapter Thirty-Four

Mr. Webb's body was loaded into an ambulance. One of the EMTs shouted through the door, "Detective Pat Ransom, we're leaving for Cape Cod General." The police officer marked the time on her notepad.

She stepped outside to the front landing. "I want a full autopsy on that subject," she yelled.

"Why? Look on the kitchen counter at the pills that the guy was taking! His fingernails had dug into his chest from a heart attack or deliberate OD. He was eighty-seven! The coroner would have come, but there's a fatality on Route 6," the EMT commented.

"Doug," the detective addressed the EMT, "have you ever heard the statement, 'yours is not to question fucking why'?"

"No, ma'am, not worded quite like that!" He snickered.

"Have that report on my desk in 48 hours, or you'll be picking up dead cats on Route 28. Got it?"

Doug thought for a moment, looked at her, and nodded.

A police officer outside lit a cigarette. He looked at the ground and kicked some dirt with his boots.

"*Kline!* What the hell are you doing; stirring dirt, destroying evidence like a mule? Get in here and put that cigarette out!" Ransom barked at him. "And don't touch anything!"

"Yes, ma'am," Officer Kline replied.

"And don't give me that ma'am shit! I'm at least ten years younger than you! I'm a detective and will be addressed that way."

"Yes, ma'am," he replied jokingly.

"I want forensics to dust everything in here and take pictures," she informed Kline.

"I was the first one on the scene at eleven a.m., so my fingerprints will be on both sides of the doorknob," said Kline. "The neighbor who found him will have prints everywhere, too. Who knows who else?"

"That's who we may be looking for," Ransom stated. "What do you see in here, Kline? You were the first one on the scene, weren't you?"

"Yes, after I received the call, I spoke first with the neighbor who found him. She saw two newspapers on the porch landing and figured something was wrong with Mr. Webb. When I entered the kitchen and found Mr. Webb on the floor, his eyes were open but clouded over. He was deceased."

"Did you move or touch him?"

"I put my fingers on his left forearm to check for a pulse, but there was none. I then called it in to dispatch."

"And did you touch anything else in the room?"

"No, I waited outside until you arrived. The ambulance came right after you."

"Look around this room. Do you see anything odd or out of place, Kline?"

"Not really. It's a little unkempt, but the guy was eighty-seven years old, right?"

"Okay, let's start with these kitchen chairs around the table. Did you push them in?"

"No."

"Did you notice the black scuff marks on the floor? He has dock shoes on with white soles."

"No, I didn't notice that."

"Did you bring a black cherry soda in and leave that bottle cap on the counter?"

"No, I didn't."

"Where's the bottle to that cap?" Ransom asked as she wrote on her pad.

"I guess I don't know where the bottle is. Did you check the trash or fridge?"

"Yes, I did," Ransom said quickly. "Did you notice that yellow stain on the wall?"

Officer Kline walked to the stain on the wall and examined it. "Looks like mustard to me."

"Don't touch it! We'll have the lab check it. Did you notice his partially eaten sandwich?"

"There's only one bite taken," Kline observed. "It looks like baloney with mustard to me."

"Don't you think it's strange a possible mustard stain on the wall is the exact size of that sandwich bread?" Ransom quizzed him. "And isn't it a little odd the sandwich is back together on a paper plate after it may have made a mark on the wall?"

"I didn't think about that."

"Come in the living room. Two chairs are away from the table as if he was going to play checkers with someone."

Kline disagreed. "I think that's stretching it."

"Do you think he played by himself and switched chairs every move?"

"No, I'd probably spin the board around after each move," Kline answered smugly.

"You *are* brilliant!" Ransom mocked him. "Maybe you will pass the sergeant exam on your fourth try!"

"C'mon, that's hitting below the belt!"

"I have a strong feeling that someone else was present while Mr. Webb had his medical emergency," Ransom stated.

"Hey, wait a minute. Maybe those two guys who stopped by earlier saw something the other day."

"What two guys?"

"Those two delivery guys," Kline paused. "That's it! The two guys who had a baloney sandwich for Mr. Webb! I told them he died, and they left."

"*Are you kidding me?*" she reamed him. "What did they look like? What were they driving?"

"One older man and a young kid, but his head almost touched the roof of the van. He was so big. It was a plain white van. They seemed surprised and saddened when I told them Webb was dead."

"Great, there must be a million white vans on Cape Cod! Get an APB on any suspicious white vans right now. I can't believe this, Kline!"

"Sure, seemed like they didn't know anything when they got here, Detective," Kline said.

"You stay here until the lab comes and dusts," Ransom ordered. "I want everything fingerprinted, including the kitchen sink. I'll go to the DMV in Hyannis and run a report for every white van registered on the Cape. That'll take all day and weeks to track them down. Don't touch anything else when I leave!"

Officer Kline knew he was in deep trouble for his mistake and would probably be assigned to desk duty. He waited for the lab to show up and stayed out of their way. They dusted for fingerprints on the chairs, fridge, pill bottle, switch, and even the soda cap sitting on the counter. They removed a stain sample from the wall, wrapped the sandwich, and enclosed the garbage bag from a kitchen waste basket. They photographed footprints and tire marks in the sandy driveway. One of the lab technicians said it might take months to decipher the info gathered because of such a backlog.

This was not good news for Detective Ransom. She scolded Officer Kline again for no reason.

Chapter Thirty-Five

Lewis got to the pizza parlor a half-hour early to meet Emmie. With the Webb incident behind him, a burden was lifted from his shoulders.

Emmie was on time but hobbled in on crutches. Lewis jumped up and pulled a chair for her to sit. They shared a tasty pizza and talked for hours, getting to know each other. Lewis didn't bring up any details of his mother's recent passing or his father's. He wanted to keep the conversation upbeat.

Time passed so quickly that when Emmie finally looked at the clock, she exclaimed, "Oh my gosh, Lewis! It's nine-thirty. We've been here three and a half hours!"

"This has been the best time I've had in years!" Lewis crowed. "How about taking a boat ride on the Bass River tomorrow?"

"I've never been on the river, just the beach. There's one thing. I can't swim – especially with this foot!"

He laughed. "You were born and raised on the Cape, live within eyesight of the ocean, and you don't swim?"

"Yes, my parents thought going to the beach and swimming were things only cheesy tourists from Boston do!"

"Well, when your foot's better, I'll take you to the kiddie section of the beach, where it's only knee-deep, okay?" Lewis teased her. "C'mon, I'll give you a ride home in the luxurious brown bomb." Lewis helped Emmie onto her crutches.

"What's the brown bomb?"

"It's just a nickname for my mom's old car that I kind of inherited. That's it right there." Lewis pointed to it. "Don't worry. I have a pair of sunglasses and a hat so that no one will recognize you." She broke out laughing.

It was a five-minute ride to Emmie's house. Lewis was nervous as a cat, wondering if he should kiss her when they got to her house. Emmie broke the silence with a question that was hard to answer.

"What did you mean this car was inherited? Did your mom get a new one?" Lewis was caught off guard and didn't want to spoil a good night, so he pulled over just shy of Emmie's house.

"Emmie, I didn't want to bring up any of my past ghosts. I don't want to ruin our night," he confessed painfully.

"Lewis, nothing could ruin tonight! Please tell me what's wrong."

"My mother didn't get a new car. She died last month from a heroin overdose." Lewis started to tear up. "I haven't shed one tear yet but look at me now!" he sniffled.

"Oh, Lewis, I had no idea. That's so sad. Can I do anything for you?"

"I'm doing okay, but every time I turn myself around, there are more complications everywhere."

"I know how you feel. My stepfather's in jail for drugs, and my mother has been in rehab three times," she admitted.

"She probably met my mother there, too!"

"How is your father taking it?" Emmie asked.

"Well, I don't know."

"What do you mean you don't know?"

"My mother's ashes were scattered beside my father's in the ocean. He died in an accident almost ten years ago, on my eighth birthday."

"No way!" Emmie wanted more information. "How have you been able to cope with this?"

"I don't know. It seems every day is a new challenge for me. As I said, I didn't want to ruin our night. This is the most fun I've had in years!"

"Do you live with any relatives?"

Once again, Lewis was stumped. "No, I live by myself."

"You live by yourself? Aren't you lonely?"

"I do get lonely now and then. I've been picked on and bullied all my life because of my size and looks. Everything about me has been a disaster. Hey, I should get you home before your mom starts looking for you."

"Her? Look for me? She probably won't be home until Sunday afternoon. She goes on a three-day bender every weekend. So, there's no one at your house?" Emmie asked shyly.

"Nope, even my dog died. It's just me."

"Well, why are you dropping me off at my house? Why don't we go to yours?"

Lewis almost hit his head on the car roof. He was so surprised and excited he could hardly find the words to say a simple yes. Emmie piped in.

"I have to run into the house, get a few things and check on my two little brothers, okay?"

"Please, go right ahead." Lewis pulled the car closer into the driveway. Emmie stepped out gingerly as he tried to make it to open the door for her, but it was too late. She hobbled to the front of the car, then paused a moment, looking at him. He was watching her closely, leaning on his open door. She came around the car and stretched her arms onto his shoulders. She planted a long, wet kiss on his lips.

"I'll be back. You won't leave me here, will you?"

"Leave you here? No way! I'm not that crazy!" he said, laughing. He was psyched. He didn't have to break the ice for a kiss, too.

Lewis wasn't sure how he could drive to his house because he could hardly contain his excitement. She changed into a beautiful sundress and wore a scarf. Lewis could see two little heads peering from a window on the second floor.

It seemed like an eternity while he drove to his house, but it was only a few miles away. Lewis pulled into his driveway and hustled to open the car door again for Emmie.

"You certainly are a gentleman, Lewis," she praised him as he just smiled.

"C'mon into my mansion."

"This is so cute in here!" She admired the miniature doll house. "Can I have some ice water?"

"Sure, help yourself to anything."

"Lewis, I have to tell you something," Emmie said nervously.

He thought she wanted to go home. "What is it, Emmie?"

"I wanted to let you know that I've never been with a man before. You're going to be my first," she said with her hand on his lap.

"I've never been with anyone either. I'm a little nervous, too," Lewis admitted.

Lewis's bedroom was still upstairs. He did have plans to move into his mother's room on the first floor, but he appreciated a glimpse of the ocean he got from his bedroom window.

Emmie sat on the edge of his bed when they entered his room. She slid her sundress over her head and unbuckled his pants. They slid to his feet.

"Oh, my gosh, Lewis, I didn't know these things came in extra-large!" She couldn't believe how excited he was. She laughed. "I don't know if you'll fit!"

Lewis might have been a novice and awkward on his feet, but nature spontaneously took over.

She lay back on the bed and opened her legs slowly. Lewis moved awkwardly on top of her and let out a pleasant moan. For hours they pleasured each other until exhaustion set in, and they fell sound asleep.

Morning came, and they showered together in an old clawfoot tub.

"Can you give me a ride home in a bit? I should check on my brothers and feed them. They can't do anything for themselves," Emmie said.

"Sure. Do you still want a tour of the river later?"

"Definitely. Do you have life jackets? Remember, I can't swim."

"I have four – that's how many people I can take on the boat. It's only a fourteen-foot Boston Whaler. I'll drive you home and come for you in a couple of hours."

"Can't wait! It's a beautiful day for a ride and my first time in a boat ever! Hey, just think, Lewis, I'll have two *firsts* with you in one day!"

He looked at her, puzzled, "I don't get it."

"Oh, never mind! Just give me a ride home."

Lewis dropped Emmie at home and took the shore road to his house. The ocean never looked so good, he thought. Were things going to change for the better, finally? He was used to things going sour pretty quickly. This particular Saturday wouldn't be any different.

Chapter Thirty-Six

Lewis pulled onto his street and waved to his neighbor. Entering his driveway, he didn't like what he saw. His heart and adrenaline started pumping madly. The three motorcycles that visited him months ago were parked on his lawn again. He slammed his car into park as he slid to a stop.

There was no one in sight, but Lewis knew they were inside. He was fuming as he flung the kitchen door open and found Honch and two different sidekicks seated at the table.

Honch laughed. "Welcome to my humble abode, you little fuck!"

"That'll be the day. I told you never to come here again, and I meant it," Lewis said angrily.

The two new prospects stood up on either side of Honch to protect him. "I gave you a short reprieve, seeing how your Mommy isn't with us anymore. I figured you'd be crying yourself to sleep every night."

"Yeah, you figured wrong, asswipe." The prospects took a step toward Lewis.

"You've got one week! One week to give me that money. Next Friday night, you bring it to the old cement factory, the last building on the left."

"I'll be there, but I won't have any money. It's between you and me," Lewis stated. "I won't have anyone with me, but I know you will because you're a coward. There'll be no guns, no knives, just you and me."

"You want to fight me?" Honch broke out laughing again. "Okay, kid." He looked at Lewis. "Loser *buys!*" Honch and his lowly cohorts howled.

"You don't fucking get it, do you? You've been sniffing and booting too much of that shit you sell." Lewis pointed his finger at Honch and took a step closer. "Loser," he paused. "Loser *dies*. Now get out of my house."

Honch stood up and extended his hand to Lewis. "Loser...dies," he repeated. They shook hands firmly. Honch and his pals left quietly on their bikes.

Lewis couldn't believe he had made that threat to him. It came out so easily. Would he be able to fight someone to the death? He'd been beaten up so many times as a kid he'd lost track. Would he take out his revenge on just one man? He knew he could.

Lewis became very hard inside and was in excellent shape. He thought the condition he had growing up would work to his benefit. If he couldn't feel pain, he would have an advantage over Honch. He knew one thing: he needed to get some advice, but from whom? He couldn't think of anyone he could turn to. How did he get himself into this? Could there be any good ending?

Finally, it came to him – Tank Belmont! He had scuffled with the gang before. Maybe he could get the lowdown on Honch – any weaknesses or faults he may have.

Lewis would see Tank on Monday at practice and planned to approach him then. He was feeling confident, more confident than ever before. He had six days to get in even better shape. Lewis was a strong young man, just coming into his prime with testosterone levels peaking. Honch was a worn-out drug addict who used club members at his mercy.

Lewis walked into his bathroom, tore his shirt off, and admired himself in the mirror. His biceps and forearms were chiseled. He started to develop rock-hard stomach muscles from sit-ups. The results of his daily running workout and two hundred pushups were noticeable.

He was pumped and wished the fight was tonight. He knew his mother and father would be watching to keep him safe. His father always reminded him to use words to settle a dispute. This time, it was different. Honch killed his mother with illegal drugs. Where was the law then? Lewis quickly dismissed the idea of a peaceful ending with Honch.

*****

Lewis picked Emmie up for the boat ride around noon. She came out of the house in a stunning pink bikini and sunhat, bouncing her way to the car on crutches. Her two little brothers came out, sat on the front steps, and started to make fun of Lewis's car. He gave them a big smile and a thumbs-up as he drove away.

It couldn't have been a better day on the Bass River. He brought his Hibachi grill and cooked a feast like his father used to on the beach. They ended up at his house again for an all-nighter in bed. Emmie couldn't believe his stamina could endure that long. Lewis felt like an alpha lion of his pride. Nothing was going to get in his way ever again.

*****

Monday morning came, and Lewis went to track practice. How hard could it be to practice running? Boy, was he wrong. Coach Gibbs had them doing ten, twenty, and fifty-yard sprints for an hour. The runners were sucking air like goldfish.

Lewis was on the lookout for Tank but didn't see him on Monday. He wasn't too concerned. Lewis ran to the beach after practice for more push-ups and sit-ups. He figured the only day off exercising would be Friday. Lewis told Coach Gibbs that he had an appointment and couldn't come to practice. He lied. He wanted to conserve his energy before the fight on Friday night.

Tuesday morning at practice, Lewis spotted Tank Belmont across the track field while performing wind sprints. "Coach Gibbs, may I take a breather? I need to speak with Coach Belmont for a few minutes."

Gibbs knew something was up between Tank and Lewis, but Tank wouldn't tell him. "Sure, go ahead. You got five minutes. And it'll be tacked on at the end of today's practice."

"Thank you, Sir, thank you." Lewis bolted across the track in seconds.

"Tank! Tank!"

"Hey, Lewis. What's up?"

"I had a visitor this weekend. Honch and his crew stopped by."

"I had a weird feeling. Was it Saturday afternoon?" Tank asked intuitively.

"Yeah, I've been invited to their clubhouse this Friday night to square things up."

"That's a dangerous move, Lewis. Are you sure you want to do that?"

"Look, I've been bullied all my life. One way or another, it's going to end this Friday!" Lewis raised his voice in anger.

"Okay, okay. I did get some dirt on Honch. Don't be mistaken, he may be over fifty, but he's still in excellent shape. He rules that bike club with fear and an iron fist. He has two weaknesses, though."

"What? What?" Lewis was itching to hear.

"His nose has been broken so many times; there's barely any bone left between his nostrils and brain. It may take him out if you hit him dead square on the nose. And don't let him get you in a bear hug. He has arms like a gorilla and will pop you like a tin can."

"Yeah, what else?" Lewis wanted the lowdown.

"He has a steel rod and dozen screws holding his left leg together from a motorcycle accident. If you kick him in that knee, he'll drop in a second."

"You mean—kick him—like a girl?"

"Like a karate kick, it's done all the time in combat. Honch will come at you with everything, but he's a heavy smoker and tires quickly. Try to wear him out, take a few shots and then make him miss. He'll be exhausted within three minutes."

"You mean let him hit me? *No way!*"

"He throws haymakers, wide looping punches. They should be a snap to duck under."

"Easy for you to say, Tank!"

"Don't waste your time throwing body shots. He's hard as steel and has been known to wear a bulletproof vest under his clothing. One other thing – I'm coming with you."

"Nope, no way, end of subject. I got myself into this, and I'm not dragging anyone else in."

"Okay, kid. If you change your mind by Friday, I'll have more muscle there than you can imagine."

Lewis raised his t-shirt and flexed his biceps proudly to impress Tank. He exposed his near-perfect six-pack abs. "I think these will do me okay, Tank."

"Good luck, kid. I don't want to see your obituary in next week's paper. You hear me?"

"Don't worry. It won't be mine," Lewis said solemnly.

When Lewis finished his conversation with Tank, he walked to the squad with his head down. He had butterflies and wondered if he should go through with it. As he approached his teammates, he noticed Gibbs and the squad staring. Coach Gibbs was clicking his stopwatch nervously over and over. They knew something was up.

Lewis looked at Gibbs, trying to break the tension. "Do you want to time me? Two laps against anyone?"

There weren't any takers. Gibbs looked at his stopwatch. "Okay, Lewis, you were on pace to tie the school record before you stumbled last time. It's you against yourself. Got it?"

"Coach Gibbs, it's been me against myself since I was born. I'm ready."

Lewis approached the starting blocks. He bent over and put his feet squarely in them for the first time. Coach Gibbs was impressed.

"I don't have a starter pistol, Lewis. When you're ready, launch. The clock will start then. Two laps, one-half mile."

Lewis nodded in acknowledgment. He knew a lot was riding on this. He sprang from the blocks and ran with more pep than usual. He quickly got into a groove with each stride and kicked track dust from his sneakers. After one lap, as he passed his teammates, they started shouting and pulling for him.

"Come on, Lewis! You can do it!" they screamed.

It was ages since anyone applauded him. He was so used to getting beaten down. He used this energy and turned it on. He rounded the final corner as Gibbs looked at his stopwatch.

"You're one second up!"

"Step on it!" Everyone hollered. "Go, Lewis!"

Lewis stretched across the finish line and almost tumbled out of control.

"Two seconds! You shaved two seconds off the county record!" Gibbs exclaimed. Lewis's teammates hugged and tossed him around. "If you keep that up, we'll take the first-place trophy this year! I'm giving you all a break. Go hit the showers."

Lewis was still bent over, trying to catch his breath. For a change, a few tears of joy were rolling down his cheek. He had never felt this type of comradery before. He knew one thing: he didn't want this feeling to end. He looked at his chest and felt something he had never done before. He was dripping wet.

"I'm sweating!" he yelled out. "This is great! I'm sweating!"

Coach Gibbs gave him an odd look. "Well, Lewis, most people would sweat their ass off after breaking a school record!"

"Never mind, Coach." He tried to contain himself and walked into the locker room, rubbing his hand over the greasy sweat. He looked at himself in a mirror, admiring his carved body, and smiled. "You're mine, Honch."

*****

Lewis and Emmie were together every night that week. On Thursday at her house, she asked him, "Hey, Lewis, wouldn't it be nice if we made a date for pizza every Friday night?"

"Well, maybe," Lewis was stalling and caught off guard by her question. He couldn't even think of some cheap excuse to give her.

"Isn't that a good idea? Lewis, are you listening?" Emmie was demanding an answer.

He wasn't going to bullshit her. "Do you remember last week when I said I have some ghosts in my past?"

Emmie looked puzzled. "Yes."

"One of those ghosts has come looking for me, and it's tomorrow night."

"Who is she, one of your old girlfriends?" she asked nastily.

"That's not it at all! I said I've never been with anyone except you, and I meant it. I've never kissed another girl besides you. I hope what I'm going to tell you won't change things between us."

"Well, I don't know, Lewis. Are you gay?"

"I wish it was that simple." Lewis gulped. "On Friday night, I have to meet the man who gave my mother the drugs that killed her and three other people from town!"

"What do you mean you have to meet him?"

"I have a score to settle!" Lewis shouted, pointing his finger at her.

"You mean you're going to − fight him? Who is he? Where?"

"Hey, only one question at a time!" He paused. "He runs the motorcycle gang from the abandoned cement plant. My mother started dating him six months ago. They met in some stupid bar and got her hooked on booze and drugs."

"She sounds like my mother," Emmie said. "Go on."

"I threw two thousand dollars of cocaine down the sink at my house. It belonged to him."

"Why don't you just pay him and end it?"

"Believe me. I have the money. But I'm not giving him one cent! He's come to my house twice and tried to rough me up with his sissy friends. Last Saturday, after I drove you home, they came into my house and threatened me again. It will never end unless I ...."

"Unless you what, Lewis?" Emmie begged for an answer.

"Kill him."

"*What? Kill him?* You'll end up in jail! Never mind that killing someone is wrong! I don't know about this. It's crazy. If he wins, does he kill you?"

"Yes, but it's too late to stop it. I can't back down."

"It's not too late. I'll go there and pay him. I have money too."

"You'll do no such thing! Don't worry. I'll be back. I guarantee it. I'm not going to let myself down. It will haunt me the rest of my life if I don't stand up for my family."

Emmie turned away and looked at the sky.

"I have a confession to make as well," she said, looking directly into his eyes. "I have a heart condition. That's why I missed school so much last year and stayed back."

Lewis hugged her. "What a pair we are! Why didn't you tell me?"

"That's why my stepfather's in jail. He tried to make some money selling drugs for my operation and got caught. He was ratted out by some guy named Jerry."

"Jerry?" Lewis immediately knew who it was but didn't let on.

"That's why mom has been in and out of rehab. The pressure with dad and me, she couldn't take it anymore. I need fifty thousand dollars to have an operation in Boston for a chance to live," Emmie admitted.

"I don't know how I'll get it, but if I have to sell my house for you, I will!"

"No way!" she reprimanded Lewis. "There's more. I can walk only one lap around the track for therapy. I meant it when I said I was the team's water girl and mascot. They've taken me in for my support."

"I'm going to fix everything for us. I am. I won't be able to see you tomorrow night. I need to be by myself." Lewis changed the subject. "Did you say, stepfather? What happened to your real dad?"

"My real dad? He doesn't exist! When Mom was sixteen, she went to a party, spent the night with some hitchhiker, and got pregnant. She didn't even know his name. Mom never wanted me to be born, especially a girl."

"How do you know that?"

"Last month, Mom told me she was disappointed that I was born a girl and would end up like her."

"Emmie! I'm so sorry."

"She hated me so much that she used to make me sniff ammonia in a saucepan! She only ever loved my two half-brothers!"

"Come off it!"

Emmie looked at him with tears in her eye and hugged him for what could be the last time.

"You know something, Lewis? After spending this past week with you, I wanted to die in your arms after making love with you."

"Oh, my gosh! Don't ever say that! I think I'm in enough trouble right now!"

"You've twisted me up pretty good, Mr. Duncan!" Emmie cried on his shoulder. "I'll always be here for you."

"I'll make good on that pizza. It might not be tomorrow night, but I'll be there for you. I may get banged up, but you have my word. I'll see you tomorrow night." He kissed her forehead, then walked toward the brown bomb, not saying a word.

Lewis took the beach road home and pulled into a parking lot that was his parent's favorite spot. He sat at the old picnic bench they had frequented when he was growing up. He observed some happy seagulls and terns making a racket at the water's edge for *Last Call*. The waves gently lapped the sun-kissed shoreline. As his hands moved along the tabletop, his fingers stopped as he felt some deep grooves. He looked down. Carved into the table were "BD and JD forever." Bruce and Jen Duncan forever!

He couldn't believe it. He sat at that same table dozens of times every summer and had never seen this before. Was this a sign or just a coincidence? Lewis took it as a powerful omen from them. He jumped onto the tabletop from his seat and screamed, *Look out, world! Lewis Clark Duncan is coming for you!*

Lewis attracted the attention of a few beachgoers wrapped in blankets, who gave him an odd look. Lewis did a backflip off the table onto his firmly planted feet. He got back in the brown bomb and lit the tires on the sandy pavement.

Lewis would never know it, but he probably stirred a few souls. Bruce Duncan yelled those exact words the day Lewis was born.

Chapter Thirty-Seven

Lewis started the day in his usual manner, but instead of four scrambled eggs, he doubled it to eight. He ate two bananas instead of one. He devoured four pieces of wheat toast instead of two. That was it — nothing else to eat for the rest of the day. He was determined to have a pizza later that night. He did some stretching and shadowboxing in his backyard. He sped off in the brown bomb after working up a good sweat.

His first stop was the local real estate office. He was pleasantly surprised by how much a sales agent said his house was worth. She told him beach access homes were skyrocketing in value, even if they needed work. He possessed the legal documents to prove he was the rightful owner, and there wouldn't be any repercussions if he sold it. One thing he insisted on with the realtor — no sign was to be placed on his property. He didn't want any flak from Emmie or a curious neighbor. The agent was confident she could bring him an offer within a month.

Second stop: the family lawyer, Attorney Theodore Kane. Lewis requested him to draw up a simple will, leaving his money in the bank and the house sale to Emmie. The lawyer thought it was strange. Lewis had known her only a month, but he insisted. The lawyer informed him the papers would be ready within a week. Nope, no way! Lewis demanded they be prepared by three o'clock and offered the lawyer four times what he usually charged. The lawyer was easily swayed, and the papers were ready by two.

*****

Lewis felt remarkably at ease all day. Five-thirty rolled around. He knew it was time to go. Lewis closed the kitchen door behind him and didn't bother to lock it. He knew he'd be back. As he started the car, he looked up at his bedroom window. The curtains were blowing from a late afternoon breeze in the bay. He did a double-take as he thought he saw a goofy-looking kid with thick coke bottle glasses hanging out the window. The boy was staring at him as he held a small dog in his arms. Once he gathered himself, he slowly idled down the street, heading to the abandoned concrete plant.

Six o'clock sharp. Lewis saw five men standing across the entrance approaching the last building on the left. He couldn't believe what he saw: Jerry Alfonso's new Corvette and the Gallagher brother's GTO parked in an open bay. He now knew they were involved in getting drugs from the motorcycle club.

The men parted in the middle and guided Lewis on where to park. No words were exchanged. One of the larger men walked sternly to the car and opened Lewis's door for him.

"Get out and follow me," he said in a deep, raspy voice.

Lewis obliged and followed him into a dark warehouse filled with old industrial parts and broken-down trucks.

"Wait here," he said. Lewis could hardly see anything. Suddenly, one by one, he could hear the clicking sound of what he thought were large circuit breakers as lights slowly came on.

He was surrounded by twelve men, all members of the club. Jerry and the Gallaghers were standing to one side. He could hear some heavy boots slowly walking toward him from a dimly lit hallway. It was Honch. He appeared under a single floodlight and stopped.

"It's your last chance, kid. Bring the money?"

"No. I told you why I was coming here. I don't have any money for you, ever. Let's get this over with. You got *first* punch."

"Mighty nice of you, dork." Honch tore his shirt off. A hulk of a man with tattooed, bulging muscles stood before Lewis, drooling.

Lewis ripped his shirt off also, uncovering a physique resembling an Olympic athlete.

Honch circled Lewis before throwing a wild overhead right he easily avoided. Lewis was on the defensive. Honch unloaded a straight jab and missed again. Lewis returned a left hook to Honch's nose. His eyes began to water.

"You little mother fucker," Honch scolded him. "Nice one, you damn southpaw!"

Lewis could stand further out because his arms were so long and fast. He peppered Honch again in the nose. Blood appeared. Tank was right. Honch returned a right uppercut to Lewis's body that momentarily winded him.

"Nice one back to you," Lewis applauded him.

"C'mon! When's this fight gonna start?" one of the club members yelled. "Let's go, Honch! Let's go, Honch!" They were chanting in unison. This fired Honch up. He charged directly at Lewis with his arms wide open as if to grab a hold. Lewis hit him again in the nose with all his might and knocked Honch back. He regained himself quickly, peppering Lewis with a combination of punches to open a massive gash on his cheek that covered him in blood.

"OWW!! I felt that!" Lewis moaned. For the first time in his life, he experienced severe physical pain!

"You better have, you fuckin' freak!" Honch shouted proudly.

This pumped Lewis up more. He took another swing at Honch and yelled. "You'll never understand!"

Honch delivered another punch to Lewis's left eye. It quickly swelled shut, blocking his vision.

The gang members raucously shouted for Honch to finish him off. Unlike what Tank mentioned, Honch didn't show any signs of fatigue yet. Lewis could see with just one eye, and Honch knew it as he kept circling to the left. He threw a flurry of overheads and haymakers, missing Lewis every time. He finally started to huff and breathed heavily through his open mouth.

Lewis hit him with a hard right to the chin, possibly breaking his jaw. Honch yelled in pain, which silenced his entourage. He lowered his hands to his knees for a deep breath, but Lewis showed no mercy. He hit him with a knee to the nose as hard as he could. Honch was blinded by tears and had blood in his eyes.

Lewis walked to Honch's left side. He thought about kicking him as Tank suggested but felt such crap was for girls. Instead, he got a running start and leaped shoulder-first into Honch's left knee. He heard it snap. It was bent at a ninety-degree angle. Honch was writhing in pain, clutching his leg on the ground.

Lewis thought he dislocated his shoulder on that move but tried not to show the pain. What was he going to do? Was he just bullshitting himself and Honch, saying it was a fight to the death? He couldn't kill him. But if he didn't, Honch would come for him again and again. The men were swearing and throwing beer cans at Lewis. One club member knelt beside Honch, lying on the hard-concrete floor, unable to get up. He pointed his finger at him.

"Kill him," he said quietly and paused. "Kill him, Lewis!" Another member joined in. "Kill him!" The entire club started chanting, "Kill him, kill him!"

Lewis looked around at the salivating crowd of animals waiting for a kill. He saw something that caught his eye, a large piece of concrete with metal rebar protruding from it everywhere. Lewis struggled to pick it up with his only good arm. He walked over to Honch with the large block in his arms.

"*Kill him. Kill him. Kill him!*" They were screaming wildly, reminiscent of a fight between two gladiators in the Roman Coliseum.

Lewis raised the concrete rubble over his head and fully extended his arms. He let out a primal scream that almost shattered the windows. He looked down at Honch.

"Go ahead, kid," Honch said weakly. "Do it."

Lewis dropped the humongous block but deliberately missed Honch's head by a foot.

The wild pack of bikers silenced, stunned by the turn of events.

Lewis looked down at Honch and pointed to every club member.

"The fight is over."

He approached Jerry and the Gallaghers.

"Your time is coming soon! Be warned."

Lewis picked up his torn shirt and wiped the laceration on his cheek under his eye. His other eye was black and swollen shut. The men separated as Lewis hobbled between them. None of them said a word. Lewis was weak and knew he needed medical attention. He slid into his car. A number of the men stared intently in disbelief as he started his car and left the plant.

*****

Lewis drove to Emmie's house and collapsed on the front lawn. His face was swollen, almost beyond recognition. Her two brothers found him and called an ambulance.

As the paramedics loaded Lewis onto a stretcher, he came to. Emmie was crying uncontrollably.

"Looks like we'll have to take a rain check on that pizza tonight," he said with a smile.

Emmie returned the wisecrack. "Someday, Mr. Duncan, very soon. I'm going to kick your ass!"

Chapter Thirty-Eight

Lewis received twenty stitches to close the cut under his eye, leaving a scar that would take years to heal. The track team would be on hold indefinitely.

The hospital released him Saturday afternoon. He spent a quiet evening at home with Emmie. He slept on the living room couch all night, hugging a pillow in the fetal position. Emmie slept in a recliner beside him, keeping a close watch.

Around eight o'clock Sunday morning, Emmie went upstairs to shower while Lewis slept. As she turned the faucet on, she heard a car pull into the driveway. "Oh, no!" She thought it was the gang coming for Lewis.

It wasn't. It was a police cruiser. An officer and a well-dressed woman with a badge hanging from her top left pocket got out. Emmie pressed her naked body against a wall next to the window and tried to hear what they were saying.

The officer pounded on the door, startling Lewis from his sleep.

"Come on out, Lewis! We know you're in there!" the officer yelled.

Lewis approached the torn screen door on his weakened legs and stood on the porch.

Lewis peered at the woman. He knew he had seen her before. "Is there a problem, officer?"

"Well, well, Mr. Duncan. We meet again!" she wise-cracked. "At least you have clothes on this time!" The officer laughed out loud. Emmie heard every word. She was ready to explode but remained silent, listening carefully.

"I thought this house looked familiar as we pulled in. Remember me? I'm Detective Pat Ransom. I gave you a ride when you got tarred and feathered!"

Oh, no! "I thought you looked familiar, ma'am. I've tried to forget everything about that day. What brings you here?" Lewis asked cautiously.

"I'm here to question you about this past weekend."

"Looks like you ran into a buzz saw!" the other officer stated humorously.

Ransom folded her arms and asked Lewis, "Does the name Spencer Plant mean anything to you?"

"Spencer Plant?"

"That's what I said. You must have gotten your bell rung pretty good Friday night."

"No, Spencer Plant doesn't mean anything to me, and what about last Friday night?"

"Spencer Plant, also known as Honch? Sure, you don't know him?" Ransom drilled him.

"Honch? Well, unfortunately, I do know *him*. I guess you could say we had a score to settle."

"Looks like you did more than settle a score, Lewis. Last night, he was found dead on a beach in the Bass River at low tide. A ten-foot-long chain was wrapped around him along with a small-caliber bullet hole in the back of his head."

Lewis's heart was pounding. Emmie was still upstairs, listening to every word being said.

"When I left him at the concrete plant, he was alive. He was banged up but alive."

"We know that," Ransom said.

"How do you know that?"

"We've had an undercover officer in that club for six months, and he verified you left. Did you go back later and finish him off?"

"Hell, no!" Lewis got upset. "I went to my girlfriend's house after the fight and spent the whole night in the hospital. I didn't get home until two o'clock yesterday afternoon. I spent the whole night on the couch until you just woke me up. That mole you had in the club was the one with a fake scar on his neck, wasn't he?"

"Yeah, how'd you know?" Ransom asked.

"He didn't have any dirt or grease under his fingernails. He was too clean to be a biker, just a little pussy. Ask him how he liked getting his ass kicked last month at my house, too!" Lewis stated smugly. Ransom didn't think that was funny.

"Your undercover cop was in that club for the past six months while they were selling drugs and killing people, including my mother?" Lewis barked.

"We were ready to bust the whole gang this weekend until you stepped in, Lewis! Now we can't find any of them, thanks to you. We'll need your girlfriend's name and address to verify where you've been since Friday night," Ransom ordered him.

"No reason to drag her into this. You've got no proof. If you ever bother her, I'll...."

"You'll what? Kill me too?"

"Don't worry, we'll find her," the other officer retorted smartly.

Ransom jotted down a few more notes.

"Mr. Duncan, we may need you for more questioning, so stick around, got it?"

"I think it'll be a while before I can go anywhere, ma'am." Lewis hated to be bossed around like that and was already planning an exit out of town.

The two officers returned to their cruiser and sat for a few moments, talking before departing. Lewis went inside to hear Emmie charging down the staircase with a towel wrapped around her.

"I heard every word, Lewis! Did you kill him? What the hell happened Friday night?" Emmie demanded an answer.

"I told you everything! I don't know how he ended up in the Bass River. I'm as confused as you are!"

"And what did she mean? It was nice to see you wearing clothes. You didn't have to cover for me either. I'm a big girl."

"The last thing I wanted to do was to drag you into my messed-up life! I've had people after me practically since I was born, and I'm never going to take shit from anybody again!" Lewis started to cry.

Emmie put her arms around him. "I don't need an explanation from you, Lewis, today or any other day. This will all work out. I can't get myself too upset, either. If I get my heart racing, it'll put me back in the hospital." She tried to laugh.

Lewis broke the moment of silence.

"What do you say we go get that pizza for an early lunch? They'll be open soon. I don't think I've eaten anything since Friday. I'll grab a shower, too."

"I'd love that! If anyone makes fun of you, they'd better look out for me," Emmie smiled. "Can we eat it at the beach, away from everybody?"

"Just what I was thinking, Emmie. Let's get out of here."

Chapter Thirty-Nine

Lewis tormented himself with the thought of getting even with Jerry and the Gallaghers. He knew their drugs killed his mother and other local residents. He also had to avenge the tar and feathering of Phil, who then tried to commit suicide. Jerry couldn't keep a low profile very long, and chances were he'd step in to fill Honch's shoes for drug orders.

Lewis figured Jerry wouldn't be able to stay away from his girlfriend. She lived a stone's throw from Emmie. He was right. A week later, Lewis drove through Emmie's neighborhood and saw an old Ford Maverick parked at Jerry's girlfriend's house. Lewis pulled onto the grass a hundred feet away and sat for a while, watching.

Bingo! After a half-hour, Jerry strolled out of her house with a brown shopping bag, jumped into his Maverick, and sped off. Lewis was so excited he yelled, "Gotcha now, you piece of shit!"

Lewis didn't act prematurely and watched as Jerry took a right at the end of the street. He presumed he could find the Gallaghers, too. What plan could he devise to get rid of them without getting into more trouble? It was coming to him slowly.

*****

After a week of tailing Jerry, Lewis found the Gallaghers were living on Route 28. Jerry always brought in at least one shopping bag and came out with two. What a perfect place to deal drugs, practically right on Main Street, where 10,000 cars a day pass by. No one would ever complain about vehicles pulling into the Gallaghers. They got rid of their high-profile GTO and bought a Plymouth Satellite.

Within a week, Lewis memorized the routine of Jerry's dealings. The Gallaghers were picking up large quantities of drugs at an auto scrap yard and dividing them up. Jerry would always stop at his girlfriend's house before a major drug deal. He would pick the brothers up along the way to the scrap yard for another shipment.

Lewis knew he was in hot water already with the police and figured out a plan. He followed Jerry to the Gallaghers at dusk. Lewis parked across the street at the supermarket and hustled to Jerry's car, dodging traffic. There was a briefcase on the rear floor he had never seen before. He checked the car doors, which were all locked up. He wiggled the vent window until he could fit his skeleton house key into the rubber. The latch popped open. He stuck his arm in and pulled the door lock up. This is way too easy, he was thinking.

Loads of people walked by, and not one person asked him what he was doing. He grabbed the briefcase and placed it on the front seat. He carefully pushed both buttons at the same time. It sprung open an inch.

Lewis eyeballed outside the car. He knew Jerry would be in the house for precisely fifteen minutes. Lewis opened the briefcase enough to peek inside. He couldn't believe his eyes. He thought he would find a large cache of drugs, but this was even better.

Stacks of twenty-dollar bills were banded together one inch thick. There were so many he couldn't count them. Stealing the money at that point would have been very easy, but it didn't give Lewis the satisfaction he was looking for. He closed the briefcase, returned it to the backseat floor, and locked the car.

About three minutes passed before Jerry returned, right on cue. Jerry bounced down the side staircase, obviously very high, with the Gallaghers in tow. They jumped into the Maverick. Lewis hadn't observed this before. Where were they going, to the scrapyard? He didn't want to follow them in his notorious brown bomb. Jerry operated like clockwork, and Lewis would be ready for him next week. This time, in another vehicle.

*****

Lewis bought an old Pinto for two hundred dollars from his neighbor. He waited until the following Monday night when Jerry made his purchases. As usual, Jerry stopped at his girlfriend's house for a *quickie*. He then left on time for the Gallaghers.

Lewis parked at the market again. He went inside and bought five newspapers. He saw Jerry park his car and hurry up the staircase as he came out.

Lewis made his move and ran across the street to Jerry's car. This time, Lewis brought a coat hanger to pop the latch and was inside the vehicle in a flash. The briefcase was in the same spot. He jumped in the backseat and opened the case. There was more money in it than last week! Dumping the cash into a paper bag, he put the newspapers inside with a hand-scribbled note. He closed the briefcase and exited the back seat as fast as possible. A side porch door opened. It was Jerry. He was five minutes early leaving with the brothers. They were laughing hysterically at something.

Lewis briskly walked across the street, ducking traffic. He fired the Pinto up and tailed behind Jerry's vehicle by three car lengths. They were heading out of town toward the scrap yard again.

Jerry turned into a parking lot of the scrap yard. There was a fifteen-foot-high metal door. He beeped his horn in some code, and the doors opened. Once he drove in, the monstrous doors closed.

Lewis parked three hundred feet shy of the scrap yard and slithered along the chain-link fence. He could hear voices on the other side. One man's voice was not American. He could easily tell.

"Welcome, welcome, my young friends," Lewis heard a man speaking over a few other unintelligible conversations.

"I see you wish to make your usual purchase, amigo?" he addressed Jerry.

"No, Sir. We would like to double our amount this week. Your fine product is in high demand on the Cape. We no longer have a middleman, as you well know!" Jerry and the Gallaghers cackled together.

"Double it? You want to double it?" the man roared. Lewis could hear many voices but knew they weren't Jerry or the brothers. "Oh, I think we can accommodate you." The man in charge snapped his fingers. Two more shopping bags of drugs were removed from an oil tank nearby.

The drug kingpin was pleased, and Lewis could hear him bragging with Jerry.

"We are making each other very rich! It is a pleasure to do business with you three. Now, please put the money on the hood, and we count, no?"

"Of course, of course!" Jerry quickly put the briefcase on the car hood as everyone smiled and joked.

Lewis heard the latches pop open. His mouth was dry as a desert.

"What is this, a joke?" Lewis heard the man yell at Jerry. "A fuckeeng joke?" Lewis could hardly contain himself from laughing. He listened as the briefcase spun around on the hood.

"Today's newspapers? That's what you give me, today's fuckeeng newspapers?"

Jerry and the Gallaghers looked at the briefcase in disbelief and horror.

"Angelo, Angelo, I don't know anything about this!" Jerry pleaded.

"And what is this note, 'You've been dunced!' *Me? I've been dunced? Marco! Pauly! Juan! Take them inside!*"

"Please, Angelo! I can explain!" Jerry cried out.

Lewis heard a scuffle as the Gallaghers were quickly subdued and brought deeper into the scrapyard. Jerry could be heard begging for his life.

"Their car, Marco, *crush it!* Better yet, *burn it in the pits!* We don't want any record of it here!" the leader ordered everyone.

Lewis ran to his car and knelt behind it as the squeaky metal doors of the scrapyard opened. There were so many junk cars around him; his Pinto blended right in. Two cars sped past him as his heart beat madly.

The metal doors closed. Lewis could hear some painful yelling from within the scrapyard walls.

He started his car but didn't turn on the lights. He quietly left the street, not knowing their fate. He did know Jerry and the Gallaghers wouldn't be selling their poison on Cape Cod anymore. He realized the drugs were coming from the scrapyard, and maybe the police would catch up with them eventually. He knew not to mess with these men and wished he had never met Jerry Alfonzo or the Gallaghers. Emmie might find out someday who the man was that set up her stepfather. Jerry Alfonso wouldn't be bothering anyone again, ever.

Chapter Forty

Lewis bypassed Emmie's house on the way home. He was physically and mentally exhausted.

He went inside and threw the paper bag on the couch. He started counting and couldn't believe his eyes. There was over $45,000. *What am I going to do with it? I can't possibly spend this much cash in my lifetime.*

He assumed it was dirty money in unmarked used twenties. How perfect! He didn't want to think about it. He pulled up a floorboard in the kitchen and nailed the paper bag onto a floor joist.

It had been three weeks since his showdown with Honch. Lewis was mending quite well and saw Emmie almost every day. He could tell she was feeling down but couldn't figure out if it was her health or maybe she decided he might not be the one for her. He wanted to do something special but couldn't think of anything. Maybe it was his imagination. He decided to sleep on it.

*****

Lewis awakened to the sound of someone knocking on his kitchen door. He didn't want to look but cracked his bedroom shade and took a peek. It was his realtor. He opened the window, "I'll be down in a minute!" He threw on some shorts and a tee-shirt and jumped down the stairs.

"Well, do you have any good news?" Lewis asked the somber-faced realtor.

Her phony scowl evolved into a smile.

"You have two offers! Both are over what we're asking. I can't believe it!" she said happily. "It's a bidding war!"

"Is that good? I don't know what it means!"

"One buyer has to get financing and can close in two months."

"That seems like forever to me," Lewis replied.

"The other offer is all cash and twenty thousand dollars over your asking price."

"*What?* That sounds amazing!" Lewis said.

"But that offer comes with two conditions," she informed him.

"Two?"

"They want to buy the house with all the furniture."

"Are you kidding? Do they want all this junk? No problem! What else?"

"I tried to get more time."

"More time? What?"

She paused again. "They want to move in this Friday. Only four days away."

"Friday? Holy cow!" Lewis sat down at the kitchen table and rubbed his head. "Friday?" he asked again.

"Here's the offer." She put it on the kitchen table for him to read.

He looked at it carefully, shaking his head in disbelief.

"That's all mine?" he asked while looking at the closing statement.

"Minus our five percent commission, you will still net over $150,000."

"Do you have a pen?" He beamed. "I'll close tomorrow if they want!"

"I'll run it by them. They've already done a title search."

"A what?"

"It proves you own the house free and clear."

"I can't believe it. I'll pack my clothes tonight!"

"You don't have to be in that much of a hurry, but I'll call you later. You may want to call a lawyer to examine the sales agreement."

"I was in touch with my family lawyer not too long ago. For once, maybe things *are* going my way! Thank you for everything!"

"I'll call you by day's end, I promise!"

"I'm packing now!" Lewis told her joyfully.

He was going to make this a positive thing and not look back. How could he keep this secret from Emmie? Where was he going to live?

Lewis decided to surprise Emmie and show up at her house.

"Wanna get a pizza tonight?" he asked her.

"It's not Friday night, is it?" Emmie asked.

"Aww, c'mon. It doesn't matter."

"Sure. I've been feeling a little down lately. Let's go!"

"I was worried you were mad at me or something. I can tell something's bugging you," Lewis said as he opened the car door for her. He started the brown bomb and backed out of her driveway. She put her hand on his leg.

"Lewis, unless I have that operation on my heart, I won't live through my senior year in high school."

Lewis pulled the car into a parking lot. How could his mood go from high to low just like that?

"Your family can't help at all?"

"Lewis, the bank is about ready to take our house. Nobody's made a payment in four months."

"I can fix that!" he smiled happily.

"Lewis, I don't even have a doctor yet. Mine here in town diagnosed me three months ago. They don't do heart operations anywhere on the Cape."

Lewis pulled back onto the street and headed toward the pizza parlor.

"Remember, I told you a couple of weeks ago I'd do anything for you and not to worry, right? I meant it."

"I truly believe you, and I do feel a little better. You've had every piece of crap thrown at you in the world. I may have a bum heart, but let me tell you, it's full of love for you."

"Hey, you're going to make me cry," Lewis said seriously.

"I've lived my life so much the past two months. I can't believe how boring it was before I met you. You may be a freak of nature, but it certainly has been interesting when I'm with you!"

"Well, I guarantee if you hang around me much longer, you *may* die of a heart attack!" He laughed.

"Let's get that pizza and a coke. I'm famished!" Emmie said.

*****

The closing on Friday morning went off without a hitch. Per Lewis's request, Attorney Kane deposited the check in a statewide bank.

Lewis asked his lawyer if he knew any doctors in Boston. Attorney Kane smiled as he nodded. He made arrangements for Emmie's operation without her knowledge; it was a surprise from an anonymous donor. Lewis also requested his lawyer research the mortgage on Emmie's house and pay all past debts incurred. Lewis had one last favor. He gave the lawyer ten thousand in cash and asked if Phil and his parents could get it. Lewis knew they had moved back to Worcester but didn't know how to find them. A shady lawyer can find anyone.

Kane leaned forward in his chair with a serious expression on his face. He told Lewis fifty thousand might not pay for an operation and past debts on Emmie's house. "This must be one special girl!" he remarked.

"Well, that's not all the money I have, Sir," Lewis informed him.

"What do you mean?" Kane asked him.

Lewis dropped a paper bag of *twenties* on his desk.

"You never cease to amaze me, Lewis! Where did this come from? How much is here?"

"Forty-five thousand, I guess you can say it's payback. I'll leave it at that. I need only five thousand to live on. That will give you almost two hundred grand, right?" Lewis asked Attorney Kane.

"Holy shit, Lewis! I've done some crooked deals in the past. But this is the granddaddy of them all. I think I can hide it." Attorney Kane slid his reading glasses down his nose. "Sure, I can help you. Meet me at Franklin Savings Bank in half an hour. We have to find a home for this cash. I have a safe deposit box, and the bank president knows me well. I suppose you want this girl, Emmie, to be on the account, right?"

"This is a surprise for her, so it's on the hush for now. I'll see you at the bank."

Lewis departed the office, jumped up, and clicked his heels. It was the best he had felt in years. Although he had no place to call home yet, he felt very secure.

On the way to the beach, he stopped by Emmie's. She was resting on the couch.

"Hey, Emmie! Come on. Let's pack it up and go to the beach today!"

"Lewis, this is one of those bad days for me. I have to get some rest, doctor's orders. I have a monitor on my chest to keep track of my heart."

"I was hoping we could get off this sandbar for a couple of days, maybe go to Boston or something like that."

"Babe, I wish I could so bad. Maybe next week after a few days of rest, okay?"

Lewis reluctantly agreed. "Well, I think I'm gonna visit my cousin over the Bourne Bridge for a few days, okay?"

"I didn't know you had any cousins?" Emmie asked.

"He's a second cousin. I guess you could say. Can you do me a favor?"

"I'll do anything. What?"

"If anybody comes looking for me, say you haven't seen me in weeks."

"Are you crazy? Why?" she asked him.

"Again, it's a long story. For once, everything is perfectly fine! I'll call you from Jeff's house on Saturday."

"You can't call us. The phone's been shut off."

"I bet it's a mix-up, and it'll be back on by the end of the day."

"Are you a magician too, Lewis? Can you make anything happen the way you want it to? Stop dreaming!"

He looked at Emmie with a glow in his eyes.

"Emmie, from now on, I *can* make anything happen! I'll never stop dreaming! If I do, life is over for me. I've been wondering what it's like to be someone else my whole life!" Lewis bent over and kissed her forehead, trying to change the subject. "I'll call you later."

Emmie shook her head in disbelief.

Oh, Lewis, how did I ever get so crazy about you? She thought and tried to get comfortable on the couch for a nap.

*****

Lewis started the brown bomb and went past the beach. He knew there was a day to kill before his lawyer could make arrangements for Emmie's operation. He needed to find a place to hang his hat for a few nights before making long-range plans.

He drove for hours and ended up at the harbor where his parent's ashes were scattered. Later, he found his way to the sandpit where he was tarred and feathered, even to his doctor's office where countless appointments pestered him. He ended up at the entrance to the abandoned concrete plant, where the showdown with Honch went down. He slowed to a crawl.

"Hey, that's it! Perfect!"

He put the car in reverse, eyeing the decrepit building. He nailed the gas pedal down the half-mile straightaway into the plant.

"Welcome home, Lewis!" he shouted. He hit the brakes hard and slid perfectly into an open bay. "Excellent! I've never had a garage all to myself before!"

The gang's motorcycles and belongings were long gone. Lewis strolled through the plant with newfound confidence.

"Man, when I was here last, it was pitch black. This place is pretty cool! Even a bathroom and an office with a cot! Running water?"

He turned a bathroom sink faucet. It came on!

"This is too much!"

He knew the electricity was on because the lights had worked a few weeks ago. He found an old coke machine in the men's locker room. Surprised that it was still running, he put his quarter in the slot. A nice, cold soda dropped out.

"I'm never leaving this place!" His voice echoed through the hollow building.

He walked through the rest of the plant and found a manager's office. He pulled a chair from the long, dust-covered desk and put his feet up to relax.

"Okay, men, we've got a lot of work around here today!" He imitated being a boss for a change, slamming his fist on the table.

Would this freedom and newfound wealth be something Lewis could handle? Most dreams and goals his entire life were squashed. A lot was hanging in the balance for Lewis, and it was just a matter of time before the starter's pistol fired again.

Chapter Forty-One

Wednesday, eleven a.m. Third Precinct, Yarmouth Police Department. The phone rang. "Officer Kline speaking. Yes, I was present also. Thank you very much for the lead. I'll give Ransom a shout-out." He made some notes on his hand and turned to see her glaring at him.

"Ransom? Is that how you address your superiors?" She scolded. "Ransom?"

"Oh, give me a break. We have some info on the case where that old guy died in a cabin on the tidal flats. Mr. Webb, remember him?" Kline informed her.

"I sure do! Whatcha got?"

"Forensics pulled a sandwich wrapper in the trash can. It seems it came from someplace called Meals for Seniors. It had an obscure logo stamped on it, so it took a lot of time to trace."

"Good work, Officer Kline, not that you did anything, but good work anyhow. You *may* make sergeant someday."

"You certainly know how to build someone's confidence, Detective Ransom. That makes me feel a whole lot better."

"Get my car ready. Let's get over to Meals for Seniors right away and see what we can stir up," Ransom ordered.

It was a short drive to the all-volunteer center. Unassuming plain white delivery vans and pickup trucks dotted the parking lot, just like the one Officer Kline spotted leaving Mr. Webb's house.

"Pretty interesting. Isn't it?"

"What's that, Detective Ransom?"

"I've driven by this place a hundred times and never saw it."

"You know, that's weird. The same thing for me, too. I've been driving by this place the past four years and haven't seen it either."

"Let's see what we can find out," Ransom stated.

Walking through the double doors, they first noticed a sticker on the front window. It was the same logo forensics forwarded to Officer Kline. It said, "Proudly serving the elderly and disabled for over thirty years." They were greeted kindly by a small woman who was cleaning the floors.

"He-he-hello," she stuttered. "Ca-ca-can I help you-you-you?"

"Hello, ma'am," Kline piped in. "Is there a supervisor here we can speak with?"

"Why-why-why yes. That'd be Ba-Ba-Ben. I'll go-go ge-ge-get him."

"We may be here a long time," Ransom whispered to Kline.

It seemed an eternity for a small black man to emerge from the kitchen.

"Hello, folks. I'm Ben. Oh, I see you must be police officers!" He was rather startled. "We've never had the police in here before. How can I help you?"

"I'm Detective Ransom, Sir. This is Officer Kline, soon-to-be sergeant. Right, Kline?" He blushed.

"Is there someplace private we can talk?" Ransom asked.

"My office is in the back of the kitchen. Please follow me through the mayhem!" Ben joked.

Detective Ransom and Officer Kline followed Ben closely and couldn't believe the activity that was going on. It was loud as a high school cafeteria with over twenty workstations. Many disabled and mentally challenged workers cheered them on as they walked through. All were busy making sandwiches and filling paper bags with lunches to go.

Ben opened his office door.

"Here. Please, sit down. Well, I only have two chairs in this small office," he admitted.

"I'll stand," Kline said.

"Now, what can I do for Yarmouth's finest today?" Ben asked them.

Ransom spoke first. "Ben, we are here on a rather odd case."

"Oh?" Ben was caught off-guard.

"Did your company service a gentleman by the name of Mr. Webb who lived on the tidal flats?"

"Why, yes, we certainly did. We brought him a baloney sandwich three times a week until he passed away."

Ransom looked at Kline and nodded, confirming her suspicions.

"Do you have a record of the last time one of your drivers was there?" she asked.

"Yes, I certainly do. We were there five weeks ago today, a Wednesday, I believe. A police officer was there and asked us to leave. We talked with you, didn't we, Sir?" Ben addressed Officer Kline, who agreed. "A neighbor said Mr. Webb was probably dead a few days. It looked like a heart attack. Was it?"

"It may have been. Did you say *us*? You make it sound like there were two of you in the truck."

"Yes, ma'am," Ben said. "There *were* two of us in the truck. It was one of my employee's last days on the job."

"It was their last day on the job?" Ransom quizzed Ben.

"Yes. It seems he's a budding track star and decided to further his talents on the oval."

"And does this track star have a name?" Officer Kline asked Ben.

"Why, yes, of course. His name is Lewis Duncan," Ben said cheerfully. "He was one of our best employees. It's such a shame to lose him!"

"You're kidding me, right? Lewis Duncan? Seven feet tall, who lives by the Bass River?" Ransom said in a high voice.

"Yes. Do you know him?" Ben asked curiously.

"Let's say we've had some dealings with him in the past," she firmly stated.

"Is he in any trouble?"

"It's an ongoing investigation, Sir," Officer Kline piped in.

"Boy, that's hard to believe. Everyone here just loved him," Ben reiterated.

"Thank you very much for your help, Ben. If we have any other questions, may we contact you again?" Ransom asked Ben.

"Of course, I hope I haven't gotten Lewis in hot water."

"Oh, no, I'm sure it's just a coincidence," Officer Kline stated. "Our many thanks, Sir."

Ransom and Kline departed, once again, to a standing ovation from the workers as they passed through the kitchen.

"That's pretty odd, isn't it, Kline? They gave us a standing ovation. I've never had that happen before!"

"Me neither, but I kind of like it!" Kline joked.

They made their way to the unmarked cruiser and pulled away.

"What a waste of time that was!" Kline remarked.

"Are you kidding me?" Detective Ransom screamed at him. "Lewis Duncan was working there and quit two days after someone on his route died? Open your eyes, Kline!"

"I think it's one of those weird things, that's all! You can't dispute that. The coroner said Mr. Webb had advanced heart disease, and a massive heart attack probably killed him. Skin was found under his fingernails from five-inch-long scrapes on his chest! There's no evidence Duncan was involved," Kline stated confidently.

"What about the mustard on a wall from the sandwich? Scuff marks on the floor? How'd they get there? That's probably where the bottle cap came from, Lewis!" Ransom fired away.

"How should I know? He was an old hermit living by himself for decades! I still don't think we have anything on Duncan."

"Well, my instincts and woman's intuition tell me differently, Officer Kline. What do you say we pay Mr. Duncan a visit and see what he has to say for himself? I'll show you how a real investigation is done!"

"Oh boy! I can't wait!" Kline said mockingly.

"You just watch and take a lesson, kid!" she snapped back.

*****

It was a quick five-minute ride to Lewis's house. The cruiser pulled into the driveway slowly.

"The kitchen door's open. Let's see if Lewis is home," she quietly said to Officer Kline. "We were here a few months ago after Honch died. Remember?" He shook his head, agreeing.

They walked up the driveway toward the side yard. Kline knocked on the porch door. A middle-aged woman appeared.

"Why, hello, officers." She was startled. "What can I do for you?"

"I'm Detective Ransom, and this is Officer Kline. Might you be related to Lewis Duncan?"

The woman laughed. "Oh, no, hardly! I don't know any of the Duncans."

Kline and Ransom looked at each other, baffled.

"May I ask who you are then, ma'am?" Detective Ransom politely asked.

"Of course, I'm Courtney Grant. I just bought this house today. Isn't it cute?"

"*You what?*" Ransom said in shock.

"Yes, Detective. I closed on it this morning. It's my first house! I paid cash for it, too! I hit the Keno for a big jackpot!"

"I don't believe this!" Ransom said, glaring at her.

"Do you know where the owner went to live?" Officer Kline asked her.

"No, I don't." She thought for a moment. "I met him briefly at the home inspection, but he wasn't at the closing. Only his lawyer was there."

"Do you remember the lawyer's name?" Ransom asked.

"No, I'm horrible with names, but he was a very handsome and distinguished man."

"Did you go through a real estate agency?" Ransom asked.

"Yes. It was Beach and Sea Dreams on Route 28."

"Well, thank you very much, Ms. Grant. Good luck with your new home. And should Mr. Duncan ever stop by, please give us a call," Ransom said as she handed a business card to her.

"Of course, goodbye now," Courtney addressed both of them.

Ransom sat in the cruiser with Kline and stared him down. "Still think nothing's fishy, Officer Kline?" Ransom asked smartly.

"Nope, I think it's all coincidence. There's still nothing on Duncan."

"What?" Detective Ransom tried to pound it into Officer Kline. "He was involved in the murder of the biggest feared bikers on Cape Cod. He delivered sandwiches to Mr. Webb, who died mysteriously of a heart attack! What's next for Mr. Duncan? Now he has a large sum of money and could go anywhere!"

"I still think you're wasting our time on this."

"You're going to the real estate agency and get that lawyer's name. Find where Beach and Sea Dreams is, Kline."

"Yes, ma'am. Right away!" He scoffed at her.

"Did you verify Lewis Duncan's story of his girlfriend the night Honch was killed?" she asked.

Kline paused a moment and admitted, "No, I never did. We didn't have anything to go on. I didn't think it was important. He was in the hospital Friday night when Honch died."

"You'll be walking the beat again if you don't smarten up, Kline! Put a soft APB on Lewis Duncan. The last thing we need is for him to know we're looking for him. He's always one step ahead of us."

"I don't think...."

"*Kline*! Just do as I say!" Ransom ordered. She rifled for a fresh pad of paper from the glovebox and jotted some notes. The two-way radio in their cruiser then addressed her.

"Dispatch to Detective Ransom, dispatch to Detective Ransom, over."

"This is Ransom. Go ahead, dispatch."

"Missing person's report filed today, three male teenagers from Yarmouth reported missing since last week by one of their girlfriends. Over."

"Send subject descriptions and address of the person who filed the report. Over," Ransom requested.

"Will do. Dispatch, over and out."

"Still think there's nothing strange going on in this town, Kline? It's like the Twilight Zone around here!"

"Oh, yeah, sure!" Officer Kline laughed. "And little green men landed on the dunes in Truro last week, too!"

Ransom frowned and shook her head as he drove.

Officer Kline defiantly stated, "Yeah, before I know it, you're going to try and convince me Lewis Duncan had something to do with the disappearance of those three kids from Yarmouth, too!" He broke out laughing.

"Kline, just shut up and drive," she snidely remarked.

Chapter Forty-Two

"*Kline*, get in here!" Ransom yelled.

He ran into her office from the coffee machine, spilling half his cup down the hall.

"Yes, ma'am?"

"I'm going to check out the report filed this morning on that missing person. The woman lives off Barnes Road. Go to the real estate company that sold Duncan's house. Dig up what info you can on the agent and Duncan. We also need the name of his lawyer who did the closing. Duncan could be in Florida by now, for all we know. Got it?"

"Yes, Detective Ransom. You can count on me."

"Yeah, right! Just like you never looked into Duncan's girlfriend's name?" she reminded Kline and laughed. "We'll meet in one hour and take it from there."

"Yes, ma'am. On my way." Kline raced down the hall, spilling the remainder of his coffee. He proceeded to Beach and Sea Dreams Realty to question the real estate agent who sold Lewis's home. She gave Officer Kline the sale price but never asked Lewis where he was going after the closing. His whereabouts were unknown.

Unwillingly, she gave Officer Kline the name of the lawyer who represented Lewis. Kline beat Ransom to the precinct and ran a rap sheet on Lewis's lawyer, Theodore Kane.

"Hmm, I thought I recognized that guy's name," Kline said loudly at the teletype.

"What name?" he heard a voice from behind. It was Detective Ransom.

"You won't believe what I found!" he said enthusiastically.

"You go first," she said, letting Officer Kline fill her in.

"Duncan's lawyer?" Kline paused and smiled, "Does Theodore Kane – Teddy Kane – ring a bell?"

"No, not really."

"Yeah, you were probably still in diapers!" He laughed again. "Teddy Kane, aka The Casher? Indicted in 1975 along with the Rizutti family for loan sharking, money laundering, witness tampering, and aiding criminal activity." Finally, Officer Kline knew something she didn't for a change.

"What happened to them? Why aren't they in jail?"

"Get this. Nobody on the state's witness list would testify against them, so the DA had to drop all charges."

"Great work, Kline. There's hope for you after all. Sit down. You'd better take some notes on what I have to say."

Officer Kline obliged. Taking a seat, he broke out his notepad. "Go ahead, shoot."

"I don't know where to begin," she said, practically drooling. "Those three missing teens were involved with Honch and the motorcycle club that sold drugs in town. A kid named Jerry Alfonso and some twin brothers called the Gallaghers were in high school with Duncan."

"That girl told you this?" Kline asked in disbelief.

"Yep. It seems she got hooked on drugs, too. She begged for help, so I sent DHS to her house. But get this, Alfonso and the Gallaghers were at the concrete plant the night Honch fought Duncan!"

"No! You have to be shitting me!" Kline yelled. "How do you know that?"

"I called the informant we planted in the club on the way here. He said those three were present at the fight, and Duncan pointed at them and said something on his way out."

"So that means you've got jack shit on Duncan in their disappearance, big deal!" Officer Kline stated.

"Wake up and smell the coffee, Kline! What don't you see? Honch is dead, and Duncan had *a beef* with three other missing kids. His mother died of a heroin overdose from drugs they supplied!"

"Well, fifteen gang members are missing, too. Did Duncan kill them after he was in the hospital Friday night and before we got there Sunday morning? No, they're on the lamb, on the run! You're just picking on this Duncan kid. You have absolutely nothing on him!"

Detective Ransom sat back in her chair and took a deep breath. "I guess you may be right, Kline. I just don't like him! Maybe I'm getting carried away a little here. Let's regroup and see what our lawyer friend, Mr. Theodore Kane has to say, and afterward, I'll buy you a beer at Skippy's. We can put our thoughts together, okay?"

"Sounds good, but I can't go into Skippy's. I had a dispute there a couple of months ago."

"Forget it!" Ransom said. "We'll grab a six-pack and go to the beach parking lot."

"But there's no drinking on the...."

"Kline!" Ransom screamed.

*****

Ransom and Kline proceeded to Attorney Theodore Kane's office. They were greeted by a beautiful, buxom woman who caught the wandering eye of Kline.

"How may I help you this morning? Both police officers, I presume?" the knockout receptionist asked them.

"This is Officer Kline, and I'm Detective Ransom from Yarmouth Police. Is Attorney Kane in today?"

"Yes, he is. Do you have an appointment?" she asked politely. "He's with a client and will be free shortly."

The foxy receptionist looked Kline up and down. "I've always admired a man in uniform!"

"No, we *do not* have an appointment," Ransom said firmly. "This is official business. We can request that Mr. Kane come to the precinct, or you can interrupt his appointment and save him the bother."

The previously smiling face on the receptionist quickly morphed into a scowl. Officer Kline's desires got dampened.

The receptionist stood slowly and tapped quietly on Attorney Kane's door. The door opened about two inches. Detective Ransom strained to listen but could hear only faint mumbling.

"He'll be with you in a moment," the receptionist told them. She sat at her desk and removed a nail file from the drawer.

Officer Kline let out a bemoaning sigh.

The door opened as a gigantic man, well over six-foot-six and smartly dressed in a fine black suit, walked out. He snarled as he walked by Kline, staring intently at him. Another well-groomed man appeared in the doorway.

"Come in, please," a deep voice said to them. Attorney Kane walked to his jet-black leather chair behind his spotless mahogany desk and took a seat. "And how may I help Yarmouth PD today?" he asked politely.

"I'm Detective Ransom, and this is Officer Kline."

"Your bodyguard?" Attorney Kane asked and grinned devilishly.

She did not find that amusing, and it showed. "It seems you have quite a checkered past, Attorney Kane, don't you?"

He leaned forward in the chair and clasped his hands.

"I hope you are not here to discuss a matter that I was found completely innocent of years ago."

"Innocent? It seems nobody would testify against you or the Rizuttis. I wouldn't call that being found innocent," Ransom shot back.

Attorney Kane immediately began to get perturbed by this line of questioning.

"You are correct, Mr. Kane," Ransom continued. "I'm not here to harass you about something that happened years ago. We're seeking information about your recent client, Lewis Duncan."

"Oh? Yes, he was a client of mine recently. I served with his father in Viet Nam. I represented him in the sale of his family home. He's a fine young man," Attorney Kane stated.

"Do you know he is under investigation for the death of a local biker?" Ransom asked.

"No."

"Do you know he is under investigation for the death of an elderly man in Dennis?"

"No."

"Did you know he is a suspect in the disappearance of three teens from Yarmouth?"

"No, I didn't know that either."

"What happened to the money from the sale of his house?" Ransom drilled Attorney Kane.

"I don't know what Lewis did with the money. Even if I did know, I couldn't disclose that to you. It falls under attorney-client privilege."

"Have you seen Lewis recently?" Ransom began again while looking at her notepad.

"No."

"Did he leave a forwarding address?"

"No. Detective Ransom, I believe I've answered enough of your questions concerning this matter for today. I'm a rather busy man." He reached across his desk and buzzed the receptionist. "Candy, please show Yarmouth's finest the door."

"We may be subpoenaing your records on Lewis Duncan," Ransom informed him.

"Records? It was a simple closing. I don't have any records on Lewis. The real estate agent has them. Good day to you both."

Candy led Detective Ransom and Officer Kline to the front door.

"Boy, talk about the fox in a hen house," Officer Kline remarked once out of earshot. "What did you think?"

"That's mighty perceptive of you, Officer Kline. I know he's hiding something. I can't quite put my finger on it, but I don't trust any lawyer. Did you notice he didn't have one file or piece of paper on his desk? That's pretty odd for a lawyer. Put a tail on Kane for a week. Maybe Lewis will show up here again."

Attorney Kane walked over to a file cabinet and thumbed through a large stack of manila folders. "Here it is." He went to his desk and spread a few documents on it. "Lewis, you certainly have been a busy man!" He laughed. "You should be working for me!"

Attorney Kane buzzed Candy again.

"Could you come in here, please, Candy?"

"Yes, Sir."

Attorney Kane handed the file to Candy.

"Candy, please dispose of these documents in the usual manner. They are never to be seen again."

"Understood, Sir." Candy politely replied. "Do we still have our lunch date for today?" she asked coyly.

"I wouldn't miss it for anything, Candy. And do me a favor, please."

"What's that?"

"Keep a lookout on the street in front. It'll probably be an unmarked Crown Victoria or an Impala. I'm sure the junior detective will have eyes on us soon."

"Will do, Sir." Candy spun on her stiletto heels and departed the office with a swagger that would kill most grown men.

Attorney Kane opened a desk drawer, pulled out a bottle of Johnny Walker, and poured himself a shot. He stretched back in his chair, put his feet up on the desk, and downed the shot in one gulp.

"Ahhh," he remarked and snapped his lips as Johnny's bite of alcohol hit him. "Lewis, you certainly have me puzzled. I wish I could get in touch with you. I really do."

Attorney Kane thought for a few moments and buzzed Candy.

"Could you come in here again, Candy?" he requested.

She came in and practically floated across the floor at her usual gate.

"Have a seat. I think we will have to cancel our lunch date for today," Attorney Kane stated, disappointing Candy immediately.

"Oh, no! I was so looking forward to it!" she said.

Kane leaned over his desk. "Pack your bags."

"What? Pack my bags? I don't understand?"

"We have to find Lewis somehow, and obviously, I can't go to his girlfriend's house. I'd lead Detective Ransom right to him. Emmie's operation is scheduled for next week, and I have a hunch Lewis will be making a trip to Boston. We made that donation from Lewis to Dr. Drury today. It's time for a road trip," he said slyly. "We're headed to Beantown, and the Yankees are in Fenway for three days. Please cancel our appointments for the next week."

"Are you kidding me?" Candy ran around the desk and gave Kane a big kiss. "I haven't been to Boston in years! What should I pack?"

"How about that nice lace dress I bought you and that beat-up Red Sox tank top? We'll take in a game or two while we're there. After I call Petey, we'll be wining and dining in one of the upper box suites."

"On my way!" Candy said enthusiastically.

"Here are the keys to my Caddy. Park at the bus station and take a cab back to your house. Give me your keys, and I'll pick you up in one hour. That'll confuse those junior gumshoes when they find my car at the bus station!" Kane bent over, laughing. "Candy, get your Chevette ready!"

"That's why I love you so much! You're always ten steps ahead of everyone!" Candy built him up as he pretended to shine a medal on his suit.

"One hour, *sharp!*" he reiterated.

Kane sat in his chair again, poured another shot, and iced it down. This time, he puckered his lips as the Johnnie Walker chilled his throat.

"Damn, you're good, Lewis!" he said, looking into a small mirror on the wall. "I'll find you before they do. I make that promise! You're in a heap of shit, but so am I!"

Attorney Kane got on the phone and made a few calls to some close friends in Boston. He drew the blinds in his office and stuck a sign on the front door visible from the street. "Closed for vacation," it read. Kane put some ratty clothes on from a closet, sneaked out the back door, and jumped in Candy's Chevette. He made his way from the rear parking lot through an alley. Theodore Kane was looking forward to a nice quiet week, but it would be one that would change many lives forever.

Chapter Forty-Three

Lewis took off from his new home at the concrete plant and put down fifty feet of rubber as he left. He felt like a million bucks. Lewis had a large pile of cash, money from his father's death settlement he could collect in a few years, and a monthly check from social security until he turned eighteen. It was a beautiful day driving along the shoreline to Emmie's house. Emmie was sitting on the front steps when he pulled into her driveway. She was crying. Lewis ran from his car.

"Oh my gosh, Emmie! What the heck is wrong?" He put his arm around her, trying to comfort her.

"Lewis," she sobbed uncontrollably. "These aren't tears of pain."

"What? I don't get you!"

"These are tears of joy! A doctor's office from Boston called today." She paused.

"Yeah, well?" Lewis tried to look surprised.

"Someone has paid for my operation! I can go to Boston in two days! I can't believe it!"

Lewis picked her up and spun around in a twirl. "I told you something great was going to happen for us! Did you tell your mother yet?"

"I haven't seen her for two days. She must be on a bender somewhere. I've sworn I'll never follow what she's done and ruin my life with booze or drugs. I have so much to live for!" she said, crying louder.

"I've made that promise to myself, too. I will never follow in my mother's footsteps either and go down that road! Let's get a pizza tonight before we go to Boston."

"Love to! But there's one more thing, Lewis. No more bikinis. I'll have a foot-long scar on my chest!"

"What? Are you kidding me?" Lewis interrupted her. "Look at my face! I'm going to have this scar from that fight for years! I'm proud of it, and besides the fact, I already look like a caveman! I've been stared at, picked on, and scrutinized my whole life. I consider it a badge of honor! I finally stood up for something I believed in and defended my family! Emmie, hon, you're gonna be fine."

"You don't mind giving me a ride to Boston for the operation?"

"I'd love to escort you to Boston. The bomb may look like a piece of junk, but it has only twenty thousand miles on it. It'll fit right in on those city streets!" he joked. "I'd enjoy meeting your doctor, too. But there's just one thing."

"What's that?"

Lewis laughed at himself a moment. "You're not going to believe this, Emmie."

"What? What now?" She begged for an answer.

"I don't have a license," he admitted. "I've been driving without one."

"You what? You don't have a license?"

"I know, I know. I was scheduled for my final picture the week my mother died. All I had was a paper license. I think it went through the wash or something. Since then, I've been driving everywhere and haven't given it a second thought. Heck, I look like I'm thirty years old! I pass cops all the time. At least I have my old learner's permit."

"If we get stopped, we're done!"

"I left stickers from the Air Force and Marines on the brown bomb. We won't get stopped! I'll just plead stupidity!"

"Well, I have to be in pre-op for a physical at eleven a.m. on Thursday. It's just a standard checkup to make sure I can withstand the procedure. The operation is Friday morning at eight. I'm kinda nervous," Emmie admitted. "This is a lot for me to absorb."

"I'll be with you every step of the way. Wait, I don't know if that's a good thing!" They both laughed and hugged.

"My little brothers are here, so what do you say we go to your house for a little, you know, celebration!" Emmie said enthusiastically.

Lewis hesitated, knowing he was in a pickle. "Ah, well, we really can't. The inside of my house is, uhh, being painted. I can't go in there because the fumes make me sick."

It didn't dawn on Emmie that Lewis was handing her a line of crap. She was so happy with the news of her pending operation.

"I can sleep at a friend's house or in my car at the beach. I haven't done that in months."

"You'll sleep at a friend's house? You don't even have any! And you'll get eaten alive at the beach. You can sleep on our couch, but we'll have to set a good example for my brothers, you know?"

"Oh, that's okay. I'll rough it for one night, and we'll leave for Boston tomorrow. We can get a hotel room somewhere close to the hospital. You have to be there bright and early on Thursday, right?"

"A hotel? That's expensive!" Emmie replied.

"I do have some money, you know. I worked all summer and banked the money from my father's passing. I haven't touched a cent. No need to worry about that!" he tried to convince her.

"I guess so," Emmie agreed. "Okay. I've already called Aunty Barbara to watch my brothers if Mom doesn't come home. It's lucky I just turned eighteen. I don't need her permission for the operation."

"Boy, that was close! Let's ride out to Provincetown and maybe catch a whale watch. Have you ever seen a whale?"

"Are you kidding me? My parents never even took us to the beach just two miles away! That stuff's for tourists, remember?" She reminded him again.

"Mine, too," Lewis told her. "Looks like we'll be tourists today. Sounds great!"

Lewis and Emmie had a wonderful afternoon on the ocean in what's known locally as 'P-town.' They shared their usual pepperoni pizza in Yarmouth and planned to depart the Cape around nine the next morning. Lewis wouldn't take long to pack his few belongings at the concrete plant. He liked his new home. It felt very secure to him, and most people were afraid to go near the old industrial site filled with hazardous materials. Would he ever be able to tell Emmie this is where he lived?

Lewis picked up Emmie at noon. She had a small suitcase packed and was ready to go. She gave her brothers a kiss and aunt a hug goodbye. Her mother was still not home from her week-long party.

Chapter Forty-Four

Lewis and Emmie left sharply at noon. He punched the brown bomb as they crossed the Sagamore Bridge connecting Cape Cod to the mainland. He almost caught air in the two-ton vehicle.

"This is the first time I've been off the Cape in fifteen years!" Lewis yelled over the noise from the open windows.

"I've never been off the Cape my whole life!" Emmie screamed as she laughed.

"The last time I was in Boston was for some testing when I was a baby."

"You were probably four feet long as a baby!" Emmie joked.

"Funny, Emmie, funny," Lewis said. "We'll find the hospital first and then get a hotel room for the night. Sound good?"

"Yeah, that's great! I'll be your queen for the night, and you can be my king!"

"I didn't know royalty ran in your family, but I'll go along with it!"

It was a crystal-clear day as the skyline of Boston started to appear on the horizon of the South East Expressway. Emmie got the jitters.

"I think my stomach just turned over, Lewis. I'm terrified about this," Emmie admitted.

"Hey, come off it! Your doctor told you the success rate of this operation is off the charts!"

"I know, I know. And if I don't have it, I'll be gone within a year." The reality and severity of Emmie's condition were sinking in with Lewis.

"Hey, look, there are those famous gas tanks on the highway over there. You know, the ones you always see on the news?" He tried to brighten her mood. Emmie said nothing as she stared ahead at the skyline, approaching closer and closer.

The hospital was easy to find but locating a hotel room nearby wasn't. The Yankees were in town against the Red Sox, and every hotel was booked.

They were directed to a small, cozy hotel within earshot of the busy Southeast Expressway.

"Well, it's not the Shangri-La, but it'll do for a night," Lewis commented.

"You're staying just one night? Are you dumping me off at the hospital and going back to the Cape?" Emmie quizzed him.

"Heck no! After you get admitted tomorrow, I'm camping at the hospital! I'm not going anywhere until you come home with me!"

"Will they let you do that?"

"I don't care what they say. I'm not leaving until you get discharged in two weeks."

"I'm so sorry, Lewis, but I'm not thinking straight right now, you know?"

"Don't be concerned about me at all. I'm a big boy, not to overstate the obvious." He laughed again. "Focus on yourself for once, Emmie. Everything will be all right. I know you wanted to start college this fall at Plymouth State, but the doctor said you'll be fine to attend the spring semester."

"That's the least of my concerns right now. You're right. Let's get that room and make a little noise, okay? It's going to be a long time before we can get that close again."

"I think we're going to make a *lot* of noise!" Lewis said boldly.

Emmie looked at Lewis very seriously. "Lewis?" she asked.

"What?"

"Will you love me tonight as if it may be our last night together?" she asked shyly.

"What? Are you crazy? I asked you before not to say stuff like that!" He yelled at Emmie in anger for the very first time.

"Lewis, I'm having my chest carved open like a turkey, my ribs sawn apart, my heart stopped and diced up! Don't you think I'm wondering if I will come out alive after this operation? Survival chances are good, but nothing is guaranteed!"

"I'm sorry, Emmie. I guess I had no idea what was going to happen. I'll be outside the operating room and as close as possible."

"There's one more thing." Emmie paused. "You won't be able to come into the ICU for at least a week, germs!"

Lewis reluctantly agreed.

The hotel was full of rowdy New York fans getting primed for another legendary battle against the Red Sox. Once fans departed for the game, it was unusually quiet in the thirty-room hotel. Nor were there huge celebrations later from partygoers after the Sox crushed the Yanks.

Lewis and Emmie spent all night in each other's arms in a tangle of passion, taking very little time for sleep. At 10:30 a.m., they checked out and left for the hospital.

"Boy, this traffic is wicked!" Lewis remarked as they got on the expressway. "Imagine driving in this every day?"

Emmie gazed straight ahead and nervously rolled her fingers on the armrest. Lewis put his hand on her thigh as they pulled into the hospital parking lot and grabbed a ticket at the booth.

A grumpy, machine-like attendant addressed Lewis. "Parking is eight dollars the first day, then seven dollars a day if you don't move your car."

"Are you kidding me? That's robbery! I paid a...." Lewis caught himself before going on.

"Paid what, Lewis?" Emmie interrupted.

"Oh, nothing. Here you go, Sir. Money for two days," Lewis angrily threw a twenty on the counter.

"Park that boat down at the end on the left with the other pieces of junk, okay?"

Emmie saw Lewis was furious now and had to resist belting the loudmouth.

"Let's go, Lewis. Obviously, he hates his job. Who wouldn't? He's cramped up in that hot, little cube all day."

"Yeah, I guess so. But he didn't have to make fun of the brown bomb!" Lewis joked.

They walked what seemed forever to find hospital admissions and the pre-op staging area. Emmie signed in at both offices.

"Ma'am, your insurance card, please?" the admissions desk clerk said.

"My what? Insurance card?" Emmie was bewildered and confused.

"Her operation is paid for!" Lewis exclaimed. "Call the doctor. He'll straighten this out."

"Let me make a call, okay, folks?" she replied. An inquiry was made immediately. Lewis and Emmie listened intently but barely heard anything as ambulances roared outside.

"It seems you are correct, young man. I've never seen such a thing like this here in twenty years. I apologize. You have a very generous person looking out for you, Emmie!" She handed her a stack of papers to sign and put a wristband on. Lewis almost swallowed his tongue in relief.

"I hope that wristband doesn't say 'remove left arm' – she's here for a heart procedure!"

"Oh, Lewis! Come on!" Emmie shook her head, grinning.

"After the pre-op exam, you'll be taken upstairs and prepared for your operation tomorrow morning."

"Already?" Lewis asked her.

"Yes, she'll be admitted to her room and have an IV with antibiotics administered. You won't be able to see her until after the operation, and that will be only through a window."

The gravity of the situation finally hit Lewis.

"Yes, ma'am," he replied solemnly with his head down.

Emmie turned to Lewis. "Well, I guess this is it for now." She paused. "I'll be much stronger after this is over. You just wait!"

"I'm afraid that's all I can do, Emmie," Lewis remarked quietly. They hugged in a long embrace.

"I have to go, Lewis," Emmie said as a large tear slid down her cheek.

Emmie took a few steps toward the heavy swinging doors with a nurse.

"Emmie!" Lewis called to her before she departed through the doors. "Will you let me take care of you forever?" he yelled, loud enough for everyone in the lobby to hear.

Emmie stopped in her tracks and turned to look at Lewis in disbelief. "Yes, Mr. Duncan. I would be humbled and honored if you took care of me for the rest of our lives!" She turned around and made it through the doors with assistance from her nurse.

"My gosh!" the nurse exclaimed. "Was that a proposal I just heard?"

Emmie was on the verge of collapse and grabbed the nurse's free hand and shoulder.

"Believe me, if he could etch those words in stone, he would," Emmie told the nurse as they shuffled down the hall.

Chapter Forty-Five

"*Kline!* Get in here!" Ransom yelled.

"Yes, ma'am!" Kline said as he stuffed a muffin in his mouth.

"We're upping the APB on Lewis Duncan into a statewide case. He's nowhere to be found. We don't even have a picture of him."

"Are you sure you want to do that?"

"Go to the high school and see if they have any yearbook photos of him. Then go to the DMV and get a copy of his license. We need something other than the fact he's the tallest, goofiest looking kid in Yarmouth with a ten-inch...." Ransom stopped short as Kline began to laugh.

"You're kidding me. Right? We'll be the laughingstock of every police station in America!" Kline broke into an imitation of an APB coming over the squad car radio.

"Attention all units, attention all units. Be on the lookout for a Caucasian male approximately 18 years of age, six-foot-seven, scar on his left cheek, goofy looking, driving an unknown vehicle, but does have a ten-inch...."

"Knock it off, Kline!"

"And how would you know what Mr. Lewis Duncan is packing anyhow, Detective Ransom?"

"*Never mind!* And did you put that tail on Attorney Kane as I requested?"

"Well, I did, but it may have been a little late. An unmarked was parked outside his business for six hours yesterday before he noticed a sign on Kane's door."

"What did it say?"

"You're going to love this. It said closed for vacation."

"You think that's funny? Now we've got two more people on the run. He never told us he was going on vacation!"

"I don't think he had to, do you? We're not his babysitters!"

"Sure, we tell Kane we're going to subpoena his records, and he goes on vacation. Get someone in that office and tear it apart! Put an APB on him too! While you're at the DMV, see what kind of car he drives. This is unbelievable! Cape Cod will be a ghost town if all these people keep disappearing!"

"Why do you think Lewis and Kane are on the run?" He asked.

"Find Kane, and you'll find Lewis Duncan! Now move it!"

"Yes, ma'am!" Kline said, saluting her.

"I'm going back to the missing kid's girlfriend's house and busting her chops for some more information. She has to know more than what she's told us. You've got two hours, then meet me back here. Got it?" she ordered.

"Either she's going through menopause or needs to get laid," Officer Kline said as he left her office.

"I heard that!" she yelled.

He didn't realize she was right on his heels.

*****

Two hours later, Kline appeared in Ransom's office. "Officer Kline, what did you find out?"

"You're going to love this. Lewis Duncan – no pictures, never in a high school yearbook, doesn't have a driving license either."

"What? No license? How the hell is he getting around?"

"His mother, who passed away, has a 1970 Chevy Impala still registered in her name. Here's the tag number."

"Broadcast that statewide. What else?"

"Attorney Kane has a Caddy registered in his name but look at his rap sheet and photos from the DMV."

Ransom scrutinized both pictures of Kane.

"I don't believe this!" she yelled out. "These aren't Kane! How can this photo not be him? This is a shot of Carl Yaztremski from the Boston Red Sox in front of the Green Monster! Did he pay someone off to change it? This truly is unreal!" She scratched her head.

"Pretty clever guy, I'd say," Kline remarked.

"We'll look like idiots without pictures of these suspects if we file a statewide APB!" she muttered.

"Suspects? What are they even wanted for? Please clue me in!"

"It's just – I don't know. I don't like that Duncan kid. I told you before!" Ransom admitted as she broke down and almost cried. She composed herself. "Just find that Impala and Kane's Cadillac, okay? I didn't have any luck interviewing that girl who filed the missing person's report either."

"Really? Why not?" Kline asked.

"Now she's in rehab and can't talk to anyone without an approval order from her shrink!"

"Maybe those missing teens will show up somewhere. We were only two days away from busting that whole bike gang, and now we can't find anyone! Lewis and Theodore Kane are giving us quite a schooling lesson, aren't they?"

"I'm afraid so, Kline. I'm afraid so."

Chapter Forty-Six

Six hours after the operation started, Lewis was nervously pacing the floor of the operating waiting room. He practically wore a circular track on the carpet. The doors to the operation staging area opened slowly as Dr. Drury and a nurse appeared.

"Lewis, please follow me to my office down the hall," said Dr. Drury, pointing the way.

"Is Emmie okay? How's she doing?" Lewis asked quickly.

The nurse put her hand on his shoulder and guided him to an office. She closed the door behind the two of them.

"Sit down, Lewis, please." Dr. Drury addressed him.

"What went wrong?" Lewis demanded to know. "I've seen the look doctors give people on TV when they have bad news!"

"Lewis, it was very touchy for a while. Emmie is very weak, but she's resting comfortably. If she hadn't had that operation today, she would've died within two or three weeks."

"You're kidding, right?"

"I'm not kidding at all. Her procedure was more complicated than originally anticipated. She'll have to stay in the ICU, completely isolated, for a month. She cannot be around anyone except staff, and her immune system is shot right now."

"Oh, my gosh, I never imagined anything like this would happen."

"Lewis, she's lucky to be alive. There is one more thing." Dr. Drury paused and took a deep breath.

"What? What is it?" Lewis demanded an answer.

"Lewis, some very generous benefactor paid for Emmie's operation. Did you know that?"

"Yes, I did. It was me."

"I knew it was you. I was just seeing if you'd be honest with me. You are an amazing person, Lewis. Unfortunately, that payment isn't enough to cover hospital expenses for another month in ICU," Dr. Drury informed him.

"How much more money do you need?"

"Lewis, when this was arranged, I received a large payment from an old friend in Yarmouth. How do you know Theodore Kane?"

Lewis looked down and twiddled his thumbs for a moment. He then raised his head.

"Attorney Kane has been a family friend for a long time. He was in Viet Nam with my father. I know he may be a little crooked, but he's always been good to us. Did you ever meet Nolan?"

"Yes, he was my best friend in high school."

"I served with your father and Nolan in Viet Nam also. Now, only three of us are alive from a group of five good friends from the Cape."

Lewis was puzzled but started to put it together.

"And how do you know Attorney Kane?" Lewis asked.

"I hadn't spoken with him for a long time until he called last week. He saved my ass in Nam one blistering hot day and bailed me out of a sticky situation here five years ago. Attorney Kane said this money came from selling your house?" Dr. Drury wanted to make sure Kane's and Lewis's stories matched.

"Yes, Sir, I sold my home and paid for the operation. How much more do you need?"

"You sold your house? Aren't you a little young to own property and be able to sell it?"

"I inherited the house from my parents. My mother died this year from a heroin overdose."

"I knew your father was killed at the armory, but I didn't know your mother passed away until Attorney Kane informed me last week. I was going into surgery and had to keep my conversation with Kane brief." Dr. Drury said. "I apologize for interrogating you, but I had some loose ends to tie up."

Lewis changed the subject. "I knew when I first saw Emmie years ago in high school I wanted to be with her. You still haven't answered my question."

"What question?" Dr. Drury was still trying to fathom the context of what was going on.

"How much more money do you need?"

"I'm not sure. I'm more than just a doctor here. I'm also the financial director of operations and am sure the bill will be quite staggering."

"I have money from the house closing and another account I planned to save. But if it means caring for Emmie, there's no question what I will do."

Dr. Drury leaned back in his chair and wrapped his hands over his eyes, shaking his head.

"Lewis, in some instances, the hospital can forgive some charges in a charity case like this."

"*I'm not a charity case!* It seems I've been one my whole life!" Lewis raised his voice loud enough for a passing nurse to look through a door window.

"I didn't mean that disrespectfully, Lewis. It seems we are starting to figure each other out here, okay?"

"I'm sorry, Dr. Drury. I had no right to say that."

"The main thing is Emmie will be fine in a few months. Lewis, there is one more concerning thing," Dr. Drury leaned forward in his chair.

"Did you know Emmie may be pregnant? We have to confirm this in a few days with another test. The pre-op blood test didn't show positive, but a post-op test has."

"*What?* She told me she could never have kids! Something called endo, endo – I don't know the rest."

"Endometriosis and a CT scan showed she also has blocked fallopian tubes," Dr. Drury said. "Emmie shouldn't have told you she could never have kids. I don't know how she could have gotten pregnant. Her chances were probably one in a million."

This news almost floored Lewis. A smile came across his face. "I'm – I'm going to be a father?" Lewis ignored him.

"Possibly, Emmie still has quite a road to recovery ahead of her, but I don't feel her condition will jeopardize the fetus. We'll be able to determine the baby's health with ultrasound in a few weeks and amniocentesis at a later time."

Lewis was bewildered by this information. "Well, I haven't booked any accommodations yet. I was going to sleep in my car this week." Lewis was still baffled by this upending news from Dr. Drury.

"Where were you going to...." Dr. Drury stopped grilling Lewis. He opened his desk drawer. "Lewis, my BMW is having a new transmission installed. It's only taken a year!" He laughed. "Take my parking pass, please. It will save you a lot of walking the next couple of weeks."

"I can't! That's too much!"

"I insist. I see you have quite a story to tell eventually. There are also showers in the gym downstairs. I'll give you a pass for that, too."

"Really? You don't have to. I can get a room somewhere."

"Nope, but this isn't a free ride. You'll have to earn your keep."

"What do you mean?" Lewis curiously asked.

"My brother runs a program here in Boston and could use some help. Unfortunately, he's very ill and will be retiring soon. You can work with him for a month and apply your earnings toward the bill," Dr. Drury told Lewis.

"Seems like a month's wages could hardly put a dent in such a large hospital bill," Lewis said.

"You'd be surprised. This job may come with a hitch."

"That's fine, Dr. Drury. I guess I'll accept some help for once in my life," Lewis cheerfully agreed.

"Here's my parking pass. And don't let that frumpy lot attendant give you any trouble. If he does, have him call me directly."

"How can I get in touch with your brother about the job?"

"Oh, don't worry. He'll find *you*. What type of car do you have?"

"It's a beat-up, brown 1970 Chevy Impala, four-door."

"Good city car, right?"

"Can I see Emmie now?"

"As I said, the closest you'll be able to get is to look through a glass window. She is unconscious and won't awaken from anesthesia until tonight, but you can peek in at her."

"Thank you, Dr. Drury. There's one more thing I should mention."

"I can only imagine. What's that, Lewis?" Dr. Drury asked.

"Emmie knows nothing about me paying for the operation, right?" Lewis strictly affirmed.

"You got it, kid. And don't forget to move your car into my spot, okay?"

"Thanks again! I'll get some food in the cafeteria later, then some shut-eye."

Lewis stood up, shook Dr. Drury's hand firmly, and departed the office.

Dr. Drury sat back at his desk. *That has to be one of the strangest conversations I've ever had. Lewis is such a kind and generous young man. A little odd-looking but certainly unique!*

Dr. Drury picked up his phone. "Outside line, please, Ellen. Yes, thank you."

He pushed a sequence of numbers quickly. It was picked up on the other end after one ring.

"Hello, Mags. Remember the young man I told you about? He's here." A short pause followed. "Yes, that's right. We served with his father, Bruce. Tonight will be fine to come for him. Thank you, Mags."

Dr. Drury looked at his calendar for any more appointments later in the day.

"Nice! No other patients! It looks like I'll be chasing the little white ball for a couple of holes this afternoon!"

Dr. Drury took off his white coat and hung it on the door. He shut his light off—*what a crazy day. I can't take too many more like this! I have a feeling it's just the beginning.* He certainly was correct in his assumption.

Chapter Forty-Seven

Officer Kline burst into Detective Ransom's office, totally out of breath, and bent over, gasping for air.

"What's the matter with you, Kline?" Ransom demanded.

"We've got a lead on the whereabouts of your favorite suspect, Lewis Duncan!"

"What? Tell me, Kline!"

"I knew we struck out yesterday, but when I drove by the high school earlier, I saw the track team practicing. Remember that 'Ben' guy from Meals for Seniors told us Lewis was trying out for the track team?"

"Yeah, so what?"

"So I stopped and asked some kids if they knew Duncan. They all did and said they'll miss him on the squad this year."

"C'mon, is that it?" Ransom barked.

"I asked one kid if Duncan had a girlfriend."

"Well?"

"Bingo! A girl named Emmie, who's one year older than him. I don't know her last name, but I bet you know he likes older women!"

"Screw you, Kline!"

"I went to the school office, and the secretary gave me her address. I told her it was official business involving the missing kids from town. Get this! I went to her house, and she wasn't home. Her foxy aunt told me she's in Boston having a heart operation!"

"What hospital?" Ransom asked.

"She didn't know."

"Great! There must be fifteen hospitals in Boston!"

"The best is yet to come," Kline smiled.

"You're killing me here!"

"Guess who drove her there?"

"Not Lewis Duncan?"

"Home run!"

"That squirt doesn't even have a damn license, and he drove to Boston?"

"That's right! I had Leslie in research call five hospitals so far, but none will divulge patient information over the phone. We'll have to get Boston PD involved to make direct inquiries."

"That's unbelievable!"

"The front desks think we're pranking them for patient information."

"Gas up the Crown Vic. We're heading to Boston *now!*" she ordered.

"I'm one step ahead of you, Detective. The car's ready to go. Sure you don't want to pack a bag for your make-up?"

"Kline, one of these days, I'm gonna...." She smiled. "I have some make-up in my pocketbook already. Call Sergeant Foley on Boston PD and tell him we're coming to his town for a visit. By the way, nice work today. I'll put you in for that sergeant exam next week. I should stop by my house and throw a few things in a suitcase."

Officer Kline ran downstairs into the men's locker room for a bag of clothing. He fired the Crown Vic up and drove around front to get Ransom, who climbed right in.

"Why are you really after this Duncan kid? He hasn't done anything wrong. It seems you're just picking on him," Officer Kline said as they pulled away.

"He's the key to everything. Honch, the old man on the salt marsh, fifteen missing bikers, and three other kids. What don't you see?"

"Oh yeah, so he killed fifteen bikers all in one night? Come off it! Even our snitch told us Lewis said nothing to any club members that night. And we never told him he couldn't leave town either!"

"He drove to Boston without a license!" Ransom shouted back.

"Oh c'mon, you're sucking pond water now. You'll be demoted if you drive to Boston and arrest him for that!"

"I'm not." she paused. "I'm going to arrest him for the murder of Honch and the disappearance of those three boys!"

"Based on what evidence? Hearsay from our mole informant who already clarified he saw Duncan leave the cement plant when Honch was still alive?"

"I'll find something, Kline! Young Lewis Duncan will sing like a jailhouse bird when I'm done with him!"

"I'm going on record that you are wrong, ma'am, and we'll end up looking like a bunch of fools."

"Do you want me to schedule that exam for you next week, Officer Kline?" Ransom asked him coldly.

"I don't know. I guess I'm starting to have my doubts," Kline admitted.

Chapter Forty-Eight

Lewis checked on Emmie in the ICU wing. Sure enough, he could get only a glimpse of her in bed. She had numerous monitors and an IV hanging on a hook attached to her arms and chest. A nurse exited Emmie's room.

"Nurse, ma'am, how's Emmie doing? She's not in any pain, is she?"

"Oh no, she's resting quite comfortably. We check on her every fifteen minutes. Are you related to her?"

"Well, no, not really. I'm her boyfriend."

"So you must be Lewis, right?" she asked.

"Yes, how'd you know?"

She smiled at him, "She just whispered your name as you looked at her through the window. Honestly, I had no idea who you were."

"She's the most special thing to me in the whole world," Lewis said as a tear fell onto his shirt.

"Here, take this," she said, handing him a Kleenex. "You must be very special to her. She knew you were here. Dr. Drury is the best heart doctor in Boston. She was fortunate to get on his growing list of patients. Why don't you get some rest? You can take a nap in the family waiting room. Great recliners in there."

"Thanks for the tip, ma'am. I suppose you'll see a lot of me. She's in lockdown for a month, and she may be pregnant!" Lewis said, beaming.

"I just read her chart. It looks possible. She has a long road ahead of her, but she's in the best hospital in New England," she assured Lewis. "The time will pass quickly, don't you worry. She'll be able to talk to you by phone tomorrow afternoon."

"Oh, that's wonderful. Thanks again," Lewis said as he turned away from the window. He went to the family waiting room, grabbed a seat in one of the cushy recliners, and fell fast asleep. He had so many crazy dreams. He dreamt of this summer's events leading up to today; his mother passing away, running track, the old man trying to kill him, the fight with Honch, and selling his house. Everything was in black and white. He woke up in a cold sweat.

Lewis stood and stretched. He found a restroom to freshen up and went to the cafeteria for a hot meal. Sitting alone, he noticed some people staring at him. Nothing unusual, he thought.

He glanced out a window. It was getting dark. How long had he been asleep? He exited the hospital's main entrance and walked to the far corner of the parking lot where his car was. He hopped in and sat before starting it up. *What a nice comfortable seat.* He pulled the parking pass from his pocket and put it on the dash. *Free parking in a doctor's spot for a couple of weeks? – I'll take it!* He found Dr. Drury's parking place and pulled the brown bomb in.

It was a rather dark corner of the parking lot. Lewis climbed into the back seat and wrapped himself in a blanket he had brought from the cement plant. His tall frame barely fit between the doors without getting hunched up. He took a few deep breaths. *Everything is going to be all right,* he thought and drifted off to sleep.

Sometime later, a heavy knocking on the car window awakened him.

"Come on, get out of there, kid! Why the heck are you parked here in that piece of junk?" It was the security guard again.

"Hey, hold on there, Barney Fife! I have a parking pass Dr. Drury gave me to use. Any questions? Call him! But I doubt he'd be happy if you bothered him in the middle of the night!"

"He gave you his pass? That's a good one!" the security guard said, laughing.

"Yeah? His BMW is in the shop. How else would I know that? My girlfriend is here recuperating from a heart operation, and he gave me his pass for a few weeks."

The security guard seemed a little perplexed. "Well, you're okay for tonight, but I'm checking your phony story tomorrow. And don't you call me Barney Fife ever again. I've been picked on my whole life because of my size."

Those words struck home with Lewis. "Sorry, man. You caught me off guard. I know what it's like to be picked on, too. We should get together and talk sometime. I'm going to be here for a month," Lewis said.

"I doubt it!" he shouted back. "I'll be checking out your story tomorrow."

The guard hopped onto his golf cart and disappeared into the darkness of the parking lot.

Lewis curled up in the backseat. *What the heck else is going to happen today?*

A few hours later, he heard some light tapping on the car door. Lewis looked up but didn't see anything. *I must have been dreaming.*

"Tick, tick." Something bounced off the car window.

"What the.... I've had it! That security guard is gonna get his ass kicked!"

Lewis unlocked the car door and wiped the foggy windows. He looked around. There was nothing. *I must be going crazy!* He scrunched up again.

A few moments later, serious pinging on his doors and windows started, sounding like machine gunfire.

That does it! I can't take this anymore! He threw his blanket onto the front seat and opened the back door. Stepping into the parking lot, he didn't observe anything in the murky shadows but heard giggling. "I'm going mad!" he said out loud. Some rustling came from the bushes.

"Is anyone there?" He heard footsteps, quite a few of them. "I *must* be dreaming!" He saw some figures approaching him slowly from the bushes-little people, maybe six or seven of them. Who were they? They stopped abruptly near the trunk of his car. He rubbed his eyes to make sure he wasn't seeing things. Sure enough, six or seven small men appeared. No, they were kids! They lined up about ten feet away from him.

He squared off and tried to make sense of this.

"Are you here to rob or – perhaps kill me?" Lewis asked the mysteriously silent group.

One of the small figures walked into the light of his car door and spoke.

"Hello, Lewis. We've come for you." He was a small child, maybe eight or nine years old.

"Isn't it past your bedtime?" Lewis asked smartly. There wasn't a stir from anyone, only blank stares. "What do you mean you've come for me?"

"We mean just that; you're coming. You'll be leaving with us one way or another," the small child stated firmly.

"Well, my mother told me never to go with strangers, and I'm certainly not leaving with you kids!"

"Please don't underestimate us, Lewis. We're not here to harm you, but you must come," the small child said as they took one step closer to him.

"I'm not into beating up little kids, but I can guarantee I'm not going anywhere!" Lewis reiterated.

"Unfortunately, you have chosen a path of resistance," a larger child with bright red hair said as he stepped closer, within arm's length of Lewis. "Kyle, Squeegie, Algo, prepare for a takedown."

"Takedown?" Lewis chuckled. "Why don't you kids just go home to Mommy and Daddy?"

"We don't have a Mommy or Daddy. None of us do," the child replied.

"Yip, yip!" the red-haired boss commanded. Lewis crouched slightly. Within seconds, the tribe of children surrounded Lewis, encircling him.

"All right! This has gone too far!" he pleaded.

Four kids attacked his gangly legs, and two jumped on his back. "Oh, no!" He thought this was reminiscent of the assault by Mr. Webb. Lewis spun around, trying to deflect the many little arms and tiny legs wrapping his body, entangling him in a spider's web.

One of the children placed a wet cloth over Lewis's face, covering his nose and mouth. The tingle of a nasty chemical came over him. He didn't know what it was, but he weakened. His knees buckled as his arms went limp. He lost consciousness as he lay on the ground. When he briefly came to, he saw a group of children laughing and celebrating. It appeared as if they were chanting a primitive war dance around a Maypole. A white van pulled beside Lewis. Many little hands picked him up and gently placed him on the floor.

Lewis's life was changed—even more than his run-in with Mr. Webb, Honch, or even Jerry Alfonso.

Chapter Forty-Nine

"Kline, have you been able to reach Sergeant Foley at Boston PD yet on that new suitcase phone?" Ransom asked as their cruiser passed over the Sagamore Bridge.

"No, not yet. I can hardly figure out how to work this thing. You left him a message hours ago when we left the station, didn't you? I don't think he gives a shit about your wild goose chase any more than I do. And I don't care that he owes you a favor. Neither does he! We have no idea where we are going in a city with a half million people, no clue where this hospital is, and you want me to ask this sergeant for help? We'll look like *Car 54; Where Are You?* I'm not on board with this whole thing! All you're doing is bullying this Duncan kid!"

"Duncan is in shit so deep he'll never be able to dig himself out!"

"With all due respect, Detective Ransom, I can't disagree with you more."

Kline looked out the car window as they passed numerous cranberry bogs lining Route 3.

"I can't be a part of this anymore. Lewis has done nothing wrong."

"Do you know what you're doing to your career?" Ransom needled him. "You'll be lucky if you're a dump sheriff when we return!"

"*Return?* Pull the car over!" Kline demanded.

"Pull what? Pull the car over on Route 3? Are you crazy?" Ransom screamed.

"Right here, there's an exit. I'll thumb back if I have to."

Detective Ransom jerked the wheel cutting two cars off. She slammed the brakes onto the dusty shoulder of the two-lane highway. "Turn in your badge when you get back to the station!" she yelled as he opened his car door.

"Nope, you can have it right now!" Kline unpinned his badge and handed his gun to her as well.

"This will haunt you forever; I hope you realize that," Kline told her. He closed the door quietly and walked toward the exit ramp. He never looked back as she glared in disbelief.

"You chicken shit!" Ransom yelled. She lit up the tires and put the bag phone right beside her. She dialed the operator as she sped along.

"Operator? Get Sergeant Maxwell on the line from the state police barracks in Framingham. And step on it. This is an emergency!" she ordered. "What do you mean he's not available?"

Ransom threw the phone against the dashboard in anger. She drove toward Boston in a rage, breaking every speed limit and driving rule possible on Route 3.

She was barreling along at 75 mph when her phone started to ring. She slowed into the breakdown lane to answer it.

"Ransom here!" she yelled into the portable phone.

"You're kinda scratchy," a voice on the other end replied.

"Ransom, Patricia Ransom here! Let me pull over. I'm on Route 3!"

"Pat, the big, feisty, and horny recruit from training school? Sergeant Foley here from Boston PD! I can't believe it! The last time I saw you, well, you know, we were kind of hitched up in a dorm room together! What a night!"

"Yeah, yeah, thanks for reminding me. I told you I wouldn't tell anybody, and I never did!" Ransom laughed.

"So, to what do I owe this enormous pleasure of speaking with you again, Pat?"

"I'm on Route 3 heading into Boston looking for a suspect in a murder case. He's also wanted for the disappearance of three other men from Yarmouth. He's in Boston somewhere, hiding out while his girlfriend has some big heart operation. We don't know what hospital she's in. I realize there's like fifteen hospitals in Boston, and I know jack-shit about Boston."

"There are twenty-one hospitals, Pat, but only three specialize in heart procedures. She's in one of those; I'll bet. Hey, thinking of bets, I think you welched on one we made seven years ago! As long as you're in Beantown...."

"Yeah, that was seven years ago!" Ransom cut Foley off. "And no way are you collecting now!"

Ransom laughed. "I do need some manpower, a small team to help me track this fugitive down and his accomplice-lawyer," Ransom requested of her old flame.

"Are you kidding me? The New York Yankees are in town for a double-header night series! We have every available car and officer on the beat from noon until one a.m. There's no way, sorry!"

"Okay, okay. But I'd hate to have that little secret about you get out!"

"Oh, for crying out loud, Pat! The whole department knows about my issue. No secrets anymore! I have a friend with a vacant apartment downtown where you can hang your badge. I'll have dispatch send his address and phone number to you. He owns a bar right near Fenway. That's where he'll be, especially before a game."

"Well, thanks, Jake. I'll call you when I'm closer. Maybe have a drink later?" Ransom asked. "Just like old times, right?"

"Oh, yeah," Foley said, caught off-guard. "Just for old times, right? I'll try getting contacts at those three hospitals and save you some legwork."

"I'll be in touch. Dartmouth 20, over and out," Ransom hung up quickly. She laughed and pulled onto Route 3, doing a respectable 65 mph. Her phone rang again.

"Ransom, here!"

"Ransom? Pat Ransom? It's Sergeant Maxwell, Buzz Maxwell, State Police. I haven't seen you since the good old academy days! How the heck are ya?" he happily queried.

"Oh, fine here, Buzz. I see you've made sergeant, too! That's great."

"Yeah, I started out patrolling 495 and the Pike. I worked my way up the ladder and took the exam in June. No more long hours in the cruiser. I'm head of our shift and the youngest rookie from the academy to do so, if I may say. How are you doing?"

"I've been a Detective in Dartmouth for only a month. I'm the only woman on the force and subjected to quite a bit of scrutiny. Let me fill you in on why I called."

"Go ahead, shoot," Buzz said. "I pulled over."

"I'm trying to locate a subject in Boston wanted for the murder of a biker on the Cape," Ransom stated.

"Really? Bikers usually take care of their problems. We leave them alone. The less we know, the better, know what I mean?"

"Yeah, I do, but we have a kid gone bad and is probably armed as well. I could use some extra eyes and staffing in Boston," she informed Sergeant Maxwell.

"It's Pat, not Patricia, right?" he said, changing the subject.

"That's fine, Buzz."

"I'd love to be able to help, but we are shorthanded here right now. The mob is on the move again from Providence into Worcester, and we've got almost every available officer between the borders of New Hampshire and Rhode Island."

"You gotta be shitting me! I just called Sergeant Foley. Remember him? He graduated with us. He's on Boston PD now." She paused. "The Yankees are in town for the next three nights, and he can't spare anyone either."

"I might be able to pull a few strings. Two greenhorn rookies from the Academy just graduated. I'll let you have them for a few days, but that's all the manpower I have. Go easy, breaking them in. They're a little unique."

"I don't care who they are. I'll take any help I can get. One of our officers bailed on me today, leaving me in this pickle," Ransom informed him. "I owe you one!"

Buzz snorted into the phone. "I'll hold you to that! I remember you had the hottest little – oh well, never mind. Call me when you get to Boston."

"Thanks, Buzz! And by the way, I still have the hottest, little, *never mind!*" She broke out in laughter and pegged the Crown Vic toward Boston on the Southeast Expressway.

Chapter Fifty

Lewis woke up with a tremendous headache. He had no clue where he was but thought he was lying on a bed. No, it was too hard, maybe a cot. He could hear water dripping in the distance and a deep rumbling sound. He focused his eyes on the ceiling, old brick, and cobblestone. Dim lighting shone on his body as water slowly oozed from cracks in the walls surrounding him.

"He's awake!" he heard a childish voice.

Oh, no! Not again!

Lewis struggled to sit up and shake the cobwebs from his brain. Again, he saw what appeared to be seven or eight small children gathered around him, staring at his features.

"What is this place?" Lewis asked. He heard the footsteps of a much larger person with hard soles approaching him from an unlit corridor. A large figure with long, white hair appeared behind the children and placed a warm hand on Lewis's shoulder. The man smiled at him.

"I apologize for this rather unorthodox method of bringing you here to meet my family," the man said and paused. "You have been chosen to come here, Lewis. No harm will come to you."

"Chosen? What? I'm confused, Sir," Lewis said quietly. "And how do you know my name?"

"Mind if I sit beside you?" he asked politely. Lewis nodded. "My name is Mags."

"Mags?" Lewis affirmed.

"Yes, Mags Drury."

"Drury? Are you related to Dr. Drury?" Lewis asked.

"Yes, we are brothers. I know a lot about you. I know why you're here, and you are a very generous person. You may also be in trouble with the law."

"I've done nothing wrong, Sir, and I don't look at myself as being a very generous person, Mr. Drury. I've had a bad summer on the Cape. Nothing went right until I met Emmie, Sir."

"Lewis. Please call me Mags. I know you've lost both of your parents. None of these children have parents, either. They are victims of a cruel society shuffled around like playing cards. They've never been shown the true love of a family except for what I can offer them. Cheeto, please come here," Mags requested one of the children. Mags put his arm on his shoulder. "Cheeto's parents were killed in an auto accident. He was forced into the foster system and neglected by three different families, only in it for the money. Thank you, Cheeto." The boy stepped back into line.

Lewis tried to lighten the tense situation. "I guess you call him Cheeto because of his bright orange and red hair?"

"Very observant, Lewis. Very good! You will fit in well here. Maria, please." Maria walked over and stood beside Mags. "Maria was subjected to a house where drugs were sold daily. Her father died in a shootout with police, and her mother was sent to jail for twenty years for heroin trafficking. What you see standing before you is what I like to call The Elementary Army. I have legally adopted them. This building is an old subway station, and we are forty feet below the busy streets of Boston. We have six bedrooms, separate baths, a kitchen, a library, and a TV room. Every child attends school daily and is a model student."

"So, where do I fit into all of this?" Lewis asked.

"Ahhh, I was wondering when you would ask that!" Mags snapped his fingers and pointed. One of the children brought Mags a chair to sit beside Lewis.

"The short story is...." He swallowed hard. "I am dying." Lewis sat up further and put his feet on the floor.

"Here I am, living in the medical center of the USA, and nothing can be done for me. I have come to grips with it, but it hasn't been easy. During my days in the service, I acquired mesothelioma. It's a form of cancer. I scraped asbestos insulation from pipes of transport ships overseas. You have been chosen to take my position."

"It seems I've been around people dying my whole life. I don't know if I'm bad luck or what!" Lewis lowered his head and rubbed his eyes. "Are you asking me to take care of these kids? I'm not in the best of shape either, you know!"

"I've done a lot of research on you. Lewis, you have so much to offer. You come from a broken home also. You are a borderline genius with your high IQ. You play five instruments and are a math prodigy.

These children do not need a babysitter. They are very self-sufficient. They cook, clean, have separate sleeping quarters, and report to school by themselves. If you turn them down, they will go to a foster care program where they will be separated. Lewis, I also have a large endowment for taking care of the children until they are eighteen. You need not worry about money for them or yourself. If you stay on for ten years until the youngest child graduates high school, you will inherit one million dollars from my will."

Lewis looked around and saw eight pairs of eyes silently inspecting him. "This is an awful lot for me to absorb. One million dollars in ten years? I don't need the money and wouldn't be doing it for that reason, Mags. Can I give you my decision later? What time is it, anyhow? I have no idea where I am!"

"That's fine, Lewis. Cheeto and Kyle will escort you to platform nine on the subway route to the hospital. It is four o'clock now," Mags informed him.

"Four o'clock?! I was supposed to see Emmie at ten this morning. I've been out cold all day?"

"Yes, Lewis. You were sleeping very comfortably, so you were not disturbed. Don't worry. I know Emmie has just awoken in the ICU and is being administered some liquids as we speak. Dr. Drury asked you to meet him in his office. He will get you in to see her."

Lewis stood and stretched his tall, well-built frame. The children admired his size and cut muscles. Cheeto and Kyle approached him and extended a hand for him to hold. Lewis smiled and started walking toward the door, marked with an 'Exit to street level' sign. He turned around to address Mags.

"Mags, did your brother tell you I will probably be a father?"

"Of course he did!" Mags and all the children laughed. "Look at the number of babysitters you and Emmie will have! Be on your way now!"

Lewis returned a warm smile and nodded in agreement.

"I will send a team for you tomorrow at 2 p.m., same place. Will you have a decision by then, Lewis?" Mags inquired.

"Yes, Sir, I will, Mags. But none of those crazy tricks to get me here tomorrow, okay?"

"You have my word, Lewis. You have my word," Mags assured him. Lewis turned and departed with Cheeto and Kyle. They escorted him up a steep ramp to Boston's noisy and busy streets. The bright sunshine made his eyes water as he admired the tall buildings.

Mags paced in a circle for a few moments, then addressed the remaining children. "I have some box seat tickets for tonight's game against the Yankees. Does anyone want to go?" The children broke out, screaming and clapping. "Do you know what else?" He stood and looked each child in the eye.

Maria spoke up first. "I think Lewis is going to stay with us."

"Yes, Maria. You will have a remarkable new leader soon, very soon. Keep him in your prayers tonight." Mags crouched to their level. "Come on! Let's get some of those Fenway Franks before game time and see the warm-ups. Cheeto and Kyle are meeting us there!"

The children exploded into joyous screaming. They could be heard over a quarter mile away on the deserted subway track.

Chapter Fifty-One

Cheeto and Kyle dropped Lewis at the subway platform. He found it challenging to match their swift pace.

"Here you go, Lewis. We'll see you tomorrow, right?" Kyle asked him.

Lewis was afraid of these two little kids more than facing Honch or the Gallagher brothers.

"Two o'clock tomorrow. Meet me by my car. You know where it is, right?" Lewis tried to sound confident.

This is ridiculous! Why am I trying to impress a ten-year-old? Lewis hurried down the steps underground for the next train to the hospital. He was hoping Emmie wouldn't be angry with him. He arrived ten minutes later at a large underground terminal.

Darting up the staircase, he dead-ended in a maze of hallways, confused. "Okay, there's a hospital lobby sign," he said, relieved. He ran through the front doors to the lobby desk.

"May I help you, son?" an elderly clerk asked.

"Yes, ma'am. I'm here to see Dr. Drury."

The woman looked through her Rolodex three times. "Oh, yes, Dr. Drury. It's on the fourth floor, to the left," Lewis's patience was spread pretty thin at this point. "Don't forget your badge!" she said, handing him a nametag.

"Thanks for your help," he said, but he really wanted to say, "I know where the heck he is. Just give me the darn pass!"

"You aren't alone with Dr. Drury. A distinguished gentleman and his beautiful assistant are ten minutes ahead of you," she informed Lewis. "You might have to wait."

"Thank you again, ma'am," he said politely, but he wasn't waiting for anyone. He ran down the hall just as the elevator doors were closing. He pried it open with his fingers and entered. When it stopped on the fourth floor, he bolted down the hall so fast that he overshot Dr. Drury's office.

Taking a deep breath, he calmed himself and knocked on the door. No response. He knocked again.

"Come in, please." Relief, it was Dr. Drury's voice.

Lewis opened the heavy oak door. His jaw dropped.

"Attorney Kane, Candy! What the heck?" Lewis was stunned.

Attorney Kane stood up and hugged him. Candy did the same, to the extent that her enormous breasts almost popped out from the top of her sweater, raising an eyebrow from Lewis.

"We knew you'd come here eventually!" Candy exclaimed.

"You won't believe what happened to me," Lewis said, his voice rising.

"I know every detail," Dr. Drury said. "Sit down, Lewis. Please sit."

"How's Emmie, Dr. Drury?"

"Emmie is fine and looking forward to seeing you. She got her bearings about an hour ago."

"I know what that's like!" Lewis joked.

"Pardon the interruption, Dr. Drury, but may I inform Lewis of the past day's events?" Kane asked.

"Certainly, the floor is yours," Dr. Drury replied.

"Lewis, first of all, Emmie is in the best hands here. Dr. Drury informed you that her stay will be quite extended due to the severity of her operation and rehab."

"Yes, Sir, he did."

"Lewis, you have plenty of money to last a lifetime," Kane said. "But you may have to spend it all in the next two months."

"I don't care about the money. Whatever it takes for Emmie to get better, I'm for it." Lewis almost cried.

"I realize that, Lewis. Many outside sources are willing to help you. Your bill here could be expunged if you make a couple of decisions," Attorney Kane stated while leaning over to him.

"Ex- what? What are you talking about?"

"Expunged. It means forgiven, forgotten, adios, like it never existed in the books! Got it?" He tried drilling it into Lewis.

"Why the heck would anybody do that?" Lewis thought deeply for a moment.

"Oh, I get it now. The deal Mags offered me is tied into this?"

Dr. Drury smiled and addressed Lewis. "Believe me. His offer is not the best news you'll receive today." Lewis was stumped.

Dr. Drury paused a moment. "You're going to be a father!"

"I am? Holy Smokes! Does Emmie know? Can I tell her? This unbelievable! You told me the other day it was possible but not probable."

"She showed another positive test today, Lewis. She's probably six weeks along," Dr. Drury said while shaking Lewis's hand.

"I'm on cloud nine!" Lewis belted out.

"Okay, Lewis, come out of the clouds and back to earth," Kane reminded him. "Like Jim told you, that's the best news you'll receive today. Mags offer is very generous. If you do something for someone, they'll do something for you. It's called a 'quid pro quo.'"

"Aww, come on, there you go, talking that lawyer mumbo-jumbo stuff again. A what?" Lewis asked.

"I've reviewed the terms Mags has laid out for you. Lewis, it is a great offer. But there's a very serious matter we need to discuss. Detective Ransom from Yarmouth PD is on our hides. Remember her? She's in Boston as we speak, trying to hunt us down. There's a statewide All Points Bulletin and an arrest warrant for the murder of Honch on you!"

"I didn't kill him! I could have if I wanted to. Everyone at the concrete plant saw me leave!"

"I can confirm that through the scuzzy mole informant in the bike club," Kane stated.

"Dartmouth PD can't locate any of the bikers who were at the fight or those three missing kids," he informed Lewis.

"What missing kids?" Lewis asked.

"The Gallagher brothers and Jerry Alfonso were drug dealers for Honch, right?"

"Well, I guess you can't ask Honch where they are, can you!" Lewis broke out laughing. "Who knows, maybe they pissed somebody off and vanished too!"

"Look, Detective Ransom has some backup help from the state police, some young guns who graduated from the academy. It's not long before they find you or me."

"I'm not hiding from anyone! We're in plain sight, aren't we? We haven't done anything wrong, either of us! Dr. Drury, can I please see Emmie now?" Lewis asked firmly.

"Yes, certainly, Lewis. Ted, I appreciate the information you've provided. You and Lewis are being railroaded as I was before. I thank you again for saving my practice. May we meet tomorrow afternoon? Lewis has an important decision to make."

"Definitely, Jim. How about if we meet later in the day for a few cocktails at the Iron Keg?" Ted asked his old friend.

"I may need more than a few!" Dr. Drury laughed. "Are you coming too, Candy?"

"I wouldn't miss it! Lewis is the most exciting person who's come into our office in years," she laughed.

"I won't be there, Candy," Lewis informed her. "I'm not quite eighteen yet, and I don't drink anyhow."

"I'll see you tomorrow afternoon, Ted, Candy." Dr. Drury addressed them. "Come on, Lewis, this way." They walked to the elevator and stepped in. Dr. Drury pressed the button for the fifth floor. "Lewis, let me ask you something. Is your life always this chaotic?"

"It wasn't until I met that crazy cop from Dartmouth. She's had it in for me. I admit I got in a fight with Honch, but he killed my mother. His bike gang tried to run me off, but I stood strong for my family. I've been picked on my whole life. Nobody stops me from getting what I want anymore!"

"What do you want, Lewis?" Dr. Drury asked him.

"I want to be accepted for who I am. Maybe just some peace and quiet. That's all."

"I believe you're almost there. You'll have some more high water to go through, and I hope you make it. I've never met anyone like you."

"Is it a good thing you've never met anyone like me or bad?" Lewis asked pensively.

"Lewis, you're the finest person to come through those hospital doors. Don't ever forget it! There's just one more thing, Lewis," Dr. Drury requested. "Well, actually, two things."

"What's that, Sir?"

"We don't tell Emmie she's pregnant yet, okay? You can tell her tomorrow night if another blood test comes back positive. And also, don't mention anything about Mags. We have to go easy on her."

"I understand, Sir. That may be the final bomb if I tell her I'm inheriting eight orphans, too!"

"Come on." Dr. Drury put his arm around Lewis as they exited the elevator. "We don't want to get her rebuilt ticker beating too fast with this great news, right?"

"Let's go see my wife-to-be, okay?" Lewis said.

"Ohhh, so she's your wife now?" Drury laughed and gave Lewis a friendly shove.

"Only if she'll have me. Emmie has no idea what's in store for her!"

The elevator door started to open. Dr. Drury held his hand on the side so it wouldn't close. "Lewis, there's something else I've been meaning to tell you."

"What's that, Sir?"

"You know, I've never been married or had kids. I've been busy with my career and helping Mags with his family. I just wanted to say if I ever had a son, I'd want him to be just like you," Dr. Drury admitted.

"Well, I'll take that as a compliment, but there's a lot you don't know about me, Sir." Lewis focused his eyes sharply on Dr. Drury. "I hate to use a cliché, but you'd better be careful what you wish for."

Chapter Fifty-Two

Where the hell am I? Ransom scratched her head as she looked at a map. *These directions are crazy!* She was on Franklin Street, but the house was boarded up. There was plywood on the front door and two lower windows. She pulled over and used her bag phone to call Foley's friend.

"Cobblestone Pub," a booming voice answered.

"Hello, is this Tommy with the apartment?"

"Yeah, this is Tommy. Who's this?" he shouted over the many boisterous patrons getting primed for the Red Sox game.

"Detective Ransom from Yarmouth PD. Sergeant Foley said you had a free room for the week, but the house is boarded up," she yelled stridently. "I can't get in!"

"Oh yeah, yeah. Foley mentioned that. There's no key under the mat in front of the door?"

"There's no front door at all! It's just plywood!"

"Oh yeah, that's right. My contractor is putting in a new door and windows. Let me check with him. He's sitting two stools down from me," Tommy informed her. "Hey Marty, Shawn, youze guys didn't get that door in Franklin Street yet?"

"Nah, nah, remembah? You gave us deze game tickets last night! You musta been really hammid if you can't remembah!" he said in a heavy Boston accent as everyone around them laughed.

Tommy slapped his knee and belted, "Oh, shit, yeah! Now I remembah!"

Ransom shook her head. *What did I get myself into this time?*

"You can still get into the apartment. Just take the next alley on the right. There's a parking lot behind the building. What kinda cah ya got?" Tommy asked.

"It's an unmarked Crown Vic from Yarmouth PD. Will it fit down the alley?"

"Just barely. It's not trash pickup day, so you're in the clear."

"Oh, great!" Ransom said sarcastically.

"One other thing," Tommy paused. "The apartment is on the second floor."

"Yeah, so?"

"There ain't any stairs to the second floor. It's apartment 2A. You'll have to use the fire escape ladder to get up there. The kitchen window is always unlocked." Ransom heard a bunch of background laughter again.

"Are you kidding me?"

"Nope, and there's no way these guys are gonna put that door in today or the next three days. You'll never find a hotel room within ten miles of here either!"

"I know because of the baseball game!" she yelled back.

"I hope you weigh at least a hundred and fifty pounds, cuz otherwise you'll never be able to pull that ladder down on the fire escape!" Tommy laughed as his friends around him did too.

"Let me tell you something here, Tommy. I'm six feet tall, stocky and vivacious, not dainty. I'm more of a roller derby-type girl than a fucking nail-polished beauty queen. I have a .45 on one hip and a concealed snub-nose .38 below my tits, so I don't think there'll be any problem pulling your fire escape ladder down. Got me?" Ransom said firmly.

"Ahh, just my type of woman!" Tommy laughed. "When can we meet?"

"I do appreciate you letting me stay in your place, Tommy. This has been an awkward start. I apologize." Ransom swallowed hard. "Sergeant Foley gave you a big thumbs up, and I do too. Thanks again."

"I'll have my men ovah theyah first thing in the mawnin' so you can use the front daw, okay? I promise!" Tommy assured her.

"Don't worry about it, Tommy. Maybe we'll have a drink together some night at your fun bar?"

"Sure! Cops are always welcome here, but no sidearms! You might shoot after meeting me! I hope you catch your bad guy," Tommy laughed.

"Gotcha loud and clear, Tommy. This kid could probably rule Walpole Prison after I put him away!" She ended the call.

Oh, my gosh! Did that really happen? What else can go wrong today?

She pulled her Crown Vic into a small alley and took a right into a rather large parking lot for the tenants.

Ransom looked around and took in the sights. She was quite impressed. Two rows of three-story buildings surrounded her for a quarter-mile on each side. A nice grassy area with gardens and play equipment for children separated the backyards. Clotheslines were strung between row houses on each floor. Women were leaning from their back windows, chatting with friendly neighbors next to and across the way. Children of every race were playing with each other on finely manicured lawns.

Wow, is this what a city is all about? Ransom parked her car in the spot that said 2A.

She looked at the fire escape ladder she would have to scale. Someone pulled it down already. It was a set of rickety iron stairs scabbed onto the side of the building.

What a perfect spot for a police chase. Me, jumping from one staircase to another, just like in the movies! Chasing a hardened criminal hanging on for dear life with one hand and then being rescued by Clint Eastwood! She laughed.

"May I help you, ma'am?" an older, robust man asked through the car window, snapping her from this daydream.

"Well, I don't know. You kind of caught me off guard. I'm staying in Tommy's apartment on the second floor. I see the staircase has been pulled down."

"Yes, it has. I'm Luther, the maintenance man for his building. I think the contractors doing the repairs to the front have disappeared because there's a...."

"I know," Ransom laughed. "Yankees and Red Sox game the next three nights! I didn't know the city could be brought to a complete standstill!"

"You aren't from around here, are you?" He laughed too. "Why don't you climb up to the landing, and I'll throw your bags to you," Luther offered.

"Oh no, I'll just leave them here for now. I can handle it. This is an interesting place you have, Luther."

"I've called it home for fifty years. Tommy bought the building twenty-five years ago. He's done a remarkable job restoring this landmark to its fine brownstone condition."

"I'm sorry I haven't introduced myself. I'm Detective Ransom from Yarmouth Police Department. Please call me Pat."

"Pat? You remind me of a magpie bird. From the minute it wakes up, it doesn't stop chirping and singing!" he joked.

"I've been called worse, but that's me! Exactly! How did you know?" They both laughed. "I'm here on police business. We're looking for a murder suspect from Cape Cod. He's laying low in Boston somewhere."

"Boston's a big city, ma'am. Lots of nooks and crannies to hide under," Luther informed her.

"I'm going to let him come to me. I know where he's going."

"Well, stay safe and good luck to you. This city can gobble anyone and make them disappear, including you!"

"Thank you, Luther. I'll let you know if I need a boost getting up to the second floor."

"No offense, ma'am, but it looks like you're rugged enough to climb that ladder just fine."

Luther turned around and disappeared into the cellar of the building through an old bulkhead.

This place never ceases to amaze me! She had to get the phone plugged into an outlet soon, or it would go dead. She climbed up the ladder with ease, just like at the Academy. She steadied her feet on the thin steel landing. Tommy was right—the window was unlocked. She slipped her large frame in through the window.

She looked around at the old brick walls and beams, admiring the beautiful, high ceilings. *Wow, this place is dynamite! I could live here!* She plugged the suitcase phone into a wall socket. Feeling wiped out, she decided to get some shut-eye. She spotted a comfy couch, laid down, and kicked her shoes off before falling into a deep sleep. It wasn't long before her bag phone started ringing and vibrating.

"Yarmouth 20, Detective Ransom, here," she addressed the caller.

"Buzz Maxwell, State Police here, Pat."

"That didn't take long, Buzz. What's up?"

"I'm sending those two recruits your way into Boston. They should be in town around seven tonight."

"That's great, Buzz. I just got my accommodations straightened out here. It would be fine to meet them tomorrow morning somewhere."

"That's great because they have tickets to the...."

Ransom interrupted him. "I know, I know. The baseball game, right?" she laughed.

"Are you going? It's going to be a heck of a series. They're tied for first place. I'd give my left nut to go!"

"Ah, well, that's a little too much information for me, Buzz!"

"They'll call you at 0800 tomorrow morning. I gave them your number," Buzz informed her. "You can advise them of your game plan then."

"Game plan? I don't have one yet, but I'm sure it'll come to me," she admitted.

"I hope you have something by tomorrow. These boys are pretty gun-ho! I've briefed them on this murder suspect, and they're amped."

"Don't worry, Buzz. I'm sure something in the loop will show up. Thanks again. Yarmouth 20, over and out."

Ransom was correct in her thinking. Something was about to show up, and it would be the surprise of her life.

Chapter Fifty-Three

Oh, great! Two gun-ho cadets were coming her way, and she didn't have a game plan. *Kline was right.* She's going to look like the biggest idiot cop from Cape Cod without pictures of Lewis Duncan *or* Attorney Kane! *No wonder Kline bailed on me.*

Starving her ass off, she went to the refrigerator and peeked inside. It was empty. She noticed a corner deli with a Budweiser sign on a storefront earlier. *I could drink down a six-pack in one gulp.*

She slid down the fire escape ladder and walked through the alley toward Franklin Street.

Upon turning the corner, crowds of pedestrians dressed in Red Sox and Yankee garb made their way to the infamous Fenway Park. Admiring the camaraderie between fans, she felt she was missing something living on that forsaken sandbar.

Vendors were selling pizza, and subs on street corners filled the area with delectable, aroma-filled smoke. She went into the deli and studied the menu board. A tall, rugged, handsome worker with long wavy hair behind the counter approached her. She was still looking up at the menu, trying to decide as the worker ogled her stunning features.

"Ma'am, may I help you? Something to order, perhaps?" he asked politely.

She broke her focus on the board. "Yes, I'll have a…." Ransom looked into the darkest pair of brown eyes she had ever seen. A dark five-o'clock shadow exaggerated the man's soft skin. His stout, cleft chin was so defined you could bounce a rock off it.

"Ma'am, something to order? There are people behind you." He spoke in a beautiful accent she had never heard before. Her inner thighs were quivering.

"I'm so sorry," she apologized. "I didn't mean to hold up the line. You have so much to offer. I'll have a large Italian sub with everything on it, plenty of hots too, please."

"Anything to drink, ma'am?" he asked with a crooked smile.

She went blank again, trying to read his nametag. Antonio, of course! What hunk of an Italian stud wouldn't be named Antonio?

"Ma'am? Something to drink?" he asked again.

"I'm sorry, it's been a long day. I'll have a six-pack of Bud cans and a bottle of red wine on the second shelf, please," Ransom said so weakly; she thought she was melting.

"Having a party tonight?" Antonio asked. "You must be off duty. I see you've turned the badge around on your belt."

"My, you are very observant, aren't you?" Ransom pretended to read his name tag, "Antonio. What a sweet name."

"I can also see you are not with Boston PD, no?" Antonio remarked.

"How can you tell?" she asked him.

"Ma'am, I am embarrassed for what I am about to tell you, but you're unbuttoned to below your – ahem," he cleared his throat as he pointed to her open shirt. "I can see your gun. Boston PD does not carry .38 snub-nosed weapons. My brother is on the force."

She looked down, seeing her shirt unbuttoned. Most of her bra and holster were showing. She turned beet-red and smiled at Antonio.

Stepping aside to let other people order, she casually buttoned her blouse and waited for her sub to cook. *What a frigging idiot I am! No wonder everyone was smiling at me on the street!*

She stepped outside for some air, watching the seemingly endless crowd of people heading to the ballpark.

"Antonio, get moving," a man yelled from the kitchen. "The line is out the door!"

"Yes, Papa," Antonio replied.

"One large Italian, everything on it, one six of Bud, and a wine is ready!" he shouted.

As she went up to the cash register, her heart fluttered at the thought of facing Antonio again.

"That'll be seven dollars and ninety-five cents, please."

"You must be mistaken. Eight dollars for all that?"

"Yes, ma'am. That'll be seven dollars and ninety-five cents. If I can see you again, your debt to Gino's is forgiven."

"I feel like such an idiot," Ransom stated. "Are you sure?"

"Please don't hold up the line again, ma'am." He smiled.

She put a twenty on the counter and started to walk away before turning around. "I'll be back tomorrow for dinner again. Perhaps I'll see you?" Ransom asked seductively.

"I'll be covering the lunch crowd until two. My brother canceled on me for the Sox game tomorrow afternoon. Would you like to go?"

"Are you kidding? That sounds like a blast! I'll be in around 2:30 or 3, maybe, I'm hoping?" Antonio thought she sounded a little doubtful. "I have a surveillance case going on. I'm sorry. I haven't introduced myself." Instinctively, she almost prefaced her name with 'Detective.' "I'm Pat, Pat Ransom."

"Antonio Martinetti at your service, Pat. I'll see you at two-thirty sharp tomorrow. Next in line, please!" Antonio yelled to everyone.

Ransom walked toward the door and put a little extra pep in her step, something Antonio certainly noticed. She left the deli and mingled with a rowdy sea of fans heading to the game. She was smiling to herself. Some women even put their arms around her, "Going to the game, sweetie?" they happily asked.

Pat Ransom hadn't been this euphoric in months. No, probably years! She had a few meaningless relationships with men on the Cape and Academy but never felt this way before. Maybe it was the hot city air, she thought.

She had some soul-searching to do. She was almost a hundred miles from home chasing Lewis Duncan and wondered why she had a vendetta against him.

I feel like a damn monkey! She thought as she climbed the fire escape to her apartment and opened the window. But she didn't mind this minor inconvenience.

She opened a Bud and downed it in two gulps. She put the rest in the refrigerator and saved the wine for something special.

She looked at the bag phone as the oven heated for her sub. "Fuck sake! Three missed calls! That's Foley's number from Boston PD! Shit, I'd better get on the horn!"

She unplugged the phone from the wall, but it was only ten percent charged. *That should be enough for one call.* She redialed Foley's number.

"Sergeant Foley, here."

"Jake, it's Pat Ransom. Sorry, I missed your calls, but I grabbed a bite to eat," Ransom apologized.

"You're in luck. I just put my coat on and was going out the door to the Sox game!" Foley told her. "One of our interns did some research on hospitals in Boston."

"Great! Do you have any good info?" Ransom asked.

"There are only three hospitals in Beantown that specialize in heart procedures. Two are centers with hundreds of patients from all over the world." Foley stated.

"Yeah, so?" Ransom inquired.

"Sarah checked with the smallest one first, Saint Peters Deacon. It's right off the Southeast Expressway near you. They perform medical procedures at an absolute cost to the patient. Most doctors volunteer their time," Foley informed her. "But get this, some patients are foreign dignitaries or movie stars. They usually make a huge donation to the hospital as long as it is on the hush while they stay there." Foley paused a moment. "And get this, a teenage girl checked in yesterday for a major heart operation."

"Keep going!"

"You're not gonna believe this, but she's from Yarmouth, on the Cape!"

"*Bingo!* That's it! I don't believe it! How could some poor cowpoke girl even get admitted to that hospital?"

"I have no clue. She must have known someone."

"Yeah, she knows my fugitive! That's the best news I've heard in weeks, and I know my suspect will show up there. You're unbelievable! Thanks, Jake!"

"There's just one more thing, Pat," Foley requested.

"Anything, Jake, anything."

"Don't go shooting up my town! You hear me?"

Ransom thought for a moment, knowing who was on their way from the state police. "I'll try, Jake."

"I'm holding your ass accountable. Remember that!" Jake hung up the phone.

Ransom took her sub from the oven and cracked another beer. *I've got Lewis Duncan now!* She put her feet on the coffee table, devoured the sub, and burped. *That hit the spot!*

She unfolded her map of Boston and looked for the hospital. Sure enough, there it was, just two blocks away. She could walk there!

Thinking it called for a celebration, she cracked another beer. The six-pack was almost gone! *Who the hell drank them?*

Ransom crawled out the kitchen window to the landing and rested her arms on the railing. Barbecue smoke, grilled onions, and peppers were making her mouth water. She couldn't believe it, a city within a city. Kids were playing in their backyards. The clanging of numerous horse-shoe pits filled the air.

Everyone was so happy! *Who knew this place could exist?* Snapping from her holistic experience, she looked toward a nearly full moon rising above the city houses. Ransom raised her beer skyward, "Lewis Duncan? Prepare. Your days of freedom are over!" She felt the effects of six beers and staggered along the shaky landing toward the kitchen window. After going inside, she passed out quickly on the sofa.

Her phone rang loudly at eight a.m. precisely the following day, waking her from a deep dream.

"This is Detective Ransom." She spoke lowly with a slight hangover.

"Officer Feazel here, ma'am, State Police. I also have with me another officer. We've been assigned to help you locate a fugitive from Cape Cod?" he asked quizzically.

"Yes, thank you very much for taking time from your normal duties. I understand you both graduated from the Academy. That's great!"

"Thank you kindly. We're ready to roll. Where should we meet to discuss apprehending the fugitive?" Officer Feazel asked.

"I'm staying at 36 Franklin Street. There's a deli on the corner with a large parking lot for the baseball games. I'll meet you there at nine a.m., copy?"

"Loud and clear, nine a.m. next to a deli near 36 Franklin Street. State Trooper Feazel, over and out."

"I'll be in a grey unmarked Crown Vic," Ransom added. "Yarmouth 20, out."

She hung up the phone and plugged the cord in to charge it. She stared into a bedroom mirror, admiring her rugged and vivacious physique. *Are you ready for this, Pat?*

Chapter Fifty-Four

Detective Ransom felt apprehensive about dragging two rookies into the big city for an unclear assignment. She jumped from the shower and put on some black pants. A sharp-looking gray blazer added a nice touch to a white shirt. She concealed a holster that carried the .38 in her favorite spot. She adjusted her wardrobe and slid down the ladder to the parking lot.

Opening up the trunk, she put her .45 in a gun safe bolted to the frame of the car. *You'll be fine there until I need you, baby.* She closed the safe and double locks on the trunk.

Ransom started the V-8 Interceptor engine. Its deep rumble from dual exhaust echoed through the alley, scaring every tomcat within a hundred feet. She tried to exit quietly, but these big motors were not meant to idle without protest. They were built for high-speed pursuit at full throttle. She coasted down the alley and hooked a right toward the deli only three hundred feet away.

She pulled into the half-full parking lot. An extremely handsome attendant greeted her. "G'mawnin', ma'am. That'll be twenty dollahs for game pahkin' tonight," the young man told her.

"I'm not here for the game," she said and showed her badge. "I'm meeting some officers from the state police here. I don't have to pay, do I? Can you let me slide? We'll be only about ten minutes."

"You're not going to the game tonight? We snuffed the Yankees last night! Okay, that's fine, officer. The boys you're meeting are already heah, pahked over theyah." He pointed toward an empty State Police cruiser in the corner. "I think they went into Antonio's Deli."

"Wait a minute. You said, boys? And do you know Antonio?" Ransom fired off.

"Antonio? Yeah, he's my first cousin!" the attendant gave her an intimidating sexy grin.

"I see a striking resemblance. You are both very handsome! And actually, I met Antonio last night when I had a sub there. It was delicious! But you said — boys?"

"Yeah, yeah. They pulled in heah looking tough and official, but aftah they got out of the cruisah, I thought they were two Cub Scouts!"

"Oh, man, what have I gotten myself into?" Ransom asked loudly.

"I don't know ma'am, but my cousin, Antonio is a real lady's man. Know what I mean? He wears cologne with those pheromones and stuff that make women drool over him!" The attendant laughed. "Better look out!"

"Well, I guess that cologne worked on me. I'm going to the game today with him!"

"No way! That's you? He was talking about you last night at Billy's Bar! Thousands of people on the streets heah, and I meet you! Very pleased to meet you, ma'am. I'm Victor."

"I'm Detective – oh forget that. I'm Pat, Pat Ransom. I live on the Cape but am here on police business. I wish I could leave my car here and "pahty" with you!"

The attendant laughed at her cheap imitation of a Boston accent. "You pahk your cah right ovah theya, next to the gahd shack. I'll watch your cah while you meet up with those boys." He laughed again.

"Maybe I'll see you after the game tonight at Billy's. It's Antonio's call," she replied.

"Oh, I doubt it! After watching the Red Sox, and he has a spell on you, I doubt you'll be going to any bah!"

"We'll see about that!" Ransom laughed. "Thanks for the parking spot, Victor."

She arrived at the lot fifteen minutes early. It was approaching nine a.m. Ransom backed her cruiser into the spot next to the guard shack and got out. She leaned on the hood and observed the deli.

Sure enough, two very small men, barely five feet tall, dressed in State Police uniforms, exited the deli. Each was eating a breakfast sandwich of some type.

"Man, that walk-off home run for the Sox last night was unbelievable. Wasn't it, Roley? I've never seen it in person!"

"Sure was, man. I need these muffins to soak up those beers from last night!" Both officers laughed as they sat on a bench consuming their sandwiches. They filled each other in on every girl they wanted to bang last night.

"Hey, Roley, where do you think that bird is that we're supposed to meet from the Cape? She's late!"

"Yeah, really, it figures! Most dames I know are never on time or stand me up."

"You deserve it!"

Ransom heard every word they said and had enough. She unfolded her badge from her blazer and walked sternly toward the two seated officers.

"Uh, oh. You think that's the cop from Cape Cod walking over here?" Roley whispered. "She looks like a friggin' monster!"

"I think that's her, and I bet she heard everything we said!"

Ransom stopped about five feet away. "Hello, boys! I didn't know Sergeant Maxwell was sending two cadets from junior high school!"

Officer Feazel stood up, wiping some crumbs from his mouth. "I'm State Trooper Kevin Feazel. You must be Detective Ransom."

The other officer spoke up. "Officer Roland Topping, but you can call me Roley. Ma'am, don't let our size fool you. We are fully certified state troopers."

"Our police department in Yarmouth has a minimum height requirement of five feet ten inches for men and five-six for women. Both of you are barely five feet tall!" Ransom laughed.

"We're much taller than that! I'm five-two," Roley stated proudly.

"And I'm five-foot-three," Feazel informed her.

"Well, the fugitive we're after is six-foot-seven and has already killed the president of Cape Cod's most notorious biker gang. Spencer Plant was almost seven feet tall! Lewis Duncan is also a suspect in the disappearance of three drug dealers from Yarmouth. He has an accomplice, a renegade lawyer who served in Viet Nam for eight years. Theodore Kane is a third-degree Black Belt and has ties to the mob. His six-foot-tall bombshell secretary could probably eat both of you for lunch! Do you know what you're getting yourselves into?"

"Detective Ransom, I realize you think we may be unfit for this assignment, but me and Roley took the height restriction requirement for State Police to the Supreme Court and won. Just because we're small does not diminish our obligations to the citizens of Massachusetts!" Officer Feazel stated firmly.

She wiped her brow and took a few steps backward while trying to decipher the situation.

"Do either of you have any felony arrests?"

"Well, no, not yet."

"Have you done surveillance?"

"No, not really."

"What about a traffic stop, a fucking traffic stop?"

"No. We graduated just last week," Officer Topping admitted.

"Maxwell sent me some greenhorns that I have to train? Look, this is how it's going down. Today we're conducting surveillance at Saint Peter's Deacon Hospital to see if our suspect shows up. His girlfriend is a patient for a heart operation. I know he can't stay away from her."

"Sounds pretty easy. We're ready for anything this punk can throw at us," Feazel claimed.

"Anything? You don't know what this kid is capable of. He's also a suspect in the murder of an eighty-five-year-old man!"

"That crosses the line for me, Roley. How about you?"

"That does it for me, too, Kev. I'm all in, guns a-blazing!"

"That's what scares me about you two. I have eight years of seniority over both of you. I will always go in first so you don't get your little asses blown off! Lewis Duncan has never been known to carry a weapon, but his lawyer friend is believed to be heavily armed."

"How did he kill all these people without a gun? The APB said he was armed," Roley asked.

"His brutality, he's a freak of nature! He must be stopped at any cost. He has the strength of five men and could toss you fifteen feet. I may have stretched the truth a little on the APB," Ransom admitted.

Roley swallowed deeply, wondering what they were signing up for.

"He must be taken out," Officer Feazel declared firmly.

"This is the plan for today. We're going to Saint Peter's and keeping our eyes open." Ransom informed her two anxious mercenaries. "We'll be waiting for Lewis Duncan to show up. At that time, we'll evaluate how he'll be taken into custody."

"Do you have a poster of him?" Officer Feazel asked.

"A wanted poster? Are you shitting me? He doesn't have any pictures of himself on record; no high school, no license, no nothing. He's invisible! You'll follow me to the hospital and park your cruiser in the farthest spot you can from the main entrance. I'll do the same. Feazel, you'll cover the front door. There's a bench nearby you can sit your ass on to watch for him. Topping, cover the subway tunnel entrance next to the main lobby. It leads to the underground rail. And don't get lost, either of you!"

"What does he even look like, our suspect?" Officer Topping asked.

"He's over six-foot-six, brown hair, with a large, fresh scar on his cheek which may still have a bandage and easily identify him. He also walks with an unusual gait due to many disabilities as a child."

"What, we're after a cripple?" Officer Topping asked.

"Don't underestimate him. He's smarter than a fox and will outwit us to avoid being taken."

"I'm going into the hospital to dig up some Intel on his girlfriend, got it? I have three walkie-talkies on the same channel in the trunk of my cruiser. Stay close. This Boston traffic is a nightmare."

"We got it. How about we rendezvous at our vehicles around noon in the parking lot?" Officer Feazel asked.

"Good idea, Officer Feazel. And change out of those uniforms into some civilian clothes. Do you have any? If he spots anything, he'll rabbit."

"What the heck does that mean, rabbit?" Officer Topping asked.

"You have to be shitting me! Run, rabbit, run? Like a damn rabbit? Who am I dealing with here?" Ransom sighed. She hopped into her cruiser and gave the parking lot attendant a big smile. "Tell Antonio I'll be at the deli by 2:30 for the game if you see him. I hope!"

Ransom drove a safe distance ahead but close enough so she wouldn't lose the rookie cops. She approached the guard shack in the hospital parking lot and pulled out her badge. Officers Feazel and Topping were right on her tail.

"Hi there, Sir. Our two vehicles are here on police business. Can we get one ticket and square up tomorrow? We may be here a few days," Ransom asked the feeble attendant. He certainly appreciated the show he was getting with her partially unbuttoned shirt and exposed cleavage.

"Sure, ma'am, there's never a charge for officers, park where you'd like." It was the same attendant who'd given Lewis a hard time. Both cars went to the rear of the lot.

"Give us a few minutes so we can change out of our uniforms," Officer Topping yelled from inside their car. They took their assigned positions at the hospital.

Ransom departed her vehicle after making a few notes and walked the half-mile trek into admissions. The line inside was ten people deep. She didn't want to pull rank on anyone, so she waited for almost a half-hour.

"Yes, ma'am, may I help you?" the front desk clerk asked.

"Hi, I see your name is Jeanie. I'm here on police business." Ransom produced her badge.

"Oh, my! We don't get much of that here!" Jeanie stated.

"I suppose not, which is a good thing, right? I need some information on a patient. Maybe you can help?"

"I wish I could help you," she said, then paused. "And your name?"

"I'm sorry, Detective Ransom."

"And your badge again, please?"

Ransom frowned and showed her badge again.

"Oh, my dear! You're not with Boston PD?"

"No, ma'am. I'm from Cape Cod and searching for a fugitive. We have reason to believe he may show up here. The patient's name is Emmie. She's from Cape Cod, too. She may have had a heart procedure."

"Detective – uh, what was it again?"

"Ransom, R-A-N-S-O-M, as it sounds, just like I'm holding you for ransom!"

"Sorry to disappoint you, Ms. Ransom, but there are over three hundred patients in this hospital. It would take all day for me to look up that information. Even if I could give it to you, I can't. You know, we have privacy laws since the terrorist attack at the Olympics? Do you have a room number?"

"No, I don't have a room number! Is there anyone I can talk to in the cardiac unit? It's important." Ransom begged her.

"The head physician will be in surgery until noon and then has patient consultations for an hour after that," Jeanie informed her.

"Can I make an appointment to see him? What's his name?"

"I can't guarantee that you'll be able to see Dr. Drury, but I'll pencil you in for one o'clock, okay?"

"That would be great, Jeanie. Thank you." That might leave enough time to meet Antonio by 2:30, Ransom thought.

"Check in here at 12:50, and I will have security bring you to the fourth floor."

Security? I'm a cop! She took a seat in the admissions lobby. Removing her walkie-talkie from the holster, she pressed the button to speak.

"Yarmouth 20, Ransom to State Police Feazel, come in." She repeated herself three times but got no response.

An out-of-shape aging man in a black uniform noticed her frustration and approached her. "Can I be of some assistance, ma'am? I'm Charlie, head of security."

"You're head of security?" Ransom almost laughed. "I'm a detective from Cape Cod trying to reach my fellow officers here in the hospital."

"That contraption will never work in here. There's too much concrete and steel in this building. Plus, we jam all electronic devices." He laughed. "Are you a rookie in training with Boston PD?"

"No, Sir, I'm not. I guess you didn't hear me. I'm Detective Ransom from Yarmouth, Cape Cod."

"My apologies, ma'am. I was exposed to a lot of gunfire in the service. I can hardly hear anything, even my wife!"

Ransom felt a little embarrassed. "Funny you should ask if I'm a rookie, though. I'm with two from the state police who belong in the motor pool!"

"What are you doing here?" he asked her.

"Long story. I won't bore you, but I'm waiting to see Dr. Drury later today."

"Well, good luck to you and everyone else! You have to be pretty special to get an appointment. By the way, I've been here twenty years since I retired from Edison Power."

Holy shit! The guard had to be at least eighty if he retired twenty years ago.

"I know every square inch of this hospital," he went on. "Cameras and call buttons every fifty feet go directly to Boston PD."

"Why the high security, Charlie?"

"You may not know it, but royalty and movie stars from around the world come for their operations here. Dr. Drury and his brother founded this hospital twenty years ago and are quite the philanthropists."

"You're pulling my leg, right?"

"Nope! You must know someone special if you're seeing Dr. Drury later!"

"Oh, he's special, all right! I can't wait to meet him! Maybe I'll see you later on before my appointment?"

"Oh, no! I work only four hours a day. Well, I have to be making my rounds, ma'am. Nice meeting you." Charlie rose slowly from the chair beside Ransom with assistance from her shoulder.

How the heck did some girl from Cape Cod get an offer to come to this hospital? She had to find those two cub scouts before they got into trouble. *I'm going to regret ever coming here.* There had to be a larger piece of this puzzle she was missing.

It was time for Ransom to check in with Officers Feazel and Topping. She patrolled the parking lot until lunchtime when they met up. They didn't spot anything except many hot nurses and were dying to get their phone numbers.

"Detective Ransom, Detective Ransom! You're not going to believe this, but I think we found that brown Impala you described," Officer Feazel yelled out.

"You've got to be kidding me. Here, in this parking lot?"

"Yes! It's in the first row, parked in a doctor's spot. Someone named Dr. Drury!"

"Well, isn't that a coincidence? I have an appointment with Dr. Drury at one p.m. to shed some light on this mysterious patient named Emmie. Good work, Officer Feazel."

"This may be a stupid question, but why don't we confiscate the patient register and find out what room she's in?" asked Officer Topping.

"Don't you know what protocol is? We can't bust in and confiscate patient info! We're not in your or my jurisdiction here. Boston PD has a lot of clout here! They have an invisible hand in the security of this joint. Take an hour off in the cafeteria. I'll catch up with you in the main lobby around one-thirty after I meet with Dr. Drury."

"Yes, ma'am. Lobby, one-thirty. We'll keep our eyes peeled," Officer Feazel stated.

"Officer Feazel, that's what worries me!" Ransom laughed and gave him a departing pat on the back.

Chapter Fifty-Five

It was pure luck, but Lewis crossed paths with Detective Ransom just seconds after she left the hospital lobby.

Lewis went to Dr. Drury's office and quickly exited Emmie's room with him. They approached a viewing area with a small window opening, just large enough for Lewis to peek in. "She's sitting up drinking something!" he yelled in excitement. Emmie heard his voice through the door and radiated an ear-to-ear smile. Tears rose in her eyes. "Can't I go in? Just for a minute?" he begged.

Dr. Drury looked at him and shook his head. "Let me get a mask for you, but only three minutes! Hear me?" he commanded.

"Yes, Sir. Yes, Sir! You can make it two minutes if you have to. That's great!"

Lewis put his mask on and went through the door behind Dr. Drury. Emmie raised her arms to embrace Lewis but winced in pain immediately.

"I'm okay, Lewis! They're great in here. I'm a little sore and weak. Once I get some solid food in me, I'll be fine."

Lewis sat beside her on a small chair. He didn't have any words as he reached for her hand, only a smile behind his mask.

"I've been so worried about you!" He managed to say.

"I bet you didn't sleep a wink last night!"

"Oh, if you only knew!" he laughed and gave Dr. Drury a wink.

"Looks like you two are the best of friends already!" Emmie noticed slyly.

Dr. Drury interrupted her. "Emmie, your vitals are very stable. They're great! I attribute your condition to strong physical stamina before the operation."

"I did walk almost two miles every other day for a couple of months. Lewis made me!" She laughed but startled herself with some pain.

"Your incision and rib cage will take months to heal, but you'll be fine, Emmie. You certainly have a great guy here to take care of you."

"Emmie, unfortunately, my time is up," Lewis said. "Dr. Drury let me in for a moment, but I'll be here every day outside your door until you can walk with me, okay? I'll see you tonight and look through the window. I have something to do this afternoon, and he wanted you to rest all day without any interruptions." Lewis needed to be somewhat elusive.

"Your social calendar is booked already?"

"Dr. Drury told me you need the rest, that's all." Lewis fibbed. "I'll be in for the seven o'clock visiting hour."

"Ahh, yes, Emmie. You need quite a bit of rest and nourishment, and we have a few tests scheduled for you later today." Dr. Drury told her a tiny lie of his own, too.

"Okay," she grumbled. "I'll see you tonight. Can Lewis talk to me by phone?"

"That will be fine, Emmie. But there's a ten-minute limit," he advised her.

"That's super!" Lewis exclaimed. "I won't bug her, I promise!" They laughed, even the nurse. Lewis blew her a kiss as he left the room and took his mask off. He sat on a bench in the hall. Dr. Drury closed the door quietly and sat beside him.

"I'm wiped out," Lewis said. "I didn't think this much confusion and excitement could happen to a person in a lifetime, never mind two months!"

"I don't know how you've done it. I realize you have a big decision looming over your head about my brother's proposition," Dr. Drury reminded him.

"Yes, I didn't dare say anything to Emmie about it. I'd probably kill her with that news!"

"You're right. Emmie will be in ICU for at least three weeks and possibly four more in rehab. Lewis, I wouldn't say anything to her for a while about your predicament. It'll be enough of a shock to her if she's pregnant."

"Oh, great!" Lewis exclaimed. "I have to keep it a secret? Can we tell her tonight?"

"Maybe, hold off on telling her about your decision with Mags, but I know what it is already."

"What, that I may be inheriting eight kids for ten years? It's a lot for me to fathom, Dr. Drury. She hoped to attend college this fall. Now that's on hold until spring if we have a baby on the way. Shouldn't she know this? I have enough money tucked away to last twenty years, never mind what Mags wants to give me. And now I've got some cop from Yarmouth breathing down my neck! What the heck should I do?" Lewis begged for answers.

"Lewis, from my understanding, your whole life has been one upheaval, right? You have made more decisions as a young man than most adult men make their entire lives. You are a remarkable person, and I'm sure Emmie will understand any decision you make."

Lewis sat in deep thought. "Easy for you say, Doc. What time is it anyhow?"

Dr. Drury rolled his sleeve up, "It's 12:45, and I haven't eaten a thing since last night! How about lunch? I'm buying."

"12:45? Holy crap! I'm supposed to be at my car by 2:00 to meet Cheeto! I haven't made up my mind yet!"

"Lewis, I have an appointment at one o'clock, so I'd better be on my way. I doubt I'll see you tonight when you visit Emmie. Good luck with your decision."

Dr. Drury stood from the bench and returned to his office. Lewis put his head between his hands, going into deep thought. He walked to the end of the hall and studied the floor directory. The infant nursery was on the second floor. It was only one floor down, so he took the staircase instead of the elevator. He proceeded down the hall to a glass wall. He stopped about five feet away and gazed into a room where ten babies were sleeping. A nurse was monitoring each baby. He was mesmerized. Had he fit in one of those things a long time ago?

"Which one is yours?" a woman standing by the window asked.

"Who, me? Oh no, I'm just admiring the infants. My girlfriend is in ICU."

The small woman pointed to a pink bassinet in the last row. "That's my baby girl. This hospital saved her life."

Lewis didn't know what to say.

"She's four months old, but she's going to make it thanks to Dr. Drury and his team. I don't owe a dime, either. My debt was totally forgiven."

What type of deal was she offered? Lewis wondered.

"He operated on my girlfriend, too! What's her name, your daughter?"

"Shay, it's Shay."

"That's beautiful," he replied and then thought for a moment. "I think I misled you. I said I didn't have a child, but my girlfriend's pregnant. It hasn't hit me yet." Lewis paused and changed the subject. "Can you smell them? I love that fresh, new baby smell."

"You can smell the babies through the glass? Your senses must be a lot stronger than mine!" she laughed. "I'm sure it will take a while before everything sinks in. Your girlfriend will be fine. She's in the best of hands here. Well, I must be going—nice meeting you. And your name is?" she asked kindly.

"Lewis, Lewis Duncan from Cape Cod."

"I'm Opie, kind of short for Ophelia. I wish you well, Lewis."

She turned and slowly dragged her finger across the glass as if pointing to her sleeping daughter as she drifted toward the elevator.

This brief encounter shook Lewis. He suddenly questioned his mortality and past decisions he made and one he had to make. Every day of his life and corner he turned yielded a new challenge. Would it ever end? The next few hours would decide that fate for him.

Chapter Fifty-Six

An enormous security officer brought Detective Ransom to Dr. Drury's office at one o'clock sharp. He never said a word to her. The guard approached Dr. Drury's door and knocked quietly.

"Come in. Thank you, Tree," Dr. Drury said. Detective Ransom entered, and Tree departed without saying a word, just a firm nod.

This just keeps getting weirder and weirder, Ransom thought. She extended her hand toward Dr. Drury. "I'm Detective Ransom, Sir. I've been waiting to meet you for quite some time."

"I'll take that as a compliment. I've been waiting to meet you also," Dr. Drury returned a puzzling comment to her. "Now, what can I do for you today, Detective? Please take a seat."

"Well, I don't know where to begin, Dr. Drury. You see, I'm trying to locate a fugitive from Cape Cod. I work for the Yarmouth Police Department."

"Yes, thank you. I knew that already but go on." He stunned her again.

"The fugitive I'm looking for has a girlfriend who recently underwent an operation here."

"Does this fugitive you are looking for have any formal charges brought against him?"

"I never said it was a man," Ransom stated.

"My mistake. Please go on."

"I have two state police officers providing surveillance inside your hospital."

"You mean those the two little boys snooping around with you? And who gave you permission to stake out our private hospital? Do you realize that you're trespassing?"

"We've stayed in common and public areas of the hospital and haven't gone any further," Ransom said confidently.

"Oh, really, Ms. Ransom? May I call you Ms. Ransom?"

"That's fine."

"You and your cohorts have stayed in public areas only?"

"What do you mean by that comment?"

"Please turn around in your chair and observe the wall behind you."

Ransom obliged and spun her chair around. Her jaw dropped. Over forty monitors were hanging on the wall, recording every square inch of the hospital.

"Now let's see, one of your eagle-eye assistants looks like he is having a nap in the lobby right now!" He laughed. "And he had another doze earlier today." He flipped to another screen showing a 9:45 time stamp.

"Feazel!"

"And your other assistant, ah, let's see," he paused while flipping to another monitor screen. "He's infatuated with three of our nurses in the lounge right now! It seems both of your cronies have taken turns between the cafeteria and the sofa. They also took the privilege of a tour of the second and third floors. So, what else may I help you with today, Ms. Ransom?"

She was deeply embarrassed. "Wait a minute," she said, her frustration evident. "Isn't that the guard sitting beside Officer Feazel who brought me here?"

"Right on the mark, Ms. Ransom! That's Tree's brother, who is appropriately named Bear. I adopted them ten years ago, and they have observed the three of you since 9:30 this morning. We had to make sure you weren't up to any harm. Otherwise, the consequences would be quite severe," Dr. Drury said as he folded his hands.

"Do you realize that we are police officers on duty? And are you aware that threatening or harming an officer is a felony?" She raised her voice.

"Oh, please, Ms. Ransom. We take the security and privacy of our patients here very seriously. Any Boston Police officer who steps foot in our facility has been background checked by the FBI. I assume you will inform your men of our boundaries."

Ransom was trying to stay calm. "When I talked with the head security guard this morning, he said you have dignitaries from all over the world come for medical procedures."

"Do you mean Charlie? Who was he today, a retired insurance salesman from Prudential or the lineman from Edison?" Dr. Drury laughed.

"He conned me?"

"No, it's just harmless play! Charlie used to be the head of OSS in World War Two. Ever hear of it?"

"No, never." She was baffled someone could dupe her.

"The Office of Strategic Services existed for only three years before it became the CIA. Ever hear of them?"

"What do you think?"

"Charlie was instrumental in forming the CIA in the 1940s and stayed with them for over thirty years. I have surrounded these hospital walls with three of the most dedicated, humble, and dangerous men known to exist."

"Would those so-called dignitaries and royalty be angry if they knew a fugitive wanted for murder is wandering the halls of your hospital?"

"Does this fugitive have a name?"

"Yes, Lewis Duncan and his girlfriend's name is Emmie. Ring a bell with either of those names?"

"I've never heard of them."

"That's pretty funny because Lewis Duncan's car happens to be in your parking spot right out front. Just a coincidence?"

"It must be! I ride a bicycle to work every day or take the subway when it rains. My car has been in the repair shop for eight months. It seems nobody likes to work on a BMW! My time is running short, Ms. Ransom. Please advise your team they are not welcome here, or as I said, the consequences will be severe. That applies to you as well. Good day. Bear will see you out."

Dr. Drury's office door opened as those words left his lips. Bear was waiting to escort her downstairs. She was rattled to her core. If anything, she dug herself, Feazel, and Topping a grave to jump in.

The elevator door opened, and Bear extended his arm to hold it open until Ransom entered.

"I feel kind of helpless being in a tight spot with such a brute of a man!" Ransom said seductively.

Bear smiled at her and pointed to the upper corner of the elevator. A camera lens was focused on her with a blinking red light. He folded his hands and placed them across his chest. The door opened, and she hurried across the lobby to meet Officers Topping and Feazel.

"Get outside, both of you!" Ransom ordered them. "Follow me!"

She stormed into the parking lot about two hundred feet from the main entrance.

"You idiots! What the hell have you been doing? I told you to stay in the subway entrance and main lobby, but no! Their security cameras caught you, Feazel, taking a two-hour nap on a sofa! Worst of all, didn't you notice the seven-foot-tall guy beside you? He's security and will tear you in half if he sees you in the hospital again!"

"I'm sorry. You're right. I didn't see him, probably because I *was* sleeping. We got in real late last night from the ball game."

"Never mind! And you, Topping, schmoozing it up with nurses in the lounge! They have you on camera snooping around on the second and third floors."

"I was trying to get a feel for the layout of this place, that's all," Officer Topping tried to cover his actions.

"Didn't you notice that guy dressed in black following you every step?" she asked Officer Topping. "One wrong move, and you would have been dead. I don't know what they taught you in the Academy, but you guys better wake up, or you'll be wearing a pair of cement shoes in the Charles River!"

Both officers held their heads down while taking this tremendous reprimand from Ransom.

"I'm going to pull night duty starting at seven. Can the two of you stay out of trouble and keep an eye out for Duncan until then?"

"Yes, ma'am!" both answered.

"Feazel, here are the keys to my car. Park it in that vacant spot in the front row. It's better to have an unmarked there instead of your cruiser. Keep an eye on the front lobby door. Topping, go to the subway platform and watch it with your life! You'll have to hurry through the lobby and hope you don't get noticed. And don't be eyeing every girl that gets off those trains! Give me the keys to your car, so I can go to my place for some shut-eye. It may be a long night here by myself, and I want the two of you in your hotel room by eight. And don't leave it, either of you!"

"Is it appropriate for you to operate our cruiser? We signed it out," Roley asked her.

"Look, Roley, or whatever you call yourself. Rules are being thrown out the window right now to catch Duncan. If I let your Commander know what happened today, your probationary period will be over. Got it? Now give me the fucking keys!"

"You're right. Sorry, Detective," Roley admitted.

"I'll be back here at my car at 1900 hours. That's seven p.m. in case you don't know."

"We know, we know," Topping griped.

Ransom started their cruiser and tried to familiarize herself with an actual state trooper's car. It was loaded to the hilt with the latest communication technology and a computer screen.

Man, oh, man! It put her Crown Vic to shame! Her radio didn't even work. *Maybe I should ask Sergeant Maxwell if he needs any more troopers.*

Ransom knew she was supposed to meet Antonio at two-thirty. She wasn't about to let Feazel and Topping know what she was up to. She barely had enough time to freshen up before meeting Antonio at his deli.

*****

Dr. Drury informed Mags of Detective Ransom's visit. He booked important finance meetings and a fundraiser that started at seven. It might last well into the evening. That left limited time to call Mags. He tried four times, but the line was busy for half an hour. The first meeting had already started. He walked in late and apologized to his donors.

Lewis walked behind the unmarked Crown Vic and didn't notice the car. Officer Feazel was fiddling with the broken radio, trying to pick up a station for the Sox pre-game. Lewis saw Cheeto and Kyle standing by his car, only six parking spots away from Feazel. They had Freda and Natalie with them.

"Aww, here you guys are, trying to butter me up!" Lewis said to them. He stopped walking when he was about ten feet away and looked at four sets of eyes intent on him.

"Are you coming with us?" Cheeto asked.

Lewis thought for a moment and smiled. "You're not going to tie me up again, are you?"

"Not if we don't have to," Natalie said.

"C'mon, let's go," Lewis agreed.

"This way," Kyle pointed. "At the end of the parking lot, there's a steep hill. We'll take the express route."

Lewis didn't have any idea what was going on. Natalie and Freda put an arm around Lewis's waist as they walked toward a steep grassy embankment that led to the subway track.

Feazel happened to look in the hazy rear-view mirror and tried to focus his eyes on five people who were walking away from him. *Poor bastard.* He felt sorry for him, a father with four kids! He laughed and tried to find a station for that Sox game. "This damn radio doesn't even work. What a long day this is going to be!" He mumbled.

Chapter Fifty-Seven

Cheeto and Kyle removed some cardboard boxes from the dumpster in the hospital parking garage earlier. Unfolding them, they placed them at the top of the slick, grassy hill. "You ready, Lewis? Hop on!"

Lewis was puzzled but complied with Cheeto's request. He sat on a big Wheaties box as Cheeto gave him a shove. Kyle gave Natalie a push at the same time. Lewis gained top velocity in seconds, speeding down the hill. The combination of his weight and the wet grass helped him pass Natalie. He caught air on a small bump and held on to a folded edge for dear life, screaming with joy the whole way. Everyone on their cardboard sleds followed Lewis down the hill, filling the air with laughter and excitement.

Lewis hit the dirt hard at the end of his ride and brushed it off. Everyone landed around him, tumbling in the same manner. "Wow!" he exclaimed, "I haven't had that much fun in years! You do this all the time?"

"Whenever we can," Freda answered, out of breath.

"Okay, let's move out!" Cheeto ordered. Very little was said between the children and Lewis. Everyone picked up their cardboard sleds and carried them a few hundred yards to the next above-ground train platform.

Kyle deposited some coins into a turn style, and they entered the awaiting train. "Only two stops, then we get off, Lewis."

"Boy, you guys sure know your way around here!"

"Other than walking, it's the only way we get around. It's too dangerous to ride a bicycle in the city," Natalie informed him.

After getting off the train, the walk began to feel familiar. Cheeto and Kyle led the way. Lewis remembered a few of the intersections and an alley he was on. Kyle opened a bulkhead door attached to a deserted building and held it for everyone to descend a ladder. "Now I remember this place," Lewis told them.

Cheeto turned a few lights on to illuminate the old tunnel, dripping with condensation.

"Close formation!" he commanded, and Lewis did so. They ended beside a large steel door that took Cheeto and Kyle to open. Lewis could tell they'd done this numerous times before and didn't need help. The door opened into the same abandoned subway station where Lewis spent the night.

The kids broke into a run toward the open arms of Mags. "Welcome back, my children! Welcome, Lewis! We're so happy to see you! Please follow me into our meeting room."

Lewis followed him as the kids bolted out of sight. They entered a small cafeteria that was spotless. Stainless steel panels covered the walls, and bright subways tiles met a beautiful tin ceiling. Lewis was stunned.

"Was it always this nice here?" Lewis asked.

"Oh, no!" Mags replied. "It took Dr. Drury and me a year to restore this old subway station. Bear and Tree put in countless hours of labor also. I purchased it from the city for a dollar! They said it didn't have any potential."

"Boy, were they wrong!" Lewis gazed across the room. The 'Elementary Army' was seated neatly at a large dining table with praying hands staring at him.

"Please take a seat, Lewis, at the other end. I'll sit in my usual spot." Mags laughed as he slid his chair from under the table. "I'm sure you must be famished. We have quite a feast planned today!"

"Boy, you couldn't have picked a better day. It's been chaos. I guess that's my norm."

Lewis was sitting at the opposite end of the table from Mags. Two rows of seated children were still keeping a sharp eye on him. There was an uneasy silence among everyone.

"Well, Lewis, I don't want to mince any words. Have you made a decision yet?"

Lewis leaned forward and folded his hands like the children. "Yes, I have. As everyone knows, I am far from a model citizen. I have many flaws and seriously question whether I am the person you want to fill your needs. I still have a lot of growing up to do. Emmie will need a lot of special care, *and* we're going to have a baby!" The Army appeared nervous, wondering what Lewis might say next. "Although

I've had a rough time in my life, some of it was filled with joy and love. I sympathize with what you have gone through. Can you understand the words I am using?"

The Army nodded in agreement.

"I guess what I'm saying…." He paused and looked up. "I would be humbled and honored to join your family!"

The kids jumped onto Lewis and knocked him to the floor. It reminded him of when he jumped on the table at his birthday party and mauled Tasha after speaking her first words.

Mags stood slowly from the other end of the table, trying to hide his pain. Almost doubled over, he caught himself on a chair. He started to peel the children from Lewis one at a time. "Okay, kids, come on! Let poor Lewis up!" Mags noticed everyone had tears in their eyes, Lewis too.

Lewis straightened his shirt and took a breath. "Mags—put your hand over my heart."

"What? Are you sure?" Mags questioned why.

"Yes, I'm sure! Go ahead."

Mags complied and placed his hand on Lewis's chest.

"Feel it, my pounding heart?"

"I certainly do, Lewis! I certainly do!"

"It hasn't beat like this in years! I feel – alive!"

Mags was torn up and changed the subject. "Nat and Freda, can you turn the stove on to heat the spaghetti you made last night? And don't forget the bread! Lewis, take my hand." Mags helped him to his feet. Cheeto and Kyle were still clutching his leg.

"Boys, can you help set the table?"

"Yes, Sir," they answered politely.

"Let's start over again, Lewis. Please sit down." Mags sat in his chair but cringed in pain again, Lewis noticed. "There are some papers we have to go over and sign. I'm very happy for the children and you. It will not be an easy road to travel, but I realize you are used to that!" Mags laughed. "Children, may I have a few moments alone with Lewis? There's plenty to do in the kitchen."

The Army arranged the chairs neatly into their appropriate places and went into the kitchen.

"Lewis, I'm in bad shape, which I'm sure you've noticed. Per our discussion, I had a hunch you would accept your future here, so I've already changed my will to show you as a beneficiary."

"Really?"

"Yes, Attorney Kane has set up a college fund for each of the children. Kyle and Cheeto already have their hearts set on going into the Army or Marines. They are born leaders, so don't get in their way!" Mags laughed again. "I may only have two to four weeks left. My cancer has advanced much faster since my first diagnosis and treatment. It's too late."

"It seems everyone I get close to in my life dies. It's not fair!" Lewis moaned.

"Lewis, the only thing most of these children know of is pain, death, and their families being torn apart. You are solid as a rock. That is why you were chosen to come here."

"Chosen? What do you mean?" Lewis asked curiously.

"I've actually known you since you were born."

"Are you crazy?"

"Hear me out. Your father, Dr. Drury, Attorney Kane, Nolan, and me served in an elite unit together in Viet Nam. Soon, there will only be two of us alive."

"Yes. Go on."

"It was no coincidence that Dr. Drury did Emmie's surgery. When you went to your family lawyer, Ted Kane, for the closing on your house and offered to pay for her surgery, I knew right then you were the person to take over. Ted called Dr. Drury that day and arranged surgery for Emmie. And by the way, you will be reimbursed the money you paid for her surgery."

"What? No way! I don't want it! Like I told Dr. Drury, I'm not a charity case. Donate it to someone or something else!"

"Those are some of the finer points you can discuss with Dr. Drury after my departure, okay? Now, let's have ourselves some lunch!" Mags said enthusiastically.

"Needless to say, Mags, you just about knocked me out of my chair again!" Lewis snickered and whacked the table with his hand.

"One more favor I want to ask of you, Lewis," Mags asked quietly.

"What? I'll do anything."

"The children know I'll be leaving soon, but not why. When my time has come, I'm going to disappear. I won't be able to say goodbye. It'll be too hard on them. I've made arrangements with Jim already."

"Yes, Sir. I'll be able to handle it, I think."

A very proud Elementary Army started to bring lunch, a four-course meal for everyone.

Mags addressed the children after they sat. "Let's gather our hands together, children. Cheeto, would you like to say grace?"

"Yes, Sir." Cheeto thought for a moment but started to well up with tears. "I'm sorry, I can't, Sir."

"Juanita?" Mags noticed the children were on the verge of crying with happiness, something they hadn't felt in a long time.

"Well, Lewis, I guess it's up to me. We are grateful to you beyond words. We thank you deeply," Mags said as he teared up also. "Let's eat!"

Lewis was so stuffed after feasting he couldn't move. He let out a huge burp and got a scolding from Algo. He looked at the clock and saw it was 4:30. He knew he could visit Emmie at seven and was getting itchy. The children handled clean-up and gathered in a large room next to the dining area. They played board games and cards with each other.

"See?" Mags commented. "I told you, Lewis. They're very self-sufficient. Sometimes coming from the school of hard knocks has its advantages. They demand very little attention and don't expect a gold star put on their forehead every day."

"I guess I'm living proof of that, too, aren't I?" Lewis went silent for a moment. "Mags, I have to be going. I'm visiting Emmie at seven, but I think I'll take in some sights along the way."

"Just one more thing before you go, Lewis. I have one more piece of advice. Keep a sharp eye on Kyle and Cheeto. They are strong-willed young boys vying to be our family's dominant leader."

"They want to be a dominant leader. Why?"

"Lewis, every wolf pack needs protection, usually from a strong male like you."

"Are you kidding, a strong leader, me? Come off it!"

"Not at all," Mags responded thoughtfully. "You've overcome so much turmoil in your life. Have you ever defended or protected someone other than yourself and stood up for your beliefs? I know for a fact you have many times. Your resolve will continue to be challenged. That's what my family needs! Understand?"

Lewis thought for a moment. "You know what, Mags? I think I finally realized why I'm here. Thank you."

"Do you remember how to get back to the hospital?" Mags asked, trying to change the subject. Lewis snapped from his deep thought.

"My photographic memory may be foggy, but I'll find it." Lewis went to shake Mags's hand but got fully embraced in a hug.

"Thank you, Lewis. I know you have much to offer and will have many great memories when this is over."

"Over? Will it ever be over?" he asked Mags seriously. "Can I ask you one more question?"

"Ask me anything, Lewis."

"How did you get your name, Mags?"

He roared in laughter. "When I was born, I weighed over eleven pounds! It was quite a feat for my mother of one hundred pounds to give birth. My real name is Magnus, a folklore nickname for 'Giant.' I was almost fifteen pounds by the time I was two weeks old!"

They shared a brief moment of eye contact.

"Lewis. There's one more thing I'd like to tell you."

"What's that, Mags?"

"If I ever had a son...."

Lewis raised a finger sharply. "Don't say it, Mags. Don't even think about it!"

*****

Lewis gradually vanished into the murky shadows of the vacant tunnel that once transported thousands of Bostonians decades ago.

Chapter Fifty-Eight

Detective Ransom met Antonio precisely at 2:30 outside his deli. He dressed plain but sharply and wore an off-white cotton gauze shirt with jet-black Levis. Ironically, she was wearing something quite similar. They spotted each other from fifty feet away and snickered.

"Oh, my gosh!" Antonio shouted. "Didn't you get my message about what I was wearing?" He gave Ransom a gentle hug. She noticed that fragrance Victor warned her about.

"We look like the Bobbsey Twins!" She laughed too. "I can change my top on the way to the game."

"Oh no! I have a complete wardrobe of clothes in the back of the deli. You know. In case I spill something on myself? I'll be back in a minute. Would you like a beer from the deli while we walk?"

"Thanks, but I'm on duty tonight. We're still looking for that fugitive from Cape Cod. Maybe I'll have a soda or iced tea."

Antonio nodded and charged into the deli. His sculpted arms accentuated his broad shoulders. He was wearing a more suitable Red Sox shirt when he returned with an iced tea in a Styrofoam cup.

"That tee shirt suits you much better, Antonio. It looks like you work out a lot!"

"I do! I lift three thousand pounds of meatballs, pizza dough, soda, and beer five days a week! Plus, I'm here every morning at four, making two hundred sandwiches for the Boys and Girls Club. We charge them what they cost, about twenty cents apiece. Everyone who works here donates time for a great cause."

What the heck have I ever done to help anyone except myself? I'm such a selfish, rotten bitch!

Antonio broke her train of thought. "Well, at least we don't look like the Bobbsey Twins anymore!" he laughed as he gave her the iced tea.

Crowds of people marching their way to Fenway Park were on fire after the defeat of the Yankees last night. Pat and Antonio tried to keep pace with the crowd as they walked and talked.

"Did you see that walk-off home run last night winning the game?" Antonio asked her.

"Oh, my gosh, no. I was asleep by eight after that great sub I devoured from your place. It was a long day of travel to get here. There were a few snags, but all's well. So, tell me about yourself."

"Let's see. I'm a third-generation owner of the deli. My grandfather started it in 1947. Every day, it's the same thing, but I love the neighborhood, my family, and my customers. I can't imagine living anywhere else. My Papa helps me at the deli a few days a week. He thinks he still owns it; know what I mean? He has that dementia kind of thing. We entertain and babysit him for now," Antonio admitted. "How about you? What town are you from?"

"Yarmouth, I've been there for seven years and have lived on the Cape my whole life. I left once to attend the Police Academy in Framingham. Our family has never left the Cape for anything. You'll lead a boring life if you're not into fishing or boating!"

"What about those beaches everyone raves about?"

"Are you kidding? My Irish skin doesn't tan. I turn into one big boiling tomato! I stay out of the sun and haven't put a foot in the water since *Jaws* came out, either!"

It was a quick walk to Fenway. Antonio had seats right behind third base, foul ball alley. Ransom was stunned when they exited the tunnel leading to their seats. She stopped walking and took it in; the perfectly manicured bright green field, vendors selling peanuts, popcorn, hot dogs, and soda filled the aisles. Antonio didn't notice she stopped walking until he was thirty feet in front of her.

"Pat!" he yelled over the boisterous fans waiting for the game to start. "You coming?"

They had a great view of the enormous wall in left field known worldwide as the Green Monster. She snapped out of her daydream and moved on. By the game's end, she wiped the unbearable thought of returning for surveillance duty at the hospital.

Walking with Antonio toward her apartment after the game was as delightful as the walk to Fenway. Boston locals outnumbered the Yankee fans ten to one and hurled friendly taunts at their rivals, who'd lost another game. Pat was taking this in, too. It was 6:45.

She would be late for her surveillance stint, but it didn't faze her for some unknown reason.

"Can I talk you into playing hooky from your job tonight?" Antonio asked sweetly.

"Oh, thanks, but I already lost one co-worker on my way here yesterday. The last thing I should do is piss off these two rookies I'm working with."

"Rookies, are you kidding? I thought you were after some bad killer. I have some local firepower available if you need it. Our neighborhoods are the safest in Boston. Know what I mean?"

"Thanks, Antonio, but I'm under strict orders from the Commander of Boston PD not to shoot up the town!"

"Will I see you again before you leave Boston?"

"Well, I hope so!" Ransom replied shyly. "I may take a few days off when this case is closed. I'll come for another of your delicious subs tomorrow night! Is it a deal?"

"Deal, I'll look forward to it!" Antonio leaned over and gave her a small peck on the cheek. He turned and walked toward the deli. She couldn't take her eyes off him as he strutted away.

What a true gentleman! Most other dates would be trying to rip her clothes off by now. Was Pat Ransom finally softening her stand-off and abrasive personality embedded in her from a messed-up childhood?

While walking back to her apartment, she looked hard at herself. Pat thought of many close friends she had trampled to get where she is today. They couldn't be counted on two hands.

Can a tiger really change its stripes?

Chapter Fifty-Nine

Officer Topping was sitting in Ransom's cruiser with a perfect view of the front entry door. It was 7:15. She was late. *Where the heck is she? This time, I'm gonna bust her chops for a change!*

Officer Feazel was sitting on a bench outside the lower level of a subway stop at the hospital. It was impossible to study every person departing the trains.

Lewis stepped off one of those subway cars. He mingled amongst a crowd and stopped to look at a clock.

"Crap! I'm late!" He increased his pace breaking into a fast, stiff-legged walk. This caught Officer Feazel's attention. He stared at Lewis keenly, trying to confirm a scar on his left cheek Ransom mentioned. Feazel could see only the right side of his face. *That's got to be him!*

Lewis hurried up the stairs toward the hospital entrance and disappeared into the crowd again.

Feazel didn't know what to do. If he was spotted in the lobby, all hell would break loose. He glanced at the top of the escalator and saw a mountainous security guard. Bear was eyeing his every move.

He tried the walkie-talkie Detective Ransom gave him.

"Feazel to Topping, Feazel to Topping, over." He listened for a response but got none, just static. He tried again, but nothing. *Shit!*

During Officer Feazel's many strolls around the hospital property, he noticed an exit sign leading to the main street. Dashing up the staircase brought him to a bustling Boston thoroughfare. He looked across toward the hospital.

"Give me a break!" he yelled. A ten-foot-high concrete wall stretched in both directions separated him from the hospital. He looked down the sidewalk each way with his hand up, trying to block the setting sun.

Feazel noticed a pedestrian bridge crossing the four-lane highway. *All right!* It was a half-mile, maybe a mile away, tops. He figured this was his only way to the hospital. He tried contacting Officer Topping again but couldn't hear anything over the loud city traffic.

"Screw this piece of junk!" He ran full speed on the sidewalk toward the overpass and threw the walkie-talkie into a trash can.

*****

Dr. Drury was in donor and finance meetings since 2:30. He kept calling Mags at every break to alert Lewis about the heavy police presence. He didn't get through to him until 7:18.

"Mags, what the heck is going on? Is your phone broken? I've been trying to call you since 1:30!"

"Sorry, Jim, one of the kids must have knocked it off the hook, that's all. You sound out of breath."

"I am! I just left a meeting with those donors I told you about last week. The big presentation for them is tonight. They're worth five million dollars for our hospital! I said I had to use the bathroom. Lewis is in deep trouble here. Three cops are waiting here to grab him! Where is he?"

"For crying out loud, Jim, he left hours ago. He said he was going to visit Emmie tonight at seven."

"Not good, Mags. He's walking right into them. Gather the Army, and we'll meet at Emmie's room in fifteen minutes."

"Roger, Elementary Army on the way!"

"Bring some distraction devices along, and step on it!"

Mags slammed the phone down and yelled, "*Code Red!* Let's move it! One minute, kids!"

The Army assembled in an orderly fashion and loaded into Mag's van in two minutes flat. They were briefed on the ride to the hospital.

Chapter Sixty

Lewis approached the front reception counter in the lobby and showed his pass to the watchman. "Know where you're going?" he asked Lewis.

"Yes, Sir, Recovery, third floor."

"That's fine, son. Just sign in here. Visiting hours end at 8:30."

"Yes, Sir. I won't stay any later than that." Lewis went to the elevator and jumped in as the door closed.

"Third floor, Lewis?" a security guard addressed him.

Lewis looked over, then up. It was Tree. "How do you know my name?"

"Dr. Drury asked me to escort you to see Emmie. I'm Tree."

"Wow, I don't get to meet many people taller than me. You must be six-eight."

"I'm six-nine without my shoes. Me and my brother didn't stop growing for a very long time."

"I know what you mean," Lewis chuckled. The elevator door opened. "Nice meeting you, Tree."

Tree nodded. He was a man of few words.

"Lewis," Tree called as the door closed, "the heat is on. You are covered from our end."

Lewis turned and looked at Tree. What the heck did he mean by that?

Lewis walked down the hall toward Emmie's room. He stopped at the window and knocked as he looked in. She was sitting, smiling evasively. He snuck in and gave her a gentle hug.

"Where have you been? I thought visiting hours started at seven?" she drilled him.

"I know, I know. You won't believe what happened today. I'm just learning the subway system and got lost!" he fibbed again.

"Dr. Drury says I'm doing great and will be in a regular room by tomorrow, complete with a color TV! I'll get to watch shows without stupid rabbit ears like at my house! He said I can have visitors for a short visit."

"That's great. I can finally be with you! Emmie, I'm sure you know TV never really interested me. My life has always been one big show, I guess."

Lewis made some idle chit-chat before Emmie finally spoke up. "Lewis, what's on your mind? I could tell something was bothering you when you walked in here. Tell me."

"Emmie, I can't tell you. I'm not supposed to, Dr. Drury's orders."

"What, Dr. Drury's orders? Am I going to die or something?" she groaned, demanding an explanation. "I can take it, Lewis! I've been through hell and back!"

Lewis moved closer and took her hand. "Emmie," he paused for a moment.

"Yes, Lewis."

He cupped his hand and whispered in her ear. "We're going to have a baby!"

A look of astonishment came across her face. She leaned and whispered in his ear, "That's impossible, Lewis. You know what I told you. I'm not fertile! I have endometriosis and blocked tubes." She leaned against the pillow, cupped her hand again, and then laughed. "What are we whispering for?"

"I don't know," he whispered back and laughed too. "Emmie, the stars and planets must have aligned since we met, but you've had four blood tests in three days, right?"

"I don't know. I've lost count! Am I going to be okay with the baby and operation?"

"That's what they were checking for, to see if you're pregnant. Dr. Drury assured me you'd be fine. Pregnant women get operated on all the time."

"Pregnant, really?" she asked again, seeking reassurance.

"One hundred percent, I know you had your heart set on college this spring, but it looks like you're due in March or April. At least it's not a Leap Year!" he laughed. "You can start school next fall; it's only one semester later, no big deal!"

"What if we can't find a sitter after the baby is born?"

"Oh, I can guarantee we'll have plenty of babysitters!" he joked. She looked puzzled but brushed it off.

"I guess my rebuilt heart took that shock pretty well, don't you think? Do you have any more surprises for me, Lewis?"

"No, that'll do it for at least half an hour!" They both laughed, but Emmie cringed in pain.

"I'm okay, I'm okay," she said. "Can you put your head on my pillow and stay here all night? I love to hear you breathe."

"Sure, just relax. I'll stay until they kick me out! I'm exhausted, too. We could use a little rest. Just close your eyes. I'll be here, always." He looked at Emmie. She was already asleep and probably didn't hear a word Lewis said.

He put his head on the pillow and placed his hand gently on her stomach. As he tried to drift off for a nap, he wondered if it would be a boy or a girl. He prayed that neither one would turn out like him. He thought he was nothing but a bundle of trouble his whole life. He tried to think of the good times he had spent as a child, but there weren't many. He remembered being ridiculed and bullied just because he was different. He had flashbacks of wearing his tortuous leg braces, special shoes, and thick eyeglasses. He recalled being bullied at school and even by the largest motorcycle club on Cape Cod. Now, it was an over-zealous cop after him. When was it ever going to end?

He leaned very carefully to whisper one more thing into Emmie's ear.

"What have I done to you? I'm so sorry."

Chapter Sixty-One

While sitting in Detective Ransom's car, Officer Feazel kept a sharp eye on the front lobby entrance. Lots of fancy limousines were dropping well-dressed people off at the door. It also seemed valets were parking vehicles and escorting these well-to-do people inside. Was this place a hospital or a fancy restaurant? It fazed him only a moment.

Feazel was getting impatient and decided to call Officer Topping on his two-way radio. "Officer Feazel—calling Officer Topping! Feazel calling Topping. Come in, over."

There was no response for a moment. He heard a few clicks on his radio. "Officer Topping, is that you? Over."

"Ah, no, man. This is Stan. I just picked this thing up out of a trash can! It's pretty cool. What's it worth? I'm keeping it! Are you the cops?"

"What is this, a joke? Where are you located?" Feazel demanded.

"I certainly ain't telling *you*. Later, dude!" The unknown trash picker shut his radio off and ran down the street with it.

Officer Feazel got out of Ransom's car and paced nervously, wondering what to do. *This is ridiculous. Where the hell is Roley?* Stomping his feet, he kicked the door panel. *What a great first assignment!*

Feazel saw another large group of cars unload as he looked down the street again. He saw a man running toward him. The guy bent over and took some deep breaths. "Holy shit! That's Topping!"

Officer Topping practically collapsed into Feazel's arms. He was exhausted and winded.

"Where the heck were you?" Feazel asked him.

"Hold on. I can't breathe!" Topping said, still bent over. It took almost two minutes for him to regain his composure.

"You're not going to believe this, but I think I saw Lewis Duncan get off a train and go up the stairs into the hospital!" Topping finally managed to say.

"Are you positive? How long ago?"

"It must be twenty minutes or so by now. I had to run almost two miles to get here!" Topping said, still gasping.

"Are you crazy? Why didn't you just go through the lobby? It's a three-minute walk from there!" Feazel reproached him.

"Ransom ordered us to stay clear of the hospital, and that security guard was standing at the top of the stairs. I know he spotted me. Where the heck is Ransom? It's way past seven!"

"I have no idea where she is. Let's sit in her car. It'll do you some good until we come up with a plan," Feazel said.

"A plan? Now you're the crazy one! Let's wait here until she shows up," Officer Topping begged.

"No way! This is our chance to shine, brother! We can show her and Sergeant Maxwell what we're really made of!" Officer Feazel crowed.

"Oh, no, don't include me in any plan you have! Remember that stunt you pulled at the Academy? We almost got killed by those other rookies from Rhode Island after they got drunk and passed out!"

"You were in on it, too! I didn't know that marker I used to draw on their faces was permanent," Feazel laughed, shrugging. "Man, that was funny!"

"Funny? Do you think running a hundred laps for punishment was funny? And having to box that Golden Gloves champ who trained with Marvelous Marvin Hagler is funny? My ribs still hurt!"

A large passenger van pulled up in front of the hospital. A man climbed out from the driver's side as eight kids piled out the back door and ran inside. Mags gave the valet his keys to park the vehicle.

"That's it!" Feazel suddenly screamed as the van pulled away.

"For crying out loud, you scared the shit out of me! What are you talking about, that white van?"

"Open your eyes! What do you see?"

"Lots of cars were dropping people off, and I think I see that big security guard by the door again."

"You flunky! What does that big sign say next to the entrance door?"

Topping squinted and focused his eyes, "Looks like it says, 'Welcome, Donor's Meeting This Way.' So what?" He read the sign very slowly.

"That's our in!"

"Oh, yeah, we're going to walk right in dressed as state police?"

"We have to get in there somehow," Feazel said. "Duncan could be long gone by the time Ransom gets here."

Feazel put his hand on the rearview mirror and started to fidget while looking at himself. He turned some lights on inside the cruiser and looked around. He smiled.

"Oh, Roley? Do you see anything we may be able to use to get inside that hospital?"

"No, not really. Do me a favor. Clue me in!"

"What's on the back seat?" Feazel asked smartly.

"It looks like a...." Topping paused. "A suitcase!"

They both jumped from the front seat and got in the back. Feazel opened the suitcase.

"Holy shit. *Jackpot!* It's Ransom's clothes. We're in!" Feazel celebrated.

"Oh no, you're not getting me into any of those clothes! Don't even think about it!" Topping rejected Feazel's idea immediately.

"Do you have any other ideas? I think you'll look stunning in this lime green dress, although it may float on you!" Feazel laughed hard.

"Screw you, Kevin. I'm not doing it. I'm not doing it!"

"Everything's here that we need! Two dresses, bras, pantyhose, make-up, a pocketbook, and three pairs of shoes. I'm pulling rank on you. We're doing it!"

"Rank? We're both just shmuck officers on probation!"

"Nope, I scored higher on every exam we took, and you know it! I'll be the first to get promoted! Look, I'll take the heat if something goes wrong, okay?"

Topping thought for a moment. "If we go in there and get caught, we're *dead*. If we let him get away, we're done for, too. I can't believe I'm saying this, but all right. You wear the pink one, though. You're more of a fem than I am!"

"I agree! And I'll do the talking too. I have a good chick voice!" Feazel laughed.

Shredding Ransom's suitcase, each came up with a complete outfit.

Ransom has good taste in clothing, Officer Feazel thought.

"What are we going to do about our hair?" Officer Topping asked.

Feazel thought for a moment. "Here, take these handkerchiefs. Wrap one around your neck like a scarf and tie the other on your head. You know, like old ladies do."

"What the fuck do you mean, like old ladies? I guess I've never noticed."

"Here, let me do it."

"Boy, you really do have a feminine side, don't you, Kev?" Roley teased him.

"We all do! Remember, let me do the talking. We'll probably have to sign in and get a pass or something. You ready?"

"I'm scared shitless, and I don't know if I can walk in these heels!"

"They're called pumps, you fool!" Feazel joked. "Stuff these handcuffs in your pocketbook. We'll need them when we apprehend Duncan. Let's go. You're Aunt Gladys, and I'm Martha, okay?"

They exited Ransom's car rather shakily on their newfound heels but got the hang of it.

As they approached the lobby, a concierge opened the glass doors. A sharp-dressed man in a tuxedo asked, "Here for the donor's conference tonight, ladies?" The disguised officers walked right past Tree without a glance from him.

Feazel cleared his throat and said in a high voice, "Yes, we are dahling. Do we have to sign in?"

"Oh, no, ma'am. The conference is down the hall, the last door on your left."

"Thank you. You are so kind," Feazel returned.

Officers Feazel and Topping made it in! They were walking about thirty feet down the hall when a doorman shouted.

"Ladies? Ladies? Just a moment, please." Both of their hearts started to pound. He approached Feazel and bent over to whisper in his ear. "I'm sorry, ma'am, but your friend has some.... " He paused. "Toilet paper hanging from her dress. I'm just trying to save you some embarrassment, ladies."

"Is there a powder room we can visit along the way?" Feazel asked again in a high voice.

"Yes, ma'am. It's the fourth door on the right."

"Once again, you've been so kind," Feazel said.

Man, these rich people keep getting stranger and stranger, the doorman thought.

"What's going on?" Officer Topping whispered to Feazel.

"Just follow me, you idiot!"

Officer Feazel almost went into the men's room by instinct but caught himself and passed by. He opened the door to the lady's room for Topping to follow.

"Really? The lady's room?" Topping asked.

"Just follow me," Feazel hissed. He checked to see if any women were in the stalls before speaking. "You almost blew it! You've got toilet paper or something hanging from your ass!"

Topping snickered. "I found some tissue paper to stuff my bra. I guess some must have fallen. Ransom must have some big ones to fill this bra! Hey, Roley, your lipstick is smeared. And thanks for the heads up."

"Kev, somehow we've got to avoid going in that door for the conference."

"When I was snooping around yesterday, I went up a staircase at the end of this hall. It goes to the fifth floor. The ICU and recovery are on the third floor. Duncan must be visiting in one of those rooms. But what if we come across him? We don't even have our guns."

"I have my .22 pocket rocket in this purse. I never go anywhere without it," Feazel replied. "Let's locate him first. He won't go down easy in here. We may have to nab him in the staircase or outside."

The restroom door opened as a very chatty woman came in.

"Oh, hello, girls! Going to the conference?"

"Yes, we can't wait!" Feazel said with mock enthusiasm.

"That Dr. Drury is such a generous and talented man. Do you have any pledge cards yet? I have a few extra. It seems they've run out. The donations are pouring in!"

"We're certainly going to give as much as we can!" Feazel replied. "Thank you for the pledge cards. What is your name, ma'am?"

"Belle, Belle Blatherwick. My husband is James Blatherwick the Third. Have you met him yet?"

"I'm Martha, and this is my sister, Gladys. Unfortunately, we've never met your husband."

"I'll save you two seats right beside me!" Ms. Blatherwick said happily. "We're at the first table on the right. See you there. Ta-ta!"

"That was close! Man, let's get out of this bathroom!" Officer Topping whispered. "Just go nice and slow down the hall. The staircase is on the right. See the exit sign?"

Feazel nodded. They peeked in the conference room window as they walked by. There were only five more feet to go until they reached the staircase. Officer Topping opened the door slowly. Of course, it was the loudest, squeakiest door in the hospital, but at least they were on their way up.

"I have to take these damn shoes off! They're killing me!" Officer Topping said. His voice echoed up the five-story staircase.

"Shhh, for Pete's sake! Anyone can be around here! I don't see any cameras, do you?" Feazel asked.

"Just try to act casual if you do see one. If anybody asks questions, I'll pretend we're lost."

"Roger, that's a 10-4 partner," Officer Topping affirmed.

Officers Topping and Feazel started nervously up the iron staircase, holding tightly onto the railing. Little did they know, but they were being observed by Tree and Bear in a security office every step of the way. Feazel didn't notice a small camera blended in with some nuts and bolts on a handrail. Tree was relaxing with his feet on a desk, casually eating an apple while monitoring their progress up the stairs.

"How far should we let them go before we drop the net on them, Bear?" Tree asked.

"Let's see where they're going, probably the third floor to look for Lewis. We have plenty of time. You know what, though, Tree?"

"What's that, brother?"

"I'm not into nets anymore. You know what I mean?" Bear asked Tree. "I'm more into sledgehammers these days. How about you?" He smiled.

Tree picked up a five-pound sledgehammer from inside his desk and started to hit his hand with it. "I know just what you're talking about, brother, just what you're talking about."

Chapter Sixty-Two

Detective Ransom arrived in the hospital parking lot at 7:30, a half-hour late. She stopped at her temporary apartment for the recharged phone and to freshen up. The drive to the hospital took no time in post-rush hour traffic. Ransom parked the state police cruiser in the fourth row and spotted her car still in the first row.

Well, it's still here. That's a good sign. "Where the heck is Feazel?" She walked over to her Crown Vic. *I thought I told him to watch the front.* "What the...? My car is unlocked!" *Those little jerks!* The keys were in plain sight on the floor! She glanced into her back seat.

"Unbelievable!" she yelled out. "My suitcase has been rummaged through and stripped! What the heck happened here?"

Furiously, she slammed the back door. She checked the trunk for her guns and Officer Kline's. They were there plus two more weapons locked in the gun safe. "Those greenhorns don't even have their firearms!"

Ransom didn't know what to do. She thought of leaving and seeing Antonio but decided that was a crazy idea. She started walking in circles, wondering where Officers Feazel and Topping were. While staring at the hospital, she wondered if they'd gone in, defying her orders.

After a few moments, she figured that must be where they were and decided to go in and see for herself. Just then, the bag phone started to ring. She raced around the car to answer it.

"Detective Ransom, Yarmouth PD," she answered.

"Catch your hardened criminal yet?" a man questioned her.

"Kline, is that you?"

"That's a big 10-4. After a long walk home, I cooled off and didn't resign."

"You didn't? That's great! But – you walked the whole way? I'm sorry for how I acted," she painfully admitted. "I've done a lot of soul-searching, Officer Kline."

"Within minutes, I got a ride from a trucker. He drove me the entire way to Yarmouth. I haven't told anybody what happened between you and me."

"Like I...."

"For once in your life, just hear me out!" Officer Kline interrupted. "You're not going to believe this!"

"What's going on?"

"Remember those three missing kids from Yarmouth? They found them today, floating in a dinghy on Buzzards Bay!"

"Dead?"

"Nope, they're alive. But get this, they were duct-taped together, *naked!*" Kline laughed. "Boy, that's gonna hurt getting peeled apart!"

"Shit! I don't believe it!" Pat Ransom sat in her car seat, totally dejected. "That means you were right all along about Lewis not being involved. What a bully I've been to you and Lewis. I'm sorry."

"Never mind, the best is yet to come." Kline threw another hook for Ransom.

"Come on, give it to me. The reception stinks here!"

"Remember that kid, Jerry Alfonso? You interviewed his girlfriend?"

"Of course I do. So what?"

"Alfonso said one of the Gallagher brothers killed Honch!"

"You're joking, right?" Ransom screamed.

"Nope, but the brothers say Alfonso did it. They're ratting on each other! And get this – they all want to go into W.P."

"Witness Protection? Why?"

"They're tight-lipped and won't say, but I think they're scared of someone. Alfonso said their lives are in extreme danger if they talk."

"They have to give us something more if they want protection. Otherwise, the Feds won't buy it!" Ransom told Kline.

"They've already given us something! Case closed on the murder of Honch! Don't you get it, or are you still chasing Duncan?"

"Yeah, I am still chasing him, and the shit is hitting the fan right now. I have to go. Thanks, Kline. I'm sidestepping your promotion to Sergeant, do you hear me?"

"I don't need your help, Pat. May I finally call you Pat?"

"That's fine, and again I apologize for being such a bitch, Detective Ransom, over and out."

A tear trickled from her eye. She hadn't cried in fifteen years, but her heart had a huge hole. She knew apologizing to Lewis was impossible. She had been on a futile, wild goose chase after him for months. Where were Feazel, Topping, and Lewis? She turned and looked at the hospital being swallowed by a full moon. Somehow she knew they were inside, bound on a collision course she had inspired and dreamt about. It was too late to stop the wheels.

Detective Ransom strapped on her .38 revolver and .45 semi-automatic one last time.

Chapter Sixty-Three

Lewis awoke to the sound of a creaking door as it opened. Rubbing the sleep from his eyes, he couldn't believe what he saw.

"Mags! What the heck are you doing here? And what's with the big cart?" Lewis spoke softly, not to awaken Emmie.

"You'll understand," he removed a sheet covering the laundry cart. One by one, Freda, Kyle, Natalie, Cheeto, Algo, and the rest of the Elementary Army climbed from the cart. Lewis rubbed his eyes again. "Lewis, you're in grave danger. Two Troopers are in the building looking for you. Tree and Bear have them in their sights, but you have to get out of here!"

"I haven't done anything wrong!"

"I know that, but they don't!" Mags pleaded while the Army stared at Lewis.

The door creaked and opened slowly again. Mags jumped behind it, ready to hurt someone. It was Dr. Drury! Mags lowered his fist.

"Hey, how come I wasn't invited to this party?" Dr. Drury said in a loud voice, stirring Emmie. "My part of the meeting is over for now."

Emmie started to moan and wake up.

Mags addressed Dr. Drury. "Jim, come outside right now with me, please. We need to talk." They went into the hall, leaving the Army and Lewis in the room with Emmie.

Emmie was fully awake by now. As her eyes focused, she saw Lewis standing in front of her. She smiled at him.

"I thought you left." Emmie groaned again and stretched. "What's the matter, Lewis? Why are you just standing there?"

One by one, small children appeared from behind Lewis until all eight were at his side.

"Whoa, am I dreaming here, Lewis? What the heck is going on?"

"Emmie! So much has happened since we got here. Someday I'll be able to explain."

"Why don't you start explaining right now?" Emmie demanded.

"Remember those babysitters I mentioned?"

"Babysitters, when?"

"You may have been a little groggy. Emmie, this is my new family, our new family. I'm not leaving Boston. We want you to stay with us."

"What? This is a little too much to comprehend right now, Lewis. Are you trying to kill me and my new heart?" She raised her voice.

"Emmie, it's such a long story. You wouldn't understand."

"You and your long, mysterious stories, I can't take them anymore!"

The Army separated and stood beside Lewis.

Natalie spoke first. "We need Lewis. Everyone in this room does. We'll help with your new baby." She stepped aside as Cheeto moved forward.

"My parents were killed in an auto accident. I've lived in three foster homes in four years."

Juanita placed her hand on Emmie's. "My father drank too much and is in jail for beating us. My mother abandoned our family." She spoke softly and stepped back.

Freda put her arm around Algo. "My brother was torn from me when we were two years old. We are together again, hopefully forever."

It started to sink in for Emmie. She was overwhelmed. "Lewis, is this happening, or am I seeing things?"

"I wish we were all seeing things, but no, this is real, Emmie. I've been carrying pain with me ever since I was born. I think that's what sees me through every day. I can finally do some good with my life!"

There was a knock on the door. It was Dr. Drury. "Lewis, we need you in the hall now."

"I'll be back in a minute, promise." The Army split, going on each side of the bed to comfort Emmie.

Lewis looked down one end of the hall and saw Tree and Bear growling. He turned slowly and looked at the other end of the hall. He saw what appeared to be two small women in dresses. One of them removed a scarf from her head, snickering when she saw Lewis.

It took a moment for Lewis to comprehend — it wasn't a woman. It was a man! One of them had a gun aimed at Dr. Drury and Mags. Tree and Bear didn't move.

"State police, Lewis! You are under arrest for the murder of Spencer Plant. Put your hands up!" Officer Feazel commanded.

"I'm not going anywhere with you, now or ever. You'll have to shoot me first!" Lewis yelled at Feazel. "My blood will be on your hands!" Feazel and Topping drew closer to Lewis.

"Lewis, no!" Dr. Drury cried out.

"There's an easy way out of this and a hard way, Lewis. It's up to you!" Officer Topping yelled.

"I'm gonna break you little motherfuckers in half!" Tree shouted in anger.

"Stand down, Tree!" Dr. Drury ordered him.

Cheeto and Kyle heard the commotion and opened the door slightly. Kyle made some hand signals to Cheeto.

Kyle put his hand in his pants pocket, reaching for something.

"We want only Duncan!" Feazel screamed. "No one has to get hurt!" It was a standoff.

Lewis noticed Dr. Drury pointing at something. What it was, he couldn't tell.

"Ten seconds, Lewis. Ten seconds is all you got!" Feazel was bluffing. His gun was fake, but nobody could tell it wasn't real.

Emmie attempted to come to the door window to look but was held back by the Army.

Dr. Drury pointed at a small sign on the wall. It read, 'Laundry Chute.'

"Five seconds, Lewis!" Feazel yelled again.

"Three, two, one." He cocked his gun.

Cheeto opened the door with Kyle and jumped into the hall. They threw hundreds of BBs onto the floor in the direction of Officers Feazel and Topping.

Lewis jumped headfirst into the laundry chute and took a three-story free-fall ride, softly landing on a pile of sheets and towels.

Feazel and Topping could hardly run across the painful BBs with their bare, tender feet and fell. "You little crumb-snatchers!" Feazel yelled at them.

Cheeto and Kyle joined Lewis and jumped into the chute for the three-story descent, yelling with rebellious laughter the entire way down.

"Get them!" Feazel ordered Topping.

"Everybody, stay where you are!" Feazel demanded as he held the gun on Dr. Drury.

"Roley, get down that chute!" Officer Feazel ordered him.

"You're crazy! No way. I'll take the stairs!"

"I'm right behind you. Get down that chute, go!"

Topping slid carefully into the chute feet first. Feazel shoved him and jumped in, yelling and screaming in fear the whole way.

Lewis climbed from the laundry cart as Cheeto and Kyle hit the pile of sheets. They screamed with excitement and delight as they jumped from the bin.

"Go, Lewis, get out of here!" Kyle yelled. "We'll meet at the hill! Go! Please! See you at the Express!"

Officers Topping and Feazel hit the bin simultaneously on top of each other.

"Man, that hurt my ass!" Topping whined.

Cheeto and Kyle waited long enough to be spotted by Topping and Feazel, then took off running toward the hill.

"There they are!" Topping yelled, charging after them.

*****

Detective Ransom was just about ready to get out of her car. She called the commander of the state police, trying to ward off Feazel and Topping. He said dispatch would take at least five or ten minutes to contact them, but they weren't even in their cruiser. It was up to her to end it.

She was leaning against the car, wondering if she should enter the hospital as Lewis sprinted by her car. He never saw her standing there.

Lewis? Was that him? It was! "Lewis, stop! *We know you're innocent!*" she yelled, but he didn't stop. He rounded a corner of parked cars in the lot and bolted toward the hill.

Cheeto and Kyle flew by Ransom. "Who the heck are they? *Wait!*" She then saw two women running at her and attempted to stop them. "Hey, those are my clothes!" She yelled out but realized it was Officers Topping and Feazel!

"Fuck sake, *stop!* Feazel, Topping!"

"This way, Ransom!" Feazel shouted as he ran by and wasn't about to stop.

Kyle threw another handful of BBs on the sharp turn and ran toward the hill.

Officer Feazel noticed the BBs on the ground reflecting in the overhead streetlight. "Uh-oh, another booby trap, Roley!" He yelled and pointed to them, avoiding the BBs.

Detective Ransom started to run in her flat, slippery shoes but quickly discarded them. She stepped on the painful BBs while turning the corner and yelled, falling to the pavement. She skinned both knees and shins to the bone, ripping her slacks to shreds. After rolling in agony for a moment, she stood to catch her breath when she heard a shot ring out.

Lewis made it to the hill's edge with Cheeto and Kyle at his side.

"Put your hands up, Lewis!" Officer Topping ordered.

"Get under there, quick!" Lewis ordered Cheeto and Kyle. They dove headfirst and slid under an old truck.

"Don't move! Turn around with your hands up!" Feazel yelled.

Lewis complied and faced the two officers. He looked toward the hospital and could see the silhouettes of Emmie, the Army, and Dr. Drury in a third-floor window. Emmie pressed her hands on the window in anguish.

"Lewis Duncan, you are under arrest for second-degree murder! Get down on the ground!" Feazel ordered him. Officer Topping took the handcuffs from his pocketbook, still dangling on his shoulder.

"I can't get down on the ground. My knees don't bend that way," Lewis said.

Ransom was painfully hobbling up from a hundred feet away.

"Let him go! He's innocent! Let him go!" Ransom yelled.

"What did she say, Feazel?" Officer Topping asked him.

"I don't know, cuff him!"

"*Feazel!*" Ransom yelled again. She was only about forty feet from both officers. "Let him go! I was wrong! He's innocent. I've been wrong the whole time!"

Feazel turned and addressed Detective Ransom. "We'll let the courts decide that! We didn't come all this way for nothing! Cuff him, Roley."

Roley was a little uncertain about this sudden change of events.

Ransom limped as she along raised her guns behind Feazel and Topping. She placed the barrels of her .45 and .38 on the back of their necks.

"Drop your gun, Officer Feazel," Ransom ordered him. "This could get real messy if you don't."

"You don't know what you're doing, Ransom! You'll be ruined for this stunt!" Feazel shouted.

Lewis gazed up at the window in the hospital. Emmie was pawing at it. He still had his hands up when he noticed two people walking up behind Ransom. He smiled and shook his head.

"What the hell are you smiling about, Duncan? You think this is a joke?" Feazel asked him.

"Drop your gun, Feazel," Ransom repeated.

Ransom felt a cold steel gun barrel against the back of *her* neck.

"Lower your weapon, Ms. Ransom," said a deep voice behind her. "No tricks either, Feazel."

"Kane? Is that you?" she asked, astonished.

"Candy, please relieve Ms. Ransom of her weapons and take that peashooter from Officer Feazel before he hurts someone." He spoke calmly.

Candy stepped in front of Detective Ransom. "Your guns, Pat?" She lowered her guns from Feazel and Topping, then handed them to Candy. "Officer Feazel, please?" she politely asked him.

"It's fake, just shoots blanks," Feazel admitted.

"And by the way, that lime green looks stunning on you, Officer Feazel!" He turned his gun around and handed it to Candy.

"It seems we are at a stalemate here, Mr. Kane."

"Not at all, Officer Topping." Kane turned and addressed Lewis. "Put your hands down, Lewis. As you've heard, it's been proven that you are innocent of all charges from Detective Ransom. The Gallagher brothers and Alfonso have confessed to the killing of Honch. You are free to go. Do you agree, Ms. Ransom?"

"Yes, I got the word from Yarmouth PD not fifteen minutes ago. Officers Feazel and Topping didn't have any knowledge of this new information." she conceded.

"I took the liberty of calling my good friend at Boston PD, Sergeant Foley. I believe you know him, Pat?" Attorney Kane informed her.

"Oh, jeez, no!" she moaned.

"Yes, they should be here any moment to sort this out." Kane holstered his gun. "Don't you have something to tell Lewis?"

"Yes. Lewis, you are free to go. Words will never repair the damage I've done to everyone here. I'm so sorry," Ransom admitted.

"Boys? Your turn," Candy addressed Officers Feazel and Topping. They acknowledged her and apologized to Lewis as well.

Lewis peered under the old truck where Cheeto and Kyle were hiding. They saw everything.

"Cheeto, Kyle, let's go," he said quietly. They crawled out and wrapped their arms around his legs.

"Are we taking the express route home?" Lewis asked them.

"Yeah! Let's go!" they replied with joy.

Three Boston police cruisers appeared at the end of the parking lot and drove slowly toward everyone.

"Attorney Kane?" Lewis asked.

"Please call me Ted. Okay, Lewis?" he requested.

Lewis nodded. "You know where to find me, right?"

"I certainly do, Lewis. *Underground*, right?"

Candy hugged Lewis. "You're more of a man than anyone I've ever met. Remember that, Lewis."

Lewis glanced up at the hospital window. Emmie and Dr. Drury were standing there still. He knew the suspense was killing them.

"You'll fill them in. Right, Ted?" Lewis asked him.

"You've got it, kid. Now get the heck out of here. Go to your family."

"Detective Ransom?" Lewis asked her. "Maybe we can get together someday, and I'll fill you in on everything. You weren't too far off."

Looking bewildered, she replied, "Lewis, you've brought something out in me I didn't know I had – a heart. I wouldn't have found it if I hadn't been chasing you these past two months and come to Boston. You've taught me a lot about myself. I'm done with police work and am turning in my badge. There's something more tangible here. I'm not leaving Boston." Her words left everyone stunned.

"You're free to go, Lewis. And as for that offer of getting together? Thank you, but no. It would be best if we never meet again," Ransom stated solemnly.

Lewis nodded and walked away, not saying a word.

Lewis, Cheeto, and Kyle made their way to the hilltop.

"Wait for us, wait for us!" a bunch of children screamed. It was the rest of the Army running through the parking lot. They jumped on Lewis and practically tackled him.

"I've never seen anything like this!" Ransom said.

"Me neither. How about you, Roley?" Officer Feazel weakly uttered as his eyes teared.

Lewis and the Army sat on some cardboard boxes left behind from their last journey. They gave Lewis a shove and sent him flying down the hill, hooting and hollering the whole way. "*Yeee haww!*" he screamed.

The rest of the Elementary Army jumped on their cardboard sleds and yelled with joy the entire descent.

Sergeant Foley and two other Boston police officers stepped from their cruisers. He wagged his pointer finger at Detective Ransom.

"I warned you, Pat! I told you, no shooting up my town!"

"I know, I know. It was my fault."

"No, Sir, it was my fault, Sergeant Foley," Officer Feazel admitted. "It was just a blank, a big cap gun."

"And what's with the dresses, boys?" Foley asked Topping and Feazel.

"Long story, Sir," Topping laughed as he turned red from embarrassment.

"Are we good here, Pat? Ted?" Sergeant Foley asked them. They nodded in agreement.

The three Boston police officers departed, shaking their heads in disbelief, along with some laughing between them.

"I have some explaining to that beautiful young woman in the window, don't I?" Detective Ransom asked Attorney Kane.

"You owe her a lot more than an explanation, Pat. But it won't be today. One other thing."

"What's that? Anything."

"If you don't return to Yarmouth, please make arrangements to have my office cleaned. Your associates seem to have ransacked and pillaged it. Candy knows where every file was kept."

"I'm sorry, will do. I'll have Kline handle it." She apologized to him sincerely.

Attorney Kane opened the Chevette car door for Candy, then went around the other side and got in. It started with its usual backfire, scaring the heck out of everyone.

Ransom turned to address Officers Feazel and Topping. "I messed this one up, guys. I'm sorry for the way I treated you. I'm not leaving this crazy town for a while. I think there's something better for me here."

"All's forgiven. Enough said," Officer Topping offered. "I hope every case isn't as whacky as this one!"

They strolled toward their cars and looked up to see Emmie and Dr. Drury still in the window. Hesitating, they stopped walking. Officer Topping politely bowed, and Officer Feazel did the same. Detective Ransom saluted them for ten seconds. They proceeded slowly with their heads hung in disgust.

"Dr. Drury, I think I'm going to pass out!" Emmie cried.

He grabbed her by the shoulders as she collapsed.

Final Chapter

Dr. Drury pushed the emergency call button next to Emmie's bed. He gently placed her on the bed. An alarm went off as nurses scrambled to take her vitals.

"Her blood pressure is above normal, Dr. Drury. Heart rate is ninety-five," a nurse said. "It's quite elevated!"

Emmie started to awaken, bringing sighs of relief from everyone.

"You'll be all right, Emmie. I think this has been a little too much for you to handle today, that's all. Take a few deep breaths. What's her heart rate now, Liz?"

"It's come down to 80, and BP is fine," Liz replied. "She's OK."

"Thank you, ladies," said Dr. Drury addressing the nurses.

Emmie took a few deep breaths. "Dr. Drury?"

"Yes, Emmie, what is it?"

"Can you put your hand on my stomach?" she asked of him.

He thought this was an odd request but did so.

"I think you must be starving. Your stomach is gurgling!"

"A part of Lewis is inside of me!"

"That's a wonderful thing, Emmie. I've never been able to experience what both of you will have."

"Dr. Drury, can you put your hand on my chest, over my heart?"

He did so. "I can feel it beating strong, even through the bandages!"

Emmie paused for another moment. "Truthfully, I've never felt so *alive!*" She had no idea Lewis said those exact words hours ago.

"I've never felt quite like this before, either," Dr. Drury said, overtaken with joy. It was his turn to ask a question.

"Emmie?"

"Yes, Dr. Drury?"

"Do you realize Lewis was sent here to save all those children?" he asked her seriously.

Emmie shifted her weight onto her hands and sat up gingerly, leaning forward.

"You are close, Dr. Drury. Very close."

"Close to what?"

"Lewis Clark Duncan from Cape Cod, born during a hundred-year storm on a Leap Year, was sent here...." she paused again to look Dr. Drury straight in the eye.

"He was sent here to save us all."

Leap Year's Revenge | 487

Epilogue

This story is dedicated to my first Cousin Mark, The Gentle Giant. Bullied his entire life, he committed suicide one day after his thirtieth birthday. His death tore his family and ours apart. Feelings of tremendous guilt haunted his parents for years. They went into self-imposed isolation from everyone. Our family does not speak to them anymore.

Bobby, another cousin, was born with a disability and had to wear leg braces for many years. He earned the nickname "Wobble" from classmates in school and was taunted and bullied for this handicap. He passed away at age sixteen from heart failure.

I had to wear special shoes due to my extremely flat feet while growing up. I could never run with neighborhood kids and was tormented by them. The pain I endured at night was unbearable from being strapped into them all day long. A doctor prescribed eyeglasses when I was young, and many kids in school heckled me.

Although Lewis Duncan is what I call a conglomerate character, the bullying and retaliation I experienced in our town and neighboring schools are true. The state police in Massachusetts were taken to court for their minimum height requirement by two residents. They won their case and were hired. Each officer had a very successful career with the state police.

The Elementary Army exists on every street corner and neighborhood in our country. Caring people devote their lives to underprivileged and neglected children. I have met many of them through decades of volunteer work. They get little recognition.

The 'real' Spencer Plant, aka 'Honch,' was found shot to death inside the trunk of his car. He sold bad heroin that killed three teenagers. He was reported missing and later found in a sandpit on a hot summer day in 1983 by police. Although someone admitted to the murder, an arrest was never made. He still walks the earth today — a free man who keeps a low profile.

It is rumored the Gallaghers went into the Witness Protection Program. One of them supposedly took a bullet in the stomach from someone he double-crossed years ago. He survived the attempt on his life. The remaining brother died from natural causes while in hiding at a young age.

Unfortunately, this book is based on many actual bullying and racist events in the 1970s and 1980s. Names have been changed to protect the innocent and the guilty. I will never be able to divulge my part in this story.

Dweeb, Four-eyes, Punk, Cripple, Wobble, Dunce,
Weakling, Pussy, Freak, Nerd, Flat-foot, Fairy, Queer
Chicken, Yellow, Geek, Squirt

Never Again

NJM